AVID M

INCLUDES CD

DATE DUE

AVID MADE EASY:

Video Editing with Avid Free DV and the Avid Xpress® Family

Jaime Fowler

Wiley Publishing, Inc.

Acquisitions Editor: WILLEM KNIBBE
Development Editor: PETE GAUGHAN
Technical Editor: DENNIS KUTCHERA
Production Editor: HELEN SONG
Copy Editor: NANCY SIXSMITH
Production Manager: TIM TATE
Vice President & Executive Group Publisher: RICHARD SWADLEY
Vice President and Executive Publisher: JOSEPH B. WIKERT
Vice President and Publisher: DAN BRODNITZ
Media Project Supervisor: SHANNON WALTERS
Media Development Specialists: ANGELA DENNY, KATE JENKINS, STEVEN
KUDIRKA, KIT MALONE, TRAVIS SILVERS
Book Designer: FRANZ BAUMHACKL
Compositor: KATE KAMINSKI, HAPPENSTANCE TYPE-O-RAMA
Proofreaders: JAMES BROOK
Indexer: TED LAUX
Cover Designer and Illustrator: JOHN NEDWIDEK, EMDESIGN
Cover Photography: JAIME FOWLER
Copyright © 2005 by Wiley Publishing, Inc., Indianapolis, IN

Published by Wiley Publishing, Inc., Indianapolis, IN

Published simultaneously in Canada

Library of Congress Card Number:

ISBN-13: 978-0-7821-4440-3

ISBN-10: 0-7821-4440-3

Wiley Publishing, Inc. End-User License Agreement

Acknowledgments

I'm pretty sure that when Eva Cassidy wrote that God blesses the child who "got his own," she was not referring to authors. Writing the book that you now hold in your hands was certainly due to my efforts, but it never would have happened without certain people.

From Sybex, I'd especially like to thank Willem Knibbe, who spearheaded the idea to produce this book. Willem offered much guidance and an understanding of the human condition. I'd also like to thank Pete Gaughan, who kept me focused, and my cyberfriend Dennis Kutchera, who has done many favors for me over the years and who personally made sure I got everything correct before it went to print.

Bud Samiljan, formerly with Avid Technology, referred me to Willem and is an excellent resource.

From Avid: Ellen Feldman for assisting in getting on the right track. David Caporale for walking into the middle of the project without fear. Steve Chazin made sure that I had all the resources in order to succeed with my writing.

There is a special group of advisors and professionals from whom I have learned over the years: Shirley Thompson, who knows pretty much everything about Avid systems and things culinary; Steve Bayes, the guru who taught me much of what I know in his quiet way; and Greg Staten, the world's best instructor.

From the Avid-L group: Bob Zelin, Terry Curren, and Jeff Sengpiehl—ringmasters, wisecrackers, and (don't tell anyone) helpful persons.

I would especially like to thank the miraculous team that put H. Dumpty together again without the king's horses or king's men: Terri Fowler and Oliver Gonzales for their couch and hospitality; Thomas De Porter, M.D., for his assurance and guidance; Bettie and David Fowler for their understanding; Joe and Liza Fowler for constant vigil, menudo, and behemoth burritos; Bek, who smiles and laughs through tragedy and comes through it without a scratch; and Deb Dreyspring for her patience with me and also for hanging in there with all the others.

The professional and personal influences on a human being in the course of even a day are significant. So for anyone I failed to mention herein I offer my deepest apologies.

About the Author

Jaime Fowler spends his time teaching, editing, and writing about video and film editing. He was formerly the lead editor at Sony Pictures Television and was the founder and director of the Film Camp program, an experimental educational experience in which students learned to edit and then worked as editors on feature films.

Jaime's credits as an editor include *Under Pressure: Making the Abyss* for director James Cameron, as well as trailers and promotional featurettes for Warner Brothers, Universal Pictures, and Disney.

Jaime was part of a team of developers who helped create Avid's Multicam software for television situation comedies and variety shows. As a result, he has been an advisor on 32 prime-time situation comedies. Noteworthy film trailers and promotionals include *Passenger 57, The Accidental Tourist, Rambling Rose,* and *Universal Soldier.*

Jaime has been the editor of seven Emmy-winning television series. He was one of the first Avid Certified Instructors on the West Coast. These days, he lives in Texas near his family and continues to edit as well as teach and write about technology and all things editorial.

Contents

Introduction

Back in the late 1980s and early 1990s, nonlinear editing was more of a thought than a reality. Most video editors were using CMX, Grass Valley, or the less-expensive Callaway editing systems. The concept of being able to edit in a nonlinear way was pure theory. Most of us doubted it would ever happen; some of us had no concept of what it was and why it would ever be of value. Even in its earliest form, nonlinear editing was cost-prohibitive, experimental, and full of pitfalls.

But now, many years later, you are given a book that has not only the instructions but also a DVD of the actual software to create edits on your own personal computer. The software is nearly flawless and easy to use. Our understanding of nonlinear use is so much better than before. What a milestone! To think of all of the technology evolving so quickly is indeed mind-boggling.

Who Should Use This Book

This book is written for some very specific purposes. If you're not sure that this is the book for you, scan through the following list and see if any matches your needs. There are a lot of Avid books out there, and I personally have written a few of them. But some will work better for you than others. Let's take a look at what this book has:

A complete discovery of Avid Free DV and Xpress. From top to bottom, we will explore these tools. Avid Free DV is available at Avid's website, and it is also on the accompanying DVD with this book for your convenience. The Xpress line from Avid is also easy to obtain—and at a very low cost. The other item we will explore is Avid's Mojo, a digital accelerator and hardware key that allows you to edit uncompressed media.

Useful tips on how to use each tool in Avid Free DV and Xpress Pro. The book covers not only what the tools do but also when you should use them. Think of Free DV or Xpress as a tool, like a drill. You need to operate a drill before you use it. You can use this book to learn how to operate Free DV and Xpress interfaces. But more important, when do you drill a certain type of hole versus another? And why do you drill different types of holes? When do you drill them? This book provides guidance as to when to use the tools and which purposes they serve best.

Advanced features and functions that are less documented. Have you ever worked with a software application only to find that *your* way of doing things could have been made easier if only the operation guide had explained it better? Yeah—me, too. This book will contain many of my own experiences, as well as those of my colleagues, on how to get the best results quickly and efficiently without pecking around and trying to figure out how to do it on your own.

A conversational style that puts you at ease. As I wrote each chapter and you read along, you'll learn everything from an experienced editor who has nothing to lose by furthering your knowledge. If you work at a post house, you might have noticed that some editors are a little less forthcoming. Of course they are! You could end up taking their place! After you know what *they* know, well, it could get a little sticky. So they don't always seem as willing to share as you might like.

Illustration of how to use the tools. Whenever possible, I'll show you—through screen captures, tables, and other visual media—what to look for on the interface and where to go to get the information. It's hard enough to understand the material without having someone in the room looking over your shoulder. The best education is done in person with another qualified person leading the way. With those limitations in mind and through the magic of the computer, I'll try to best explain *and* show critical information that will help you learn more quickly.

Finally, the tried-and-true form of education: *doing*. At the end of most of the chapters, I've organized a tutorial that you can work again and again. But it's not a blind tutorial in which you're just following directions. I'll explain the purpose before we do it. That way, you can understand what we're attempting to do and will not just be a "button pusher." Editors benefit very little by following direct button pushing and doing exactly as they are told. In fact, I've met some editors who were fired from their jobs because that is all that they knew how to do. So in the tutorials, we'll go over a function, you'll do it, and then I will give you something with that function that you can do on your own.

In all my years of teaching, the hardest part of the process is setting students free so that they can do it on their own. Some students never want to stop being students. Others seem ready to move on. But for the first few moments on their own, you never know how well things will go for students. But most students, despite an initial butterfly or two in their stomach, overcome it by picking up the required understanding that they are responsible. Get used to this feeling. It will never completely go away. Every Avid system is connected a little differently; every production has a different workflow for post.

I have found that even when a student is not quite fully prepared to work as an editor, the measure of dedication serves them well. If you want the job, if you care about it and mean to do well, you can usually pick up any missing gaps of information or any nuances that pertain to a specific production. Every editing situation is different, so there will always be a learning curve, even after many, many years. With that in mind, let's talk about the variety of Avid systems that have come into play. We'll include your own Free DV and Xpress systems as well.

How to Use this Book

The book is divided into seven chapters. With the exception of Chapter 1, each chapter concludes with a tutorial to help reinforce the things learned. The book is designed so that you can read an entire chapter in one sitting. The tutorial for the chapter should be done as soon as possible after reading it. If you cannot complete the tutorial immediately after reading the chapter, wait and skim through the material again, and then do the tutorial.

In theory, you should be able to complete this book and the tutorials in the course of a week. The idea is to get you up and going with your system so that you can create your own videos in as short a time as possible.

The Companion DVD

The companion DVD contains an OMFI MediaFiles folder that must be placed on the root directory of your hard drive. There are two Avid project folders: one for Xpress Pro and one for Free DV. Keep in mind that Xpress Pro and Free DV files are incompatible, so use only the project folder that works for your system. These folders should replace the folders already on your system if you have already installed the software. There are Read Me files on the DVD to give you further instruction.

Please also note that there are some effect demo files, effect templates, and other items in the folder called Extras. Be sure to read the Read Me files before trying them out on your system: they do have limitations.

How to Contact the Author

Any questions, feedback, or communication with me—Jaime Fowler—can be directed via e-mail at jmefowler@sbcglobal.net. Although I read all e-mails, I can't answer them all. I'm interested in your thoughts about this book, recommendations for any improvement in future editions, and any effect templates, keyboard layouts, or other information that you can share.

Introduction to Avid and Editing

After we've outlined the history and etymology of Avid, we'll take a look at basic editing workflow. Even though we can determine a proper A-to-Z outline of the editing process, you'll often find yourself repeating certain steps of the process again and again before proceeding further. This process is simple and basic at best. Every rule of editing can and will be broken. But the rules do serve as the place to start.

Chapter Contents

Into Nonlinear Editing
The Avid Product Line
Editing Workflow

Into Nonlinear Editing

Editing is fun. Even before nonlinear editing applications were invented for the personal computer, it was fun. There's a bit of empowerment that comes with determining what the viewer sees and when they see it. Controlling the pacing of visual information gives one a sense of both power and responsibility to the viewer. And the more material there is to choose from, the more exciting it gets.

Finding the rhythm of a scene is something of an art form that is frequently discussed in the digital community. Thelma Schoonmaker, editor of many Martin Scorsese movies, once mentioned that Scorsese made the cutting decisions, but she found the rhythms of scenes.

Every editor works a little differently, and the role of each editor can vary greatly, from project to project—even geographically. When I first moved from the Los Angeles area to Portland, Oregon, I was surprised at some of the things editors had to do. Much of the work was done alone. Some projects were completed alone. I had never borne the burden of being responsible for the finished project without someone else's approval. Not that it was bad…just different.

When Avid Technology created its first Media Composer, editing became even more fun. The interface was simple and primitive. Not a lot of bells and whistles. But it had the power of being able to manipulate media in a nonlinear way. You didn't have to create your projects chronologically, as with most video systems during that time. You could start in the middle of a program and cut the beginning later. As crucial scenes were shot, you could begin cutting right away, instead of having to wait until you had cut all the prior scenes together in order. Directors loved it because they could focus on any scene at any given time. Editors loved it because they could stay busy and not wait around for the next scene to be shot.

 Note: As a matter of fact, one of the first issues I faced with some of my linear clients when I switched to nonlinear is that we never seemed to have time to schmooze. For many editors, schmoozing can make the difference between their choice of one editor and the next.

As common as nonlinear editing is today, the concept of it, at least to video editors at that time, was mind-boggling. Combining two elements into a dissolve without checking subcarrier to horizontal phase with two playback machines was ludicrous. Instant access to several reels at the same time was unheard-of (see Figure 1.1). In fact, the things that most people take for granted when using modern editing equipment were very difficult in their day.

Figure 1.1 Editing has come a long way, as demonstrated by this Moviola editing system.

The history of editing is fascinating. In the old days, a film editor would work on a bench with razor blades, splicing tape, and a splicer. After making some edits, the editor would have to walk down the hall to the screening room and project it.

In 1924, a man named Iwan Serrurier came up with an idea for showing movies in homes without the use of a projector. Serrurier's device, the Moviola flatbed, projected movies inside an elaborate wooden box. It wasn't popular with consumers because the fancy wood and ornate detail made it too pricey. But an editor at Douglas Fairbanks Jr.'s studio saw it and asked if it could be used for projecting cut scenes. Serurrier said that it could, and the first editing system was born. It was called the Moviola because, like a Victrola that played music, this primitive machine could play films.

To edit videotape prior to nonlinear days, an editor required some kind of certification as a technician, a license from the Federal Communication Commission, or a high score on a standard test of engineering measurements and calculations. Those items are rarely used today, although for some circumstances, they are still mandatory for broadcast on some networks.

In fact, an old story that made the rounds on the West Coast was that a well-known Hollywood producer was dining with a network executive. "Bill," (not his actual name) said the network executive, "why are you playing around with all of this nonlinear stuff? You know the resolution will never be good enough to broadcast."

"Frank," (again, not his actual name) replied the producer, "you have been broadcasting it on your network with my show for the last seven weeks."

Is the story true? I have no idea, but it certainly made the rounds quickly. What I do know is that shortly after this story spread, networks began broadcasting Avid output openly.

The first Avid systems were pricey. A full-blown Media Composer was around $80,000 (USD). Not exactly pocket change. But through the miracle of development of technology, we've enclosed a copy of Avid Free DV on the companion DVD, an incredible application that actually does much more than the first Avids could do.

This free software from Avid has some shortcomings, and we'll discuss those in the book. Xpress Pro and Xpress DV are both very good systems and cost relatively little for the professional. For the hobbyist, they may seem pricey, but they are loaded with just about every feature Avid could think of.

The Avid Product Line

Today, Avid has several different nonlinear editing systems. They all basically do the same thing, and the interfaces are very similar. Eventually, it will become easy for you to migrate from one Avid system to the next.

 Note: The exceptions are Avid D|S and D|S Nitrus systems, which were originally created by SoftImage, a company that Avid acquired. D|S systems are primarily used for compositing many separate images into a single frame. The interface is very different.

In spite of new technological developments, older Avid systems still are in existence today, from the earliest Media Composers to the newer Adrenaline models. For the editor, it is important to recognize these because you might find yourself editing on one of these other systems, in addition to the Free DV or Xpress Pro models that are latest state-of-the-art systems.

The Days of Avid/1

In 1989, the first Avid system, the Avid/1 (see Figure 1.2), was created on an Apollo computer. It was well into research and development, but not yet released, when Apple Computer stepped in and offered technical support, development tools, and both hardware and software to Avid developers. From that development period came the first Media Composer.

Figure 1.2 An early Avid system.
Dreamy, Isn't it?

I remember a filmmaker bursting into my online editing suite with an EDL (edit decision list) that came from an Avid. He was very excited and tried in vain to explain to me the nonlinear difference. Instead of actually explaining it well, he kept screaming, "It's nonlinear! Don't you see! I edited all of this nonlinear!" The word *nonlinear* wasn't even in my vocabulary, and I had no idea what it meant. But this chap apparently had nothing short of a religious experience with a thing called an Avid.

In those days, development came slowly. New ideas were almost nonexistent when it came to the video-editing process. We editors felt that the systems that we had were "good enough." Of course, the software was updated to keep the edit system companies in business. Nonetheless, some company was always trying to develop an editing system that both film and video editors would like. No matter how hard they tried, they could never get both groups to like the same equipment. A system with lots of numbers attracted the video crowd. A system that could preview multiple images attracted the film crowd. So it came as no surprise to me that this man, a filmmaker by trade, liked the Avid. And it probably meant, to my own thinking as a video editor at that time, that I would hate it.

But no editor wants to get caught behind the times. Keeping abreast of technology is essential to the working editor. Reluctantly, I went out and took a look at this Avid.

I was surprised by how many other video editors attended that same demo, and I was even more surprised that the Avid people understood where we came from: Video editing was developed. We had been doing things the same way for years. Nothing short of a miraculous development would change our minds. On the periphery, some of my fellow video editors were working with companies such as CMX, which had developed one of the first nonlinear systems, but I was never an early adopter. Either it worked or it didn't. I wasn't interested in testing periods, and I hated going through the "discovery" process with companies. All I wanted was to be able to edit using the most efficient tools.

What Avid presented that day was a tool that was remarkably stable and had some features that took a while for an old diehard to understand. Sequences were edited on a computer (a Mac, for crying out loud!) and they could be reassembled again and again, changing one shot or another. I was still trying to figure out how one could reassemble an edited commercial to reflect a small change without having to recopy all the media. It seemed so easy to use and yet very complex to understand.

These days, it sounds so easy. But in the dimly lit world of the video editor, it was miraculous. In those days, if you started a new project, you had to edit the opening first. Then came the first sequence. Insert a commercial break and then on to the next sequence. This is how it was done. A single change usually meant a complete re-edit. Editors prayed for no changes. When the producer announced that some "changes need to be made," we all slumped in our chairs. It was hard to create a better cut without wanting it to change. To a great extent, the creative process was preempted by the desire to just get the job done.

The Avid system eliminated all of this. No worries about match-frame dissolves, effects, new opens, extending shots, and so on. It was all done in a computer, and until it left the computer, every change imaginable was possible.

And what did it take to obtain one of these little babies? At the time, the top-of-the-line Avid would set you back around $80,000. And it only did single-field editing.

For the uninitiated, a video frame consists of two fields. The picture first scans every other line of resolution and then scans the ones missing from the first scan. These two scans, which make up a composite image, are called fields. So when you used an Avid, you showed only half the resolution of a picture. Additionally, the images created were compressed. So much so that you could see "blockiness" or distortion of the picture when it was played back on an ordinary TV.

Bummer. It seemed at that time that the technology would never catch up or develop. But Avid told us that it was going to catch up and that we would eventually be able to edit without going through any online processing or re-creating of the pictures at high resolution. I didn't believe them at the time, but they proved me wrong.

NuBus Avids

NuBus systems were so named because the Apple computer that was used at the time, the Quadra 900 and Quadra 950, didn't have enough processing power to run the Avid software. As a result, Avid used additional coprocessors, which were connected to Apple's NuBus card architecture.

The basic Media Composer at that time (see Figure 1.3) used several coprocessors, including the following:

- Audiomedia or Pro Tools DigiDesign audio coprocessor
- Atto SCSI accelerator (this was used to play back the media at higher speeds so that you could actually read 30 fields per second)
- Truevision NuVista card with an Avid-made daughterboard for video
- JPEG or Advanced JPEG card for reading the media files correctly (the Advanced JPEG card was huge and connected to the NuVista)

Figure 1.3 That's a NuBus Media Composer under the desk.

All these cards were placed inside the computer. NuBus technology (as opposed to PCI technology, which both Apple and PC makers use) consisted of rows of little pins inside a plastic receptacle on the coprocessor, which were then mounted to a plastic socket inside the computer.

From this technology, we in the workforce learned two important things: First, Newton was right. You can always count on gravity. The size of the cards and the fact that they were side-mounted caused them to slip away from the sockets, eventually disconnecting themselves. There were numerous attempts to make the connections tighter, but few worked. The solution? Turn your computer tower sideways, so that the gravity of the coprocessors pushed downward on the NuBus sockets, securing the connection.

The second important lesson of the NuBus systems was this: When you use equipment connected by tiny pins, chances are that eventually the pins will bend or break. The process of connecting the cards to their corresponding sockets must be done with a firm but sensitive grip. Alignment must be perfect. Misalignment causes bent pins. Although not recommended by Avid, I frequently used a pair of needle-nosed pliers to straighten out pins. (That's me in Figure 1.4.) I suppose I was lucky because it always worked. But if you break a pin, the card is worthless.

Figure 1.4 Technology Marches On, Circa 1993. Everything you see in this picture (including the author and the telephone) is obsolete.

Why all this discussion about the NuBus systems? They were created in 1989 and were determined obsolete by the mid-90s. But surprisingly, quite a few schools and small organizations have managed to extend their lifetime. Many are still in use, and you might find yourself using one. If you do, I've told you the most important stuff.

The NuBus models incorporated different levels of video resolution, numbered AVR1-6. These single-field resolutions varied in quality from "poor" (AVR1) to "good" (AVR 6). Eventually Avid developed dual-field (full video frame) resolutions, named AVR 25, AVR 26, and AVR 27. AVR 26 was the equivalent of AVR 6, but with two fields of resolution. AVR 27 was superior to all of them—it led the way to better models and the incorporation of PCI architecture.

You might think that in those days the Avid was something of a battle-ax—and you would be right. Three-gigabyte drives went for $1,000 per GB and were heavy and cumbersome. We had "removable" storage using heavy metal drive receptacles that the government used to store databases in.

The monitors used were 20″ Mitsubishis that could give you a hernia if you lifted them. But we had a lot of fun trying to push Avid to its limits. And then by the time everyone got the hang of using the Avid and learning its secrets, Avid changed to PCI systems.

 Note: Before I go on, I have to say that those Avids had a whopping CPU speed of 33 Mhz.

PCI Avids

While Apple was using NuBus architecture for coprocessing, the PC world used PCI. These types of cards had slim metal connections (no pins!) that were firm and reliable. Eventually, Apple adopted PCI as well, and it meant a whole new period of development for Avid.

Many of the vendors that created the coprocessors used with Avids were well on their way. Truevision, the creator of the NuVista card, created a Targa card that Avid used with its own coprocessors. From this came the ABVB subsystem (also known as the Avid Broadcast Video Board). The ABVB systems were reliable and fast. Avid continued the use of AudioMedia and Digidesign audio systems as well as Atto SCSI cards to increase the dataflow.

They were all incorporated into Apple 9500 and 9600 computers, called Power PCs because of their higher speed. Although 350 MHz CPUs sound slow by today's standards, remember that the Quadra had a whopping 33 MHz speed!

The best thing about this period of development was reliability. Both Apple and Avid created hardware and software that crashed less often, created better resolutions, and made a true broadcast image. The original size of the Avid video frame was 640×480 pixels. This frame covered the visual aspects of the picture only and had nothing more than visual elements, with no blanking information for broadcasters. With the introduction of the ABVB systems, the picture was 720×486 pixels, the perfect size for broadcasting.

As a result, Avid systems were broadcast-ready. New resolutions reflecting these changes were developed. Avid named them AVR 75 and AVR 77, the "7" indicating that the horizontal picture was 720 pixels wide and thus suitable for broadcast.

During this time, things were developing at Apple as well. Apple stopped selling the five-PCI-slot computers and adapted a three-slot system (see Figure 1.5). Having only three slots made it difficult for Avid to continue development of its systems because of the four-slot requirement for all its coprocessors.

Figure 1.5 PCI (ABVB) Media Composer

I had supposed that this could cause a falling out between Apple and Avid, but one is never sure what happens behind the closed doors of two separate corporations. Suffice it to say, Avid used an external PCI expansion chassis for use with the newer Apple systems and it worked. But every new piece of hardware had to be developed. The result was less than elegant, but it worked.

I remember approaching an Apple executive at that time. He told me that the newer systems with fewer cards were created because Apple believed that video editing could be contained within the computer itself instead of using so many coprocessors.

He was right. A year later, Apple introduced Final Cut Pro.

During this time, Avid began serious development on a PC as well as Mac Media Composer. The results provided a larger user base, and the systems were identical.

Meridien Avids

Avid's next incarnation of technology was the Meridien subsystem (see Figure 1.6). The Meridien systems are still wildly popular and in use today. Avid changed its resolution names to reflect the industry standard in terms of ratios rather than Avid-specific names. For example, 10:1 resolution is truly 1/10 of uncompressed resolution. 1:1 resolution is uncompressed resolution, and so on. Meridiens were the first uncompressed video solution for Avid. The Avid Symphony, with a full set of finishing tools, including color correction, 3D effects, and uncompressed video, was created. Media Composers also had many of these options. Real-time playback of two streams of uncompressed video was made possible. It was an exciting time for Avid and Avid users.

Figure 1.6 A modern Avid keyboard

For some, it was still something of a burden to have to rely on so many coprocessors. But the reliability was unmistakable. These systems rarely failed, and when they did, the problems were almost always either processor failure or introduction of other software that was not compatible with Avid software.

The reason why so many people continue to use Meridien systems is simple: They work. The technology is all there; the tools are all available. Why change? For others, the adoption of a less-complicated coprocessing system lured them to Avid's latest line of systems: DNA (Digital Nonlinear Accelerator) with both Adrenaline and Mojo subsystems.

DNA Avids

Take a Meridien system and put it in a small box. Okay, you can't do it. The box would have to be big. For three years, Avid developed a small box with a subsystem capable of playing back uncompressed video without the need to render before viewing.

This system is the Adrenaline system (see Figure 1.7). Using Adrenaline or Avid Mojo, a user can move a small box and a hardware key from any system (Mac or Windows) to any other system. It allows you to change computers, keep up with technology, and move equipment more easily and efficiently. There is no need for individual coprocessor concerns. Adrenaline and Mojo either work or they don't. Best of all, on the Adrenaline, you can combine different resolutions, including the older ABVB AVR and Meridien resolution media with other current media types such as DV25. Mojo offers a limited selection of both Meridien resolutions and other current media types.

So what makes these systems work so well? Nobody seems to know the secret. It's all in that little box. I use Mojo, which connects to my Xpress Pro system via a common FireWire connection. The box has worked perfectly since I started with it. It's simple to connect and can create uncompressed video from any source. Sometimes I stare at my Mojo and wonder what it is actually doing. But most of the time I just use it.

This "magic box" technology is a little weird at first, but once you get used to it and see the results, it can pretty much go unnoticed. Although Avid made certain that we understood that we could now use our Adrenaline and Mojo boxes with faster, more efficient computers, I am sure that they have not cut their own throats by ending their product lines. Still to come is the introduction of an advanced Mojo, high-definition standards, and whatever else the industry might bring. Every new incarnation promises the "be-all-and-end-all" product, but it never really ends.

If you are currently using Free DV, none of these particular systems applies. What you have is a very basic Avid system without benefit of DNA acceleration. You cannot attach a Mojo to Free DV. But you can always upgrade to Xpress Pro, which is a more elaborate Avid with better features. For now, you'll learn about how Free DV works. But first, let's explore the process of editing.

Avid has a lot of different solutions for editors. You can compare all of the models here:

    http://www.avid.com/products/video/editing-finishing.asp

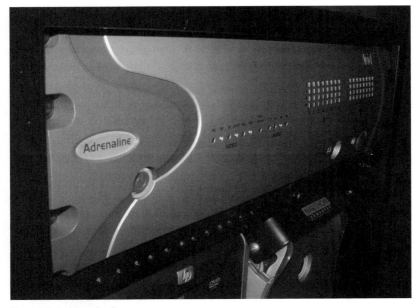

Figure 1.7 An Adrenaline box

Editing Workflow

How many times have we heard that age-old saying, "If you don't know where you're going, you'll never get there!" The same can be said for the workflow required for nonlinear editing. A little planning can go a long way. But remember, we are working in a nonlinear fashion, which presents more opportunities. Even though we might have a good cut of our program, if the phone rings and someone tells you that he or she has found a good replacement for one of your shots, you can do it with no penalty except a few extra moments.

Earlier, I alluded to the fact that video editing is something of a mutant of the creative process. Let's talk for a moment about that process and why nonlinear editing works so much better.

I know a lot of artists. Artists are, for the most part, very creative. Some don't feel that they quite fit in. They see the world differently from others. And they spend a lot of time changing things around. For example, I know one young artist who likes to rearrange her furniture. She does this frequently, much more than others. I get the feeling that she is looking for something of a perfect environment, but I am not sure that she'll ever find it. For her, the process is more important than the solution.

Take that simple idea and apply it to video editing. When we start on an edit, we have an idea of how it begins, how it develops, and how it ends. But with nonlinear editing, you have the power to do so much more! Any ideas that come during the process of editing may beg for change. If you were editing in a linear fashion, change is so much harder. From a nonlinear standpoint, any last-minute changes are easy.

Now let's look at it from an artist's viewpoint. If you read the original first draft of a screenplay or a famous novel, you would undoubtedly be disappointed. That's because (to paraphrase Hemingway) first drafts are all pretty bad. But when we edited video using linear equipment, the first draft of that edit was almost always the final draft. What a mutated way of creating! It could be so much better if we had taken the time to change it. And yet the difficulty of change necessitated very few changes. It was a compromise on creativity.

When Rodin sculpted *The Thinker* (see Figure 1.8), he started out with a big block of media. And he started carving what appeared from a distance to be a man sitting and thinking. He didn't carve the fingers perfectly or etch the toenails precisely. It was just a big hunk of rock that eventually was shaped into a man. Eventually, of course, the details were made, but his "first draft," or initial carving, didn't look all that great.

And so it goes with your nonlinear editing process. The first edit can look very bad, indeed. Most of mine are awful. But given the tools to change and mold the edit into something good, this can be done over time, whether you're dealing with just one day's work or a major months-long project. To film editors, this may sound ordinary. But any video editor who has done a machine-to-machine edit, the idea of nonlinear editing is freedom to unlock your mind to a world of possibilities.

Figure 1.8 Rodin didn't invent progressive creativity. Everything, especially nature, has a first draft.

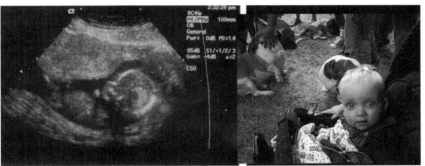

Even as you read this book, there is a certain amount of change that has taken place from its original form. We started with an outline; then I went about writing it according to the outline. This final form in your hands bears little resemblance to the outline. That's creativity at work.

So you start with a simple skeletal concept. In some cases, it is a storyboard or an animatic, or something that brings the idea forward to the editing suite. Then in the process of editing, you bring it to fruition.

There are some dangers here. If you throw out the initial backbone or ideal, you can get lost. Without some form of idea of what you're going to do, the work can atrophy quickly.

Let's say, for example, that you go to an air show. You shoot a lot of video, but you don't really have an idea of what you're going to do with it. If you don't come up with a framework for this project before the edit, it turns into a slide show. Mayhem ensues. You edit a picture of a Sopwith Camel and then dissolve to an F-14. It makes *no* sense.

On the other hand, we'll say the air show itself has a concept: "You Wouldn't Believe Our World" is the tag line for the show. Now you have an idea. You shoot some amazing footage and throw it together with the concept in mind. You start with early aircraft and rush into the latest strategic attack fighters. Your edited piece now has form and structure. In fact, it emulates the concept of the show itself.

The following sections walk you through a typical editing workflow, which looks like this:

1. Capture
2. Edit
3. Trim
4. Import
5. Effects
6. Export
7. Output

Capture

The first step in the editing process is to capture materials from their original video sources (see Figure 1.9). However, like all elements of the process, we can capture different parts of our program at different times. For example, let's pretend that you are doing a videotape of a recent visit to France. Here is the Champs-Elysées, there is the Eiffel Tower, and so on. One of your images was taken on a cloudy day. A friend who also has visited France says that he or she also has some footage but can't get it to you until Thursday. Today is Tuesday. What do you do in the meantime? You can capture all your footage and start editing. When the additional footage comes in, you can capture again. So although there is a general order of steps taken, you can repeat some steps to get what you want.

Figure 1.9 Capturing for an edit

Capturing material in this way enhances the creative process, as we discussed. All of a sudden, the project becomes bigger than the sum of its parts. You can add more—as much as you like—until it becomes better and better. It's something akin to adding tracks to a musical recording. The more tracks, the better. (In some cases, at least.)

Reading the history of modern musical artists is interesting. Paul McCartney of the Beatles didn't want to add orchestra to the piece. George Martin insisted. The result was a modern classic. It happens all the time, both in music and video. The more tracks, the better.

Note: I remember editing some promotional pieces for the movie *Tequila Sunrise*. A friend had gone to see it and mentioned a steamy hot tub scene. I replied, "Hot tub scene? *Hot tub scene? Where was I?*" It was decided to add the scene after I edited the promotionals (promotional pieces are frequently edited well before the release of the picture), so I missed out. But I am getting ahead of myself here.

Using Free DV and Xpress Capture tools, you'll need to make a few primary decisions before going through the procedure. These decisions are discussed more in Chapter 2, but here they are:

- How much drive space do I need to complete this program?
- What resolution should I use? (Not necessary for Free DV.)
- What will be the final medium for output?
- How do I name or number each tape?

I mentioned that these are done *before* capture. Again, without some form of structure, projects atrophy. If you make some of these decisions later, it will take more time to restructure the project, which gives you less time to create and complete it. As you become more familiar with Free DV and Xpress, you will highly value that creative thinking time. We'll cover capture completely in Chapter 2.

Edit

The next step in the workflow is to edit (see Figure 1.10). That may sound like common sense, but there's one thing that's different. When I mention edit, I mean to say that you will put together the elements in the order you believe they should go. The in points and out points of each picture might not be "tight" at this point. The rhythm of the scene might not match what you want yet. But there are other tools for this, as you will see.

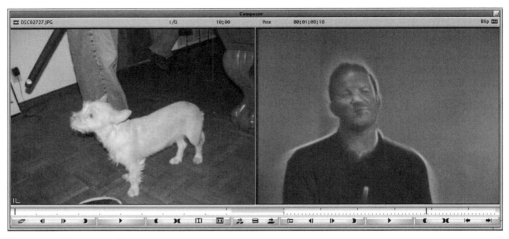

Figure 1.10 Editing the media

The important thing to remember is that your sequence should be edited loosely, leaving extra footage at the head and tail of each shot. Why? Out of sight, out of mind. If you edit the piece together in a tight manner, you might forget something that was on the original tape that you wanted to lose. In fact, you might consider this edit as an assembly of sorts, in which you throw everything in that is going to be used. It doesn't even have to follow the right order as you see it. All this can be changed later.

The author Ray Bradbury described it this way: "I throw up in the morning and clean up in the afternoon." Not a particularly pretty image, but it makes sense. In the early morning, guided by his subconscious from dreaming, Bradbury would run to his typewriter and begin pecking away. It could be anything—a phrase, a poem, the beginnings of a story, or an anecdote. After lunch, he would take all of these newly created elements and file them away where they belonged. Some would go into the wastebasket; others would be developed into short stories, novels or poetry. Most importantly, they would eventually find their place after being roughly assembled in the morning.

You can edit this way as well. Take all the elements that go into your story, assemble them into a very rough program, and then, using the next process, *trimming*, you can clean up the mess that you created into something that looks good. Chapters 3 and 4 introduce basic concepts and launch you into a new type of editing with the Timeline.

Trim

The process of trimming is the key to the nonlinear editing experience. Using the trim tool discussed in Chapter 5 (see Figure 1.11), you mold your program from the primitive elements into something that flows naturally, is appealing to the eye, and brings tears of joy to your audience. (This process would be what Bradbury referred to as "cleaning up.") The practice of trimming is basically very simple, but there are so many different ways of doing it that it might appear overwhelming at first. Not to worry, you'll adapt.

Figure 1.11 Trimming to perfection

By trimming each piece in our program, we either can extend it by adding more frames, or shorten it by reducing the number of frames for each clip in the program. Trimming gives you the power to create the overall timing of events and the flow of the program, what we call finding the rhythm of the scene. It also determines the duration of the piece. Sometimes, when editing commercials, the timing can be more important. This type of timing can mean the difference between a masterful editor and a poor editor. So trimming is very important.

Using some of the Timeline tools discussed in Chapter 4, you can replace shots, juxtapose shots (changing the order in which they appear in your program), and experiment with the final presentation. If you're unsure about whether or not this will improve the program, you can also duplicate the program and try it using the duplicate. If it fails, you can revert to your original piece.

I personally love the trim mode, which is where all my important decisions are made. It is where we take a closeup view of each clip and each transition to determine whether or not they will be used. This is also the point at which we question our original decisions, wondering if one shot would look better than the one we already chose. Although it might sound tedious, it is that level of concentration that allows an editor to really see his or her work for the first time.

If you're new to editing, keep this in mind: You've been watching television and film for years. Instinctively, you probably already know when and where to cut. But with your inexperience comes some doubt. In the trim mode, you can look closely at what you've done and determine what was necessary and what should go away from the program. The more time you spend here, the better an editor you can become.

Import

The import part of the workflow can begin at any stage of postproduction (see Figure 1.12). If you have various graphic files, shot logs, audio files, or digital media files to import, you can begin doing it right away.

But in many cases, imported files are not even created until the editor or producer realizes the need for it. For example, if someone slams a door in your program, but the audio is distorted, you might need an audio sound effect file to import a slamming door. Again, the capability of nonlinear editing shines. You can import the sound effect anytime and adjust the scene and the mix accordingly.

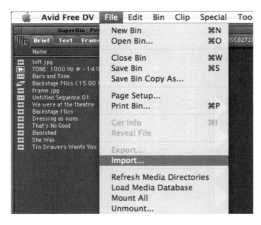

Figure 1.12 Prepping for import

If a graphical representation of what is being said necessitates a flowchart or bar graph, one might have to be created. Once created, you can import it into your project and edit it into the place where it belongs.

Avid Free DV and Xpress have the capability to import a wide variety of file formats. In addition, there are some helper applications that allow you to convert one file type to another. Importing files is relatively easy and can even be automated using Free DV and Xpress Pro software.

Effects

Normally, effects are not done until the program is basically cut together. But you might find that the timing of an effect is crucial to the program. In either case, Avid effects can be created at any time in your postproduction workflow, as long as the media for these effects have been captured or imported (see Figure 1.13). For these purposes, when discussing effects, we refer also to titles and transitional effects, such as dissolves and fades. Avid has all these available, in addition to some more elaborate effects.

Figure 1.13 Designing effects

The effects tool on Free DV is somewhat limited, but you can create and customize an effect and save it for later use. Many effects editors pride themselves on their arsenal of solutions for situations that necessitate an effect. With a disk full of templates, you will become valued as an editor who has experimented and mastered the effects palette.

Avid's Free DV effect template is pretty basic, but you can add custom effects as you go. When (or if) you should decide to upgrade to Xpress, you will find many more effects in the palette, all of which can be customized for your purposes.

Export

In many cases, you might find that to complete an effect or a composite image that Avid cannot do, you'll need to export your media (see Figure 1.14) to use on another application, such as Avid D|S Nitris, After Effects, or Smoke. Avid Free DV and Xpress allow you to export these necessary files with the simplicity and ease that the exporting tool provides.

Figure 1.14 Exporting a QuickTime

The export tool is also an excellent resource for sending still reference frames, creating storyboards, or showing examples of the work to clients. You can create simple QuickTime files that can be e-mailed or FTP'd to clients to show your progress on the program. Any visual or aural information in your bins can be exported, along with the bins and projects that you create.

Output

When your program is completed, you can output to any video recording media such as DVD or videotape using Avid's Digital Cut tool. The Digital Cut tool (see Figure 1.15) allows you to output to a huge variety of sources. It can record using a timecoded tape for frame accuracy, or assemble-edit using no timecode, or just play back to a DVD recorder. You can output for sound mixing and sweetening, special effects generation, or animatics, which, as noted earlier, are moving primitive storyboards.

Figure 1.15 Output through Digital Cut

The convenience of the Digital Cut tool provides editors with the ability to finish and refinish quickly and efficiently.

Capturing

The first step in the editing workflow that was described in Chapter 1 is the process of capturing media. But before we begin this process, let's make sure that everything on your system is ready to go.

Considerations Before You Capture

Both Free DV and Xpress Pro have certain system requirements. Although it is true that some individuals have managed to work with the application without meeting those requirements, it is not recommended that you do so. Why? Well, both Free DV and Xpress Pro are pretty elaborate applications. They have evolved from the Media Composer software developed by Avid, which is rumored to contain the biggest code-base ever used in a single application. And Avid software can be pretty quirky when the exact recommendations are not met.

Case in point: the Capture tool, which we will soon be using. I have often had to troubleshoot systems that refused to capture media properly. These systems would seem to operate correctly until you pressed the red capture button on the interface. At that point, either a cryptic error message would appear on-screen, or the system would sit and do nothing. In every case, the system didn't meet Avid's specifications. After the system was adjusted to meet those specifications, everything worked fine.

System Recommendations

We live in a world of convenience and choices, but it's really a good idea to stick with the requirements. An example is the AMD processor, which is not supported. Some people have had success using these, but Avid will not provide tech support for any system that has an AMD. Thanks to the Internet and user forums mentioned below, you can go online and share with other editors who have tried different configurations.

Free DV

Windows users:

- Windows XP Professional with Service Pack 1 or 2
- 933 MHz Pentium 3 or any Pentium 4 or Pentium M Processors
- 1 GB system memory (1.5 GB preferred)
- A qualified graphics card (as supported by system vendor); Avid recommends the NVIDIA Quadro4 980 XGL (Windows) or the NVIDIA QuadroFX 1100
- An IEEE-1394 (FireWire) port or qualified DV In/Out Card (see following)
- 20 GB or larger internal disk drive
- CD or DVD-ROM drive

Mac users:

- Mac OS X 10.3.4, 10.3.5, 10.3.6, 10.3.7, or 10.3.8
- 667 MHz G4 or any G5 (single or dual processor)

- 1 GB system memory (1.5 GB recommended)
- A qualified graphics card (as supported by system vendor); Avid recommends the NVIDIA GeForceT4 Titanium graphics card or the card that ships with G5 systems
- An IEEE-1394 (FireWire) port
- 20 GB or larger internal disk drive
- CD or DVD-ROM drive

If you do not have a FireWire port on your system or you are using the optional Mojo, here are some FireWire card recommendations from Avid:

For PC workstations:

- DS PYRO PCI 64, part #API-311
- ADS PYRO BasicDV, part #API-310
- ADS PYRO 1394 Port, part #API-300
- ADS PYRO 1394DV, part #API-1394-PCI
- SIIG 1394 3-Port PCI, part #NN-400012
- SIIG 1394 3-Port PCI i/e, part #NN-440012

For PC notebooks:

- DS PYRO 1394DV for Notebooks, part #API-601 or #API-602
- SIIG CardBus PC Card, part #NN-PCM012
- SIIG 1394 CardBus Dual, part #NN-PCM212
- IBM 1394 CardBus PC Card, part #19K5678

The ADS and SIIG cards can also be used on a Mac.

Xpress Pro

For PC

- Dual or single 2.4 GHz Xeon processor *or* Pentium 4 1.6 GHz processor *or* (for mobile configuration) Pentium M 1.8 GHz processor
- IDE, SCSI, or SATA boot drive, 40 GB minimum
- Windows XP Professional with Service Pack 2
- 1.5 GB RAM (2.0 GB recommended for "high-definition" video)
- Qualified Open GL graphics cards are Nvidia QuadroFX 1400 PCI Express, Nvidia Quadro FX 1300 PCI Express, Nvidia Quadro FX 1100 AGP 8X, Nvidia QuadroFX 500 AGP 8X or Nvidia Quadro4 980 XGL AGP 8X
- FireWire cards should be ADS Pyro PCI64 or SIIG 1394 3 port PCI
- CD or DVD-ROM drive

For Macintosh

- Single- or dual-processor G4 or G5
- Mac OS X 10.3.4, 10.3.5, 10,36 , 10.3.7, or 10.3.8
- 1GB RAM
- Graphics adapter supported by Apple
- 40 GB boot drive minimum
- CD or DVD-ROM drive

As anyone who is a computer enthusiast knows, these recommendations frequently change, so it might be a good idea to visit the Avid website at www.avid.com.

The Avid website also hosts forums for both Free DV and Xpress Pro. Here you can ask questions and get answers from others who use these systems regularly. Both professional and new users of the systems use the forums. It's also a great way to meet other editors and to trade war stories.

Note: There are a lot of good resources for editors on the Web. Some of the best forums are at www.editorsnet.com and www.creativecow.com. These are great sites for both new and experienced editors. You can get a lot of information there and questions answered. There is also the Avid Listserv, better known as the Avid-L. The "L" is notorious for cranky old editors and might not be the best site if you're new to postproduction. You can sign up for the L by going to Avid's website and clicking the Community button.

Now that you know the recommendations from Avid, let's take a look at some other important issues. Before going through the process of creating a project and digitizing, it is wise to do a little planning ahead. This sort of "pre-postproduction" works well, especially for larger projects. We talked about this in the previous chapter, but again, I must emphasize that without doing these things, you'll find yourself in a pickle. A little planning can prevent mistakes down the line. Here, then, are some of those considerations to be made:

- Do you have enough drive space to capture, import, and render media for your entire project?
- Have you determined a system of naming each videotape for this project?
- Have you chosen a resolution for the project?
- Have you determined the final medium for the finished project?
  Now we'll take a look at each of these considerations.

Allotting Proper Drive Space

Before you begin any project, you'll need to make sure that you have enough drive space to hold all the media that you create (see Figure 2.1). In addition to captured footage, you'll need space for rendered effects. There's nothing worse than being in the throes of postproduction, only to find that you have no more space on your drives. It can happen, and the results are not pretty. However, when it does happen, you have the option of deleting unnecessary files or purchasing, maybe even renting, additional drives for the project.

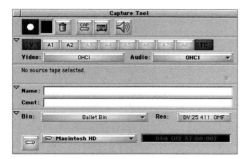

Figure 2.1 Checking for drive space with the Capture tool

Back when Small Computer System Interface (SCSI) drives were the only option for Avids, your only real alternative when running out of space was to rent drives, mostly because SCSI drives were so expensive. In 1993, I purchased 21 gigabytes of storage for a whopping $21,000. Now they're boat anchors. Fortunately, we have FireWire drives today, so drives aren't as costly. Drive space is always a good thing to have around, especially if you work on projects with high shooting ratios, such as documentaries.

Note: What's a shooting ratio? If you aren't familiar with the term, a *shooting ratio* is the amount of footage shot versus how much is actually used, For example, if you shoot 30 hours of footage for a 1-hour program, it is said to have a 30:1 shooting ratio. Because of the cheap cost of DV tapes, many DV documentaries have as much as 50:1 shooting ratios. Some even go as high as 100:1. By contrast, low-budget films shot on 16mm film can run as low as 12:1. Some television programs run less. And those crazy reality TV shows shoot using motion detectors around the clock, so you might find several hundred hours just to see who gets kicked off the island this week.

When using Free DV or Xpress Pro, it's highly recommended that you store media on a separate drive. In other words, do not store your captured media on the system drive where your operating system (OS), applications, and other materials are stored. There are a few good reasons for this.

When you press the Play button on your Free DV/Xpress Pro system, it gives a command to the clip in the database, which finds the media database, which finds the media and tells it to read back at the point where your blue position indicator or play-head is located, which also reads ahead of the media for effects and other precomputes. All this activity, known in the industry as "building the pipes," is pushing the drive to its limits. If you have other software on that same drive, chances are the drive will "time out" and not be able to properly play back your media.

This is especially true with laptops, whose drives are usually slower than desktop internal and external drives. Although you might be able to get away with capturing and playing back a short sequence, it's very likely that the drive will time out when playing back a longer stream. Laptops have drives that run as slow as 4200 revolutions per minute (rpm). By contrast, most external drives run 10,000 rpm. More revolutions per minute means more data played in a minute and less wear on the drive, although it could be argued that the drive is wearing out faster because it spins faster. Keeping your media on a separate external drive also allows you to move the project to another computer if necessary.

If you are using Xpress Pro with the optional Mojo hardware and you capture your media at 1:1 lossless compression, it will be nearly impossible to play back any media from the system drive.

Here is a rule of thumb that is easy to remember when capturing DV resolution: Every five minutes of media takes up about one gigabyte of space. So if you have a hard drive with 80 GB available, you should, in theory, be able to capture 400 minutes of media, or 6 hours 40 minutes.

Here's the Catch-22 on drive space: You could purchase one huge drive and save money, but the caveat is that when the drive fails (and all drives *do* eventually fail), you'll lose a lot more media. So it's wise to purchase just a couple of medium-size drives. Those terabyte drives are really cool for bragging rights, but when they crash, you've lost a lot of footage

In addition to the media that is captured, you'll need more space for rendering, which is the process of creating new media for effects and imported files. Any time an effect is created or a file is imported, it needs to be rendered for final output. This takes up a lot of space on the drive.

One final consideration when figuring drive space is the media database. Inside of every media drive is a file that contains a database for the media on that specific drive. Without this database, your Free DV/Xpress Pro system could not figure out what media is on the drive. This file can be fairly large, depending on how many media objects are stored on that drive. Therefore, it is recommended that you keep about 20 percent of your drives empty for rendering and media databases. Another good reason for purchasing more than one drive is that the media database files are smaller, and the system runs efficiently.

N o t e : If you are using Xpress Pro with Mojo and are using an external FireWire drive, you need to purchase an additional FireWire card for your computer because the Mojo needs the entire internal FireWire bus on your computer to work properly. FireWire cards are generally very inexpensive, from around $20–100 (USD) It is also important to remember that no notebooks work with Mojo, although there is one company that has released a notebook with multiple buses specifically for this purpose.

Logging

When using a nonlinear system, you have the choice of capturing all the media that was lensed for the project or capturing only those you feel are needed. Frankly, it is better to do the latter. By doing so, you made some choices about what is to be included in your project, which forces you to make some decisions about what you will use. More importantly, you'll end up creating fewer media objects. (Media objects are what drive your system to play back media.) Too many media objects can slow the system down.

The Capture tool has a logging option that can be used for this purpose, as shown in Figure 2.2. When you log your tapes, you are selecting only the material that is acceptable for the project. After the media is logged, it can be batch captured to a drive later. This automated function allows for a more precise workflow.

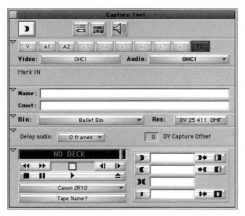

Figure 2.2 The Logging tool on Xpress Pro

It's important to remember that when logging and capturing, you should always give a couple of seconds at the beginning and end of the clip. These "handles" can last for just a few seconds. The reason for including them is that you might have to do a dissolve or an effect that uses the extra media. Better safe than sorry. This was one of my first lessons in nonlinear cutting.

Note: The logging option is available on Xpress Pro only.

Tape-Naming Conventions

Before you capture or log a tape, it is very important that you establish a tape-naming scheme. Creating an edited program is an exciting process, but you have to stay organized. There is nothing worse than an unorganized project. You want to spend your time editing, not looking for a lost tape. For example, if you have field tapes 1–5, you can name them F1, F2, F3, and so on. Studio tapes could be named S1, S2, S3, and so on. The reason for establishing tape names before capture is that these names will be used throughout the edit, and possibly for other outside work—such as 3D effects.

Without a proper tape-naming scheme, you can easily get lost. One of the more powerful features of Free DV and Xpress Pro is the database of information about each clip. That database contains the tape names (see Figure 2.3). Whatever naming scheme you choose, make sure that the name on the label on the tape matches the name you use in the database. This is an editing session, not an "I Love Lucy" skit!

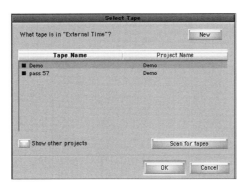

Figure 2.3 The Tape Name dialog box

Choosing a Resolution

If you're using Free DV, you can pretty much skip this section. Free DV has only one resolution, and it is DV 25. But if you are using Xpress Pro, you'll need to choose a resolution before you start digitizing.

Xpress Pro uses several resolutions, as shown in Figure 2.4. If your source is a DV tape, you should use DV 25 OMF if you want full resolution. If you're just cutting an offline version of the project, you can save drive space by selecting 15:1s.

Figure 2.4 Xpress Pro supports DV and other resolutions as well.

With the optional Mojo, you can select DVC Pro resolution (DV 50) or 1:1 resolution. If your source tapes are DVC Pro, selecting the DV 50 resolution will give you lossless quality. If your tapes are another format, such as digital beta, selecting the 1:1 compression will give you lossless quality and no compression.

For film projects that run at 23.976 frames per second (fps), you have a choice between DV 25 quality, or 14:1 and 28:1 for offline resolution. When you use 28:1 compression, the picture quality is substandard at best, but I found that it can work in situations in which drive space is precious. As long as you can detect focus in the picture and you're not planning to screen these images in front of the producer, 28:1 works well enough. However, I highly recommend that you batch digitize your completed pieces at a higher resolution before screening them.

Determining the Final Product

Before you determine which resolution you should use, it might be a good idea to determine the final product that is to be created. For example, if your final product will be original camera negative (OCN) from film, you can use low resolution for the project. For film projects, 14:1 is the de facto standard. If it is to be a DVD, you'll want higher quality. Of course, you can always capture at low resolution and then batch capture your final cut at higher resolution, but time for this will need to be factored into your postproduction schedule.

I like to ask the producer or director about the final product so that it is clear to me how the edit should be approached. In some cases, the director or producer isn't sure what the final product would be. Coaxing them to determine the final product will enable you to establish your settings, select resolutions, and determine the right amount of drive space correctly. Of course, it doesn't always go perfectly as planned, but it least you have an idea about what it will take to get the project done right.

Here's an example of what can go wrong: On a couple of occasions, I worked with a director who had a film that was determined to be cut on video, and the final product was to be video. About halfway through the edit, the director discussed the possibility of finishing the project on the original film. If you set up a project as a video project and do not use the film edge numbers as a reference, there is no way of matching your cut back to the original camera negative (unless, of course, you have window burned with the key numbers on the video). In cases such as these, you would have to write out the edit list by hand. But jogging through two hours of film is not a fun thing to do. The alternative is to reset to a film project (23.976 fps); the edge numbers can then be entered.

On other occasions when the director determined that low resolution was adequate for a cut, I have been asked to "create a DVD" of my work. Because we used low resolution to begin with, the final DVD looks pretty bad. If the director had told me that we were going to create a DVD, I would have captured the media in a higher resolution. In this case, the solution was to batch capture the finished cut at a higher resolution, taking up more drive space and wasting more time to create it.

Using a Deck for Capture

With Xpress Pro and Free DV, there is a variety of different sources that can be used (see Figure 2.5). Even with Free DV, which accepts only FireWire sources, you can add a transcoder, which converts conventional audio and video sources into a FireWire stream. Let's start by discussing some of the connections that you will be using.

Deck Connectors

Although Free DV and Xpress Pro utilize FireWire as their source, you can also use additional sources with other types of connections if you use either the Mojo (with Xpress Pro only) or a transcoder.

FireWire

FireWire, also known as IEEE 1394, is a standard for transporting data. Because it is used on so many cameras and DV decks, it is often confused as being just a DV transport. Although FireWire can transport DV data, it is not limited to doing only one thing. It can send and receive data up to 400 mbps (megabits per second) As a result, you can transport lossless quality video and DV50 using FireWire. It uses two types of connectors (see Figure 2.6): a four-pin connector, which is normally connected to the deck (this is also connected to the DV out port of the optional Mojo for Xpress Pro) and a six-pin connector, which is connected to your computer.

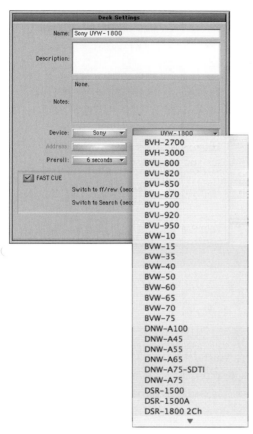

Figure 2.5 Picking a deck for capture

Figure 2.6 FireWire four-pin (left) and
six-pin (right) connectors

When using FireWire with Xpress Pro and Free DV, you can also control the source deck. In other words, FireWire not only sends the video data but also can convey information to the deck to play, fast-forward, rewind, and so on. Using FireWire to control your source deck makes it more convenient. However, there are limitations with some decks. For example, some decks convey timecode information that is one frame late. So although your video is captured, the timecode information that goes with it might be off, even as much as three frames.

Fortunately, there is a way to correct this error after the source is captured, as you will see later. You can even use a FireWire-enabled camera as a source deck when capturing.

Note: The Avid website has a complete list of "qualified" decks that can be used with Free DV and Xpress Pro. Although Avid tries to keep up with every current DV deck and DV camera that is manufactured, in some cases they might not yet be qualified. For these decks and cameras, you can select Generic Deck in the Capture tool and usually get some functionality.

RS-422

RS-422 is an older serial protocol that was created to control professional video decks. Using RS-422 allows you to control a deck and read timecode. It does not, however, transport any video data.

    If you are using a deck that has an RS-422 connection (see Figure 2.7) but not FireWire, you can connect it to your computer to control the deck. The video and audio data must be sent through a transcoder.

Figure 2.7 RS-422 connector

    RS-422 is a nine-pin connector. Although your deck uses RS-422, there is no such connector on your computer. There is a nine-pin connector on most PCs that uses the RS-232C protocol. To connect your deck to this computer connector, you need a converter, such as Addenda's Rosetta Stone. The converter takes RS-422 information and translates it to RS-232C; the information conversion flows both ways so that your deck can talk to the computer, and vice versa.

    For RS-422 connection to a Mac, you'll need either a Keyspan adapter (shown in Figure 2.8) or a Gee Three Stealth card. These tools convert RS-422 into serial language that the Mac understands.

Figure 2.8 A Keyspan adapter converts RS-422 into Mac serial.

When using RS-422 with non-FireWire decks, you need a transcoder to convert video and audio data into a FireWire signal that can be connected directly to your computer or the optional Mojo.

Transcoders vary greatly in terms of connection and quality. They range in price from as little as $295 to thousands of dollars, depending on the quality of the video signal and the manufacturer. Some transcoders can be purchased at a local computer store. Others must be purchased through a professional video products distributor.

Video Connectors

If you are going straight FireWire from your deck to a Free DV or Xpress Pro, you don't need to learn about the different types of connectors. It is a good idea to review this material, however, because you might find yourself using a different format deck from time to time.

There are three types of video connectors that can be used with transcoders and Mojo. The first is a BNC connector. When attaching a BNC connector to Mojo, you'll need an adapter from BNC to RCA, which is the second kind of video connector. A third type of connection, S-Video, will be discussed later in the chapter.

BNC CONNECTORS

BNC connectors come in different types. It is important that you use the correct type of BNC connector when connecting to your video deck. For example, a thin Ethernet connector (RG58A/U or RG58C/U; see Figure 2.9) is not recommended for use with professional video equipment, but it looks very much like a 75 ohm video BNC connector. The reason is that the center conductor of this connector (which looks almost exactly like a video BNC connector) is too thin. When you use these kinds of connectors, you lose fidelity of the video signal. Even worse, if you combine thin Ethernet and video BNCs, the signal can flutter and the quality of the video will suffer greatly.

Figure 2.9 Video BNC vs. thin Ethernet BNC

RCA OR PHONO CONNECTORS

The other type of video connector is called an RCA or phono connector, as shown in Figure 2.10. These are much more common and can be purchased in department stores. These types of connectors are considered unprofessional to some, yet they work just fine on transcoders and Mojo. The only objection that I have to these connectors is that they do not have a locking bayonet mount, as BNCs do.

Figure 2.10 RCA/phono

RCA connectors can also be used for audio. There are no strict conventions on which types of RCA/Phono cables to buy, but I would recommend purchasing thicker, more durable cables with solid connectors. Some manufacturers use "gold" cables, which they insist produce a better signal. I have not seen any difference in signal reproduction between these and the regular metal connectors.

Audio Connectors

There are three major types of audio connectors that can be used with decks. Additionally, these connectors come in two different forms: unbalanced and balanced.

UNBALANCED CONNECTORS

RCA/phono and $^1/_4''$ phono connectors (see Figure 2.11) are the two types of unbalanced connectors. They are called unbalanced because they have only two lines to transmit the audio signal: an earth line that grounds the signal, and a hot line that carries the signal.

Figure 2.11 A $^1/_4''$ phono connector

With $^1/_4''$ phono connectors, there is one additional difference. Connectors with one ring carry a single mono audio signal. Connectors with two rings carry stereo signals. Unless you have some need for running two signals through a single line, always use mono connectors. Not all $^1/_4''$ phono connectors are unbalanced; some tip rig sleeve connections can also carry balanced mono audio.

RCA phono connectors are common on consumer electronics and some prosumer decks as well as cameras. The signal comes in a bit low at –10 dBu, so you'll want to adjust audio input levels on your Free DV or Xpress system when using these connectors. If you have the optional Mojo, the signal is optimized.

BALANCED CONNECTORS

The three-pin XLR connector (shown in Figure 2.12) is an example of a balanced connection. It carries three different signals (thus the three pins on the connector). These three signals are shield (also called ground), hot, and cold. The cold signal is the same as the hot signal, but it is turned upside down, or phase inverted. That's probably a lot more information than you need right now. Suffice it to say that a balanced connection offers superior audio fidelity. Three-pin XLR connectors are common on professional audio equipment.

Figure 2.12 A three-pin XLR connector

Some transcoders offer balanced audio connections. The Mojo, however, does not (see Figure 2.13). Adapting a balanced signal to an unbalanced one can be hazardous at best. In some cases, the audio signal can cancel itself out completely. In other cases, you might notice some loss of the signal at certain frequencies. If this happens, you'll need to get a transformer so that the signal can properly conform from balanced to unbalanced.

Figure 2.13 Connectors on the optional Mojo

I've used adapters from balanced to unbalanced signals quite a few times without need of a transformer, and although there is an occasional drop in levels, I rarely have had the signal cancel out. Your results may vary.

Selecting the Best Quality Video

Before you begin the process of capturing, you'll want to determine the best quality video to send to your system. Many decks and cameras offer a variety of video output, including FireWire, S-Video component, and composite video (see Figure 2.14).

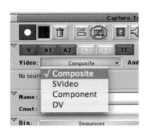

Figure 2.14 Selecting video quality

FireWire If your deck is FireWire-capable, use FireWire. It keeps the signal in the digital domain with minimal loss. However, it is important to note that although the signal is digital, rendering of effects will cause some additional loss of signal, so your effects might not look as good as the original source.

Component Professional component video consists of three separate connections, all normally with BNC connectors: R-Y, B-Y, and Y. These three separate color components produce a superior analog signal.

Component video works much like the old Technicolor three-strip film process. By separating the signal into three different color-sensitive elements, the image is far better than a single video signal. Although this is a very good signal, FireWire is better, only because it is a lossless digital signal direct from its source. Component video uses an electrical analog signal and therefore deteriorates a little with each transfer.

S-Video An S-Video connection (also called Y/C;) separates the brightness and color signals. The S-Video signal uses a special connector, shown in Figure 2.15. Although it is not the best quality, S-Video is superior to a single video signal, also known as composite video.

Figure 2.15 An S-Video connector

Composite Video Composite video uses a single RCA/phono or BNC cable as a carrier of the video signal. This signal is a combination of the entire image, thus it lacks the fidelity of the other signals.

Note: Although the Mojo appears to offer only FireWire, S-Video, and Composite video input, you can also use professional component video signals by purchasing Avid's component cable. The cable plugs into Mojo's S-Video and Composite video connectors and accepts a component signal. It's well worth the dollars for a much better signal.

The Capture Tool: Capture Controls

There are significant differences between the Capture tool used in Xpress Pro and the one used in Free DV. Because Free DV is a "free" application, some of the more-advanced capabilities of capturing are not present. For example, I earlier mentioned that Free DV has no logging capabilities. Logging isn't one of the most important aspects of capturing, nor is it entirely necessary for any project. Therefore, the folks at Avid left it out of Free DV, primarily to entice you to purchase Xpress Pro. But don't feel robbed! The features on Free DV are robust enough to work around all these shortcomings.

Note: Free DV also does not have the ability to batch capture. Which brings me to a point: There are a lot of features that are grayed-out in Free DV. This is especially annoying because you see all the features that Xpress Pro has. I suppose it's a good selling ploy, but that doesn't make it any easier to stomach.

Generally speaking, capture and output are the two things that video editors do not do well, probably because they are done so little when compared with the amount of time spent on editing. In some cases, an assistant editor does all of the capturing and output, which makes these processes even more mysterious to the editor.

Nonetheless, capturing footage is the most important process. If anything goes wrong at this phase, it can pretty much atrophy from here. Incorrect tape naming, timecode numbers, and other vital information can be lost.

Before starting the computer, make sure that all the peripherals are connected and powered up. By *peripherals*, I mean the videotape deck, speakers, monitors, and anything else that is connected to the computer. If the deck is not connected, Free DV/Xpress Pro will not "see" it when you open the Capture tool. Other operational problems might occur as well. So make sure that everything is running first.

Now you can start up your computer. If this is the first time you are using Free DV or Xpress Pro, some drivers may load automatically, particularly if you are using a Windows PC. Windows XP has some internal drivers to load, as well as the ones used with Free DV/ Xpress Pro.

If you are using Free DV, you'll see a screen that invites you to explore the advanced functions of Xpress Pro. If you're using Xpress Pro, this screen does not appear. Select Later for now. After the screen clears, you will see a Project screen in a dark gray window (see Figure 2.16); this is where your project is either created or selected.

Figure 2.16 The Project screen

Assuming that you have not previously created a project, the project selection screen should be blank. From here, we will create a new project. There are three types to choose from:

Private Project A project that appears only when you are logged into the computer.

Shared Project A project that is shared among the users of your computer.

External Project A project that comes from an external source.

First, click the New Project button. A small menu appears, in which we name our project and select the format. If you're using regular NTSC standard video, select 30i. If you're using PAL video, select 25i.

NTSC video is standard definition video for use in North America and other regions of the world. PAL video is used in Europe, Asia, and some parts of South America. Just keep in mind that the two cannot work together. If you recorded your footage using NTSC, a PAL project cannot accept it; if you recorded it on PAL video, it cannot be used in an NTSC project.

For now, name the new project "Capture Practice." After you name it, click OK; the menu will return you to the previous Project Selection menu. From here, click and highlight the Capture Practice item in the Projects listing and click OK. Your new project will open, and the interface will appear.

To access the Capture tool, choose Tools > Capture Tool from the main menu. Now let's take a look at the Capture tool and its functions.

At the top of the Capture tool, you see a row of icons, as shown in Figure 2.17. These buttons actually control the capture of your footage. Let's take a closer look at what each one does.

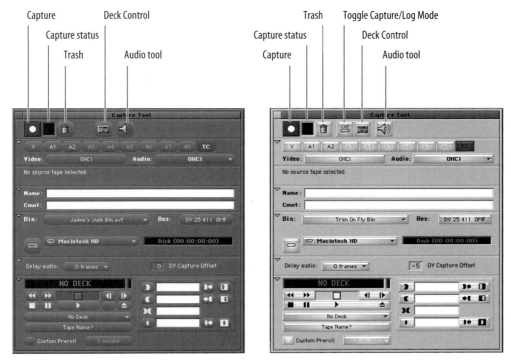

Figure 2.17 Left: the Free DV Capture tool; right, the Xpress Pro Capture tool

The Capture Button

The red button with a little white dot ⬤ is the Capture button. Click it once to begin capturing and click it again to stop. The black box to the right of the Capture button is the recording indicator. When you tell Xpress Pro or Free DV to capture, it flashes red, until you instruct your system to stop capturing.

The Trash Can Button

Clicking the trash can button gives Free DV 🗑 or Xpress Pro 🗑 an "abort mission" command. The capture process ceases and any media created during that capture is toast. Be careful when clicking this button: After you click it, there's no way to get your media back from the last capture.

There are some built-in safeguards, however. When you click the Trash Can button, it will still ask if you want to keep or discard the media that you captured. The reason for this kind of safeguard is that Avid created editing systems for the computer-challenged editor. These days, most editors know their way around a computer. Even so, the functionality of Avid systems extends across a very wide range of users. As a result, the "keep or discard" message stayed. And besides, if you're capturing at two in the morning, chances are good that you will accidentally click the mouse in the wrong place from time to time.

 Note: Sorry, users can't change this behavior to suppress the warning.

The Capture/Log Mode Button (Xpress Only)

Directly to the right of our Trash Can button is the Capture/Log button . When the button reads "Cap," we are in Capture mode; when the button reads "Log," we are in Logging mode .

When you switch to Logging mode, the Capture tool changes somewhat—it shrinks in height by a little, and the drive assignment indicators disappear. No more Capture button, flashing record light, or Trash Can. The system has switched from Capture mode to Logging mode. This is also indicated by a pencil icon in the Record button.

These changes occur because when logging, there is no need to assign a media drive, because no media are being captured. When we log from video tapes, we are only "writing" information about the clip, its timecode and tape name. When you log a tape, you're only creating clips.

The Logging Buttons (Xpress Only)

When you click the Capture/Log button, your capture interface changes (see Figure 2.18). The red Capture button is replaced by a button with a strange, cryptic icon: the Mark In button . If you're new to Avid systems, it might seem a little odd-looking. The Mark Out button shows the reverse of this icon. The way I remember these icons is that Mark In faces Mark Out; thus, the clip itself could be said to be between them. Another way to remember is that they resemble the shape of two faces looking at each other. Pretend that the clip is between them; thus, the Mark In button faces the beginning of the clip, and the Mark Out button faces the end of the clip. Too metaphysical for you? Okay, let's move on.

When you play back a tape, you can click the Mark In button to mark an in point on the fly as the tape is running. After this button is pressed, an in point appears in the register down below, and the icon on the button changes to a Mark Out button with a pencil next to it . Clicking the button again marks an out point on the fly and logs the clip. When this is done, the clip appears in a bin. We'll discuss bins a little later.

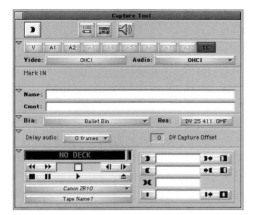

Figure 2.18 The Xpress Pro logging interface

If you don't want to mark clips on the fly, you can type in a timecode number by using the timecode registers at the bottom of the Capture tool.

The Deck Button

When the Capture/Log button is clicked again, you return to the original Capture mode, where you started. Let's continue our journey by looking at the Deck button. Clicking this button determines whether our deck will be controlled remotely through Free DV [image] or Xpress Pro [image] ; or—if it has no type of remote-control capability— whether the deck will be operated manually. An example of a manually controlled deck is VHS. Most VHS decks, including some that are used professionally, have no RS-422 or FireWire connections. As a result, Free DV and Xpress Pro cannot control them directly. Other sources that might not be controlled by FreeDV/Xpress Pro include CD players, satellite feeds, microphones, DVD players, direct sources such as studio and animation, and motion-capture cameras.

The problem is that when you have no remote control over a source, you cannot record timecode information on your clips that can be traced back to that source. In other words, if you want to recapture the material that you are using at a higher reso- lution or for any other reason, there is no way to refer to it on the source tape—other than perhaps visually. Without reference, there is no way to match the original source on the tape.

Further complications can occur when media are accidentally deleted. If you lose a media file from an unreferenced source, you'll have to find the original clip on video- tape all over again and cut it back into your sequence. How can you do this? If you named the clip or described it well in your bin, you might be able to figure out which picture was there originally. If you have a good knowledge of your source material, you might be able to figure out which parts are missing. But the precise frames will be lost because they contain no timecode reference from the original source.

There are ways of getting around this problem. I recommend copying the source material onto a videotape format that *can* be controlled by Free DV/Xpress Pro so that you have some kind of timecoded reference in the event of accidental deletion or the need to capture at a higher resolution. By doing this, some minimal quality of the source might be lost, but that is far better than having to find the original source without any timecode numbers to reference.

When you click the Deck tool button, its icon changes to the same icon with a red circle and a slash through it . This is, of course, the international symbol for "No!" When it is selected, it indicates to both you and your system that the deck has no remote control.

The interface changes somewhat when you select no remote control. All the deck control buttons—fast-forward, play, rewind, and so on—disappear from the bottom left of the Capture tool. They are not needed because Free DV/Xpress Pro cannot control the deck, anyway. All deck controls have to be done manually by jockeying the source deck rather than the Free DV/Xpress Pro interface.

When you click the deck button to indicate no remote control, you lose many of the advanced functions of digitization and also some very basic functions that you might need. Forewarned is forearmed! (Or something like that.) It is better to transfer your raw media to a remote-controlled deck and/or format. Here are the consequences:

- You cannot log any footage because the deck cannot batch capture it. (Logging and batch capture can be done only on Xpress Pro.)

- You cannot edit in low resolution and then re-create your sequence in high resolution, because the deck cannot batch capture. (Again, batch capture is Xpress Pro only.)

- Without a remote-control connection to the deck, any timecode numbers will be insignificant because the deck has no control that would give your FreeDV/Xpress Pro a timecode signal.

- In short, when you turn deck control off, this is good for capturing at final resolution with no need of reference numbers. It can work for short projects, but having no deck control is nearly impossible for long format projects with multiple changes.

Of course, there is an exception to every rule. Feel free to send me an e-mail about it.

Waveform and Vectorscope Tool (Mojo Only)

If you have an Xpress Pro with Mojo, you're in luck. The Capture interface now includes Waveform and Vectorscope tools (see Figure 2.19). If you do not have the optional Mojo, you might still read along. Waveforms and Vectorscopes are important tools to understand.

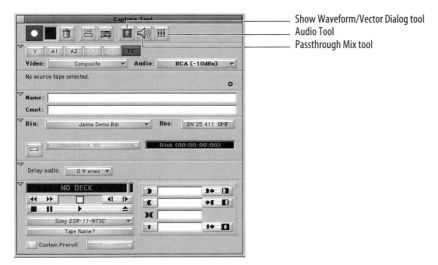

Figure 2.19 The Capture tool in Xpress Pro with Mojo

When you click the small Vectorscope icon 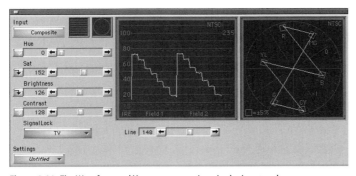 in the Capture tool, the Input tool opens. There you will find two more icons. The first is a Waveform icon; when you click it, a full-size Waveform monitor appears. The second is a Vectorscope icon; when you click it, a full size Vectorscope monitor appears next to the Waveform monitor (Figure 2.20).

Figure 2.20 The Waveform and Vectorscope monitors in the Input tool

The left side of the window is where you make adjustments. There are four video sources to choose from. Note their order as they start with the lowest quality and proceed to the best quality:

- Composite
- S-Video
- Component
- DV

We already discussed the merits of each of these, so let's move on to the Waveform and Vectorscope tools. Now that you've set up the tools, what do they do? Waveform tools are made to measure a lot of things, but here we are using them to measure the brightness and darkness of the picture. The Vectorscope tool contains many vectors, hence its name. Notice that each vector on the scope has some abbreviated notation. The abbreviations are as follows, starting at the top of the scope and moving clockwise:

R	Red
MG	Magenta
B	Blue
CY	Cyan
G	Green
YL	Yellow

Did you notice any pattern to the order of these colors? If you've studied a color wheel, you know that each color represented on the scope is 180 degrees opposite its complementary color. The six colors consist of the three "primary" on-screen colors (RGB: red, blue, and green) and their complements (cyan, yellow, and magenta).

The purpose of the Vectorscope is to make sure that these colors, when reproduced from a tape source, appear correctly in each corresponding vector box. The problem is that there are very few pictures with full representation of each color. We do have one such source, however: SMPTE color bars (NTSC) or EBU color bars (PAL). Color bars are a test signal for measuring color (chrominance) and brightness (luminance) as well as black levels in a picture.

Using Waveform and Vectorscope Monitors

Every recorded tape should begin with color bars. Okay, I didn't just graduate from tech school here; lots of field tapes are recorded without color bars. That still doesn't make it right! But if you have color bars on your tape, this is a good way of setting up the tape so that levels can be properly set when digitizing. If there are no test signals on your tapes, you can still set up the picture in pretty good fashion without them.

Now let's take a look at the Waveform monitor. As I mentioned before, the Waveform monitor will address the brightness and blackness of the picture. We begin by adjusting the black levels of the picture.

Have you ever watched television in the dark? You may have noticed that a black picture isn't really black; it's sort of a muddied dark gray. In a standard video signal, it represents black. But the signal itself is running at about 7.5 percent brightness. The first adjustment to make on your test signal is to adjust it so that the signal on the Waveform is at 7.5. We do this by adjusting the contrast slider on the Input tool. This control is a little weird. If you move the slider to the left, the black level goes up. Moving it to the right makes the signal go down. What's up with that? The contrast is actually controlling the midtones of the picture, so when you adjust the levels downward, the picture reveals less contrast, making it brighter.

Keep in mind that the first adjustment should be the contrast because the adjustment of contrast affects the brightness and saturation of the picture as well. Adjusting contrast first prevents you from chasing your tail and making brightness and saturation adjustments all over again.

The second adjustment on the Waveform is brightness. With a test signal, the brightness should not exceed 100 percent. However, if you have no test pattern and some objects are as "hot" as 110 percent, it's okay. Anything beyond 110 percent will give you a blown-out or clipped look, in which images exceed normal brightness levels, and the video has a sort of feedback effect. This might look stylish for some footage, but if that's not your intention here, keep it at 110 percent.

We'll continue with the Vectorscope. When a test signal (such as SMPTE or EBU color bars) is used, each color should show up correctly in the vector that corresponds with it. If the vectors are off to the right or left of the boxes, you need to adjust the hue setting on the Vectorscope. (Note: NTSC only: Hue adjustment is not available in PAL.) If the signal doesn't quite reach each vector in intensity (or if it is too intense and beyond the vector), you need to adjust the saturation (SAT) of the picture. If your camera source seems to be flat in color, there is a temptation to increase the intensity of saturation and "Disneyize" the picture (the color becomes vivid, like a full-blown Disney animated feature). But unlike film color, turning up the intensity of color using video can create a lot of noise in the picture. You can use Avid's color correction and color effect tools to do this more efficiently than just blowing out your saturation when capturing.

Audio Settings

Before we look at the Audio tool, we need to establish some of the characteristics of the audio coming into Free DV/Xpress Pro. To do this, look at the Project window, which has several tabs. With a click, you can analyze the Bins, Settings, Effects, and Info of your project. Click the Settings tab, and a list of adjustable settings appears in the Audio Project Settings window. Xpress Pro has more settings available than Free DV, but everything we need for this adjustment is on both systems. Take a look at the list of settings and click Audio Project. A menu appears with all the adjustments that we can make to the audio settings that pertain to the current project only.

Audio Project Settings

The first order of business is to establish a sample rate for our media (see Figure 2.21). The sample rate for DV video is normally 48 kHz. I mention that it is "normally" this rate because if you use all four audio tracks when you shoot DV, the sample rate goes down. Only two audio tracks are usually used when shooting DV. If you use four tracks, the sample rate is actually 32 kHz.

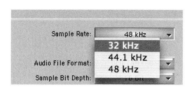

Figure 2.21 Choosing the sample rate

At the top right of the Audio Project Settings menu is the Sample Rate data. You can choose from among three settings: 32 kHz, 44.1 kHz, and 48 kHz. The higher the sample rate, the better the audio quality. It is important to note that there is only marginal difference between 44.1 kHz and 48 kHz. The default sample rate for Free DV/Xpress Pro is 48 kHz. The higher the sample rate, the more disk space is required, but audio does not take up a significant amount of drive space, anyway.

Compact disc audio recordings normally sample at 44.1 kHz. When importing audio or capturing from compact disc, you might need to upsample or downsample accordingly to make that recording properly fit the audio sample rate for your project. 48 kHz is the sample rate for many digital video- and audiotape formats, including DigiBeta. DAT can record and play back both sample rates from most players, but the typical DAT sample rate is also 48 kHz.

Note: A lot of consumer DV cameras have the audio setting at 32 kHz. Consult your owner's guide and change this setting to 48 kHz for optimum quality.

So which sampling rate is best for your project? If you used four audio tracks when recording to DV, the primary sampling rate is 32 kHz. If most or all of your material is 32 kHz, you might consider leaving it that way rather than upsampling to 48 kHz. However, if you are going to output to several different formats—CD, DVD, and so forth—it might be simpler to upsample everything to 48 kHz when you are finished editing the project so that the audio sounds the same on all formats. I tend to upsample everything to 48 kHz because it is the best sampling rate available. At the same time, upsampling does little to improve sound quality. It merely puts your audio in the same envelope as other 48 kHz audio.

Now we need to establish a rule about how Free DV/Xpress Pro will play back varying sample rates from different media. If you use audio from a variety of tape and disc formats, it's a good idea to select Convert Sample Rates When Playing and set it to Always. This setting will perform a sample rate conversion on the fly when playing back mismatched samples. Although this solution will work when playing back media, you will have to convert all of your audio to a single sample rate when outputting your final edit. If you choose not to convert sample rates while playing, the audio that does not match the Audio Project sample rate plays back as silence.

If you're using different sample rates, Free DV and Xpress Pro do not allow you to output until the rates are all converted to one standard (see Figure 2.22).

Figure 2.22 Selecting a sample rate

Setting Audio Input Levels

If you are using Free DV or Xpress without the Mojo, you can adjust your audio input levels, as shown in Figure 2.23. Normally, the audio input is set to a unity level. A unity level is a level that is optimized for best sound reproduction. But you might find yourself with some media that are recorded with very low audio or, in some cases, audio that is too hot. Audio that is too loud can be a problem. If the recording was made with a DV camera, and the audio level goes over the 0 dB level, it will be distorted, no matter what you do. For any digital recording, 0 dB is the point of no return—the edge of the universe. Whatever you want to call it, 0 dB is the point at which audio stops being audio and becomes noise. Always avoid this level if possible.

Figure 2.23 Adjusting audio levels

Note: Another caveat when capturing audio is this: Don't try to ride the levels. You can adjust them in a much more precise way when editing your project by using the Audio Mix (Free DV and Xpress Pro) and Automation Gain tools (Xpress Pro only).

To adjust input levels, select the Input tab on your Audio Project Settings window. A slider appears. Note that the slider is set to a unity level: +0. With the audio meters on your Capture tool open, you can adjust the audio on your source to an optimum level.

When monitoring audio input on the Audio tool, you should note that the right side of the meter is analog VU (volume units) and the left side is digital. In the digital domain, 0 dB is the optimum level, as we discussed. In the analog domain, the audio can go beyond zero level to as high as +14 dB. This extra space in the analog domain is what is referred to as *headroom*. Anything beyond the headroom level becomes distorted, much like 0 dB in the digital domain.

If you have Mojo connected to your system, you will not be able to adjust the audio levels. This is because Mojo will keep any incoming audio in the digital domain and "clone" it, reproducing the exact audio recorded and played back from the tape source. If this is a problem, you will need to use a deck where audio output levels can be adjusted. Normally with digital audio, the rule of thumb is WYSIWYG (what you see is what you get)—or perhaps more appropriately WYHIWYG (what you hear is what you get).

The Audio Passthrough Mix Tool (Mojo Only)

When you capture audio, you usually want the levels to be optimum. And it's always a good idea to monitor it when you capture, as opposed to going out of the room and grabbing a cup of coffee or chatting with your colleagues. When monitoring the audio, you might want to hear how it will sound when mixed.

For example, let's say you have a studio tape in which the announcer is on channel 1 and a rough music mix is on channel 2. You want to capture both at solid levels, so that you can adjust the music later, but when monitoring it, you want to be able to pull the music down to hear what it would sound like when mixed.

For these purposes, the Audio Passthrough Mix tool (shown in Figure 2.24) was developed.

On the Capture tool, select the button with sliders on it ▦ . (If you have Xpress without Mojo or Free DV, this button does not exist on the Capture interface.) This is your Audio Passthrough Mix tool. Using this tool allows you to choose between a direct mix to channels 1 and 2 or a stereo pair. You can adjust the levels of sound appropriately for monitoring or pan them any way you want. You can gang channels of audio together and adjust them as a group. But nothing you do affects capturing the media; using this tool, you can listen to the source any way you want.

Figure 2.24 Audio Passthrough Mix tool

Choosing Recording Tracks

The Capture tool will capture only the media that is selected on the track selection section of the Capture tool. Free DV/Xpress will automatically activate the tracks that were selected in the previous capture session. Before capturing, you should play back your recorded media and determine which tracks need to be captured. For example, if you find that there is no audio on track 2 of a tape, there is no need to capture it. If you decide to capture it anyway, valuable drive space will be used.

However, there might be times when one channel of audio was not used for a period of time, which is why there are production assistants and tape logs. If the project was too low-budget and a production assistant wasn't used or a tape log wasn't created, ask the director which tracks were used.

Xpress Pro and Free DV will capture two audio tracks, video, and timecode information. But when you look at the Capture screen, it looks as if you can capture eight tracks. This is an artifact from higher-end Avid software. To select or deselect tracks, click the corresponding buttons in the track selection portion of the Capture tool. The buttons toggle on and off. When they are colored, they are on; when gray, they are off. If you try to select tracks without a deck hooked up to your system, Xpress Pro or Free DV will tell you that no signal is present. Make sure you connect the deck before running the software.

Choosing Video and Audio Input Formats

After you select tracks, you need to determine what source they are coming from. Below the row of track buttons is a selection of source resolutions, labeled Video and Audio.

If you don't have the optional Mojo, your video resolution will default to OHCI. However, if you are using a transcoder or Mojo, your source can originate from any videotape format available. Transcoders allow you to go from any video source to FireWire or OHCI video. The type of connectors used with transcoders can vary from simple RCA inputs to component BNCs.

You can also use a variety of audio sources, depending upon whether you have a Mojo connected to your system. For those who do not have Mojo, the inputs are OHCI (default), MIDI, CD Audio, Line In, and Mic In (see Figure 2.25). This also depends on your computer configuration. Again, if you have a transcoder, you can originate from any audio source—a VHS deck, a professional DigiBeta deck, even a live microphone—to OHCI format.

Figure 2.25 Connectors on the optional Mojo

For those with Mojo, the audio inputs are RCA (–10 dBu) and OHCI (see Figure 2.26). Because the Mojo takes over your system, the other inputs mentioned previously—Midi, CD Audio, Line In, and Mic In—are not available. When these are needed, you can disconnect the Mojo (shutting down the computer first) and restart Xpress Pro.

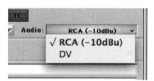

Figure 2.26 Selecting audio type with Mojo

So how do you address the issues of line level input going to RCA and RCA input going in at –10 dB? There are a couple of options to help. One is to adjust the signal of the source so that it reaches an optimum level as it passes through the Mojo. The other is to adjust your Audio Project Settings Input tab from 0 dB to +6 dB, or whatever appears to be the optimal input on your audio meters.

Naming and Commenting Clips

Somewhere along the line, you'll want to name each clip. It's better for organizational purposes to do it during digitizing and to get it right the first time. Like tape naming, the sooner you get the correct information in, the easier editing will be. The Clip Name entry box allows you to do this before or during the capture of each clip (see Figure 2.27).

If you want to add information during capture, click in the Name box and start typing. To switch from the Name entry to the Comments entry, use the Tab button on your keyboard. Any comments entered after tabbing will appear in the Comments column of your bin.

Figure 2.27 Entering clip names and comments

Note: You might think that your next project is too simple or basic to require any thorough project management. However, even though I don't know the specifics of your project, I can assure you that project management is *always* needed. For example, if you're editing together a wedding video, you might decide, "Well, it is only one camera and it's just a wedding ceremony." Then you discover that there are five hours of footage, including multiple shots of relatives, the cake, the cutting of the cake, the after-wedding dance, and so on. Even those projects that seem simple need organization.

It's a good idea to do some postproduction planning before naming clips and bins. The same conventions that apply to bin naming apply here. Come up with a method and stick with it. For example, films use Scene/Take, thus a clip named 15/11 is Scene 15, Take 11.

Video organization can be a little more tricky. On video projects, I name clips by whatever the slate reads. If there is no slate, I paraphrase the dialogue as the clip name. If there is no dialogue, I look for the primary subject in the clip or try to find the name of the element in the script or production assistant notes.

The Message Bar

Just below the input buttons is a mostly blank area used to update you with the status of the Capture tool. The message bar will tell you what mode you're in (Capture versus Logging, for example), whether you are batch capturing, currently recording, and so forth. Having some means of communication with the Capture tool is important, especially when you're new to the system. The message bar can reassure you that the system is doing what you intended.

One sure way to organize is by tape and then by subject. When you capture media, put the clips from each tape into individual bins (i.e., all the clips from Tape 1 go into a bin together). Later, organize them by subject. For example, if Tape 1 has an interview and some B-roll footage, make copies of the clips (you can do this by Alt/Opt click and drag) and drag them into subject bins (such as Interview and B-roll.) Usually your director will want to see either the clips from the tape (which you can cut together into one long sequence) or a particular subject, which can also be strung together quickly.

Setting Up Your Target Bin

In the next area of the Capture tool, you tell the program where your output is going and what characteristics it should have.

Choosing the Target Bin

Any bin that is open can be selected as the target bin for captured clips. If you want to capture to a bin that is not open, simply open it (double-click the name on the Bin tab of the Project window), and it will appear in the list of open bins in the Target Bin pop-up menu on the Capture tool.

Selecting Media Resolution

With Free DV, your only choice for Media Resolution is DV-25, described as follows. Xpress Pro has up to four different media resolutions:

1:1 (Uncompressed) Resolution This is available only with the optional Mojo. You can capture 1:1 uncompressed resolution using various methods: Composite video, S-Video (Y/C), or Component, with the optional component cable.

The optional component cable uses the signal paths from S-Video and Composite inputs for the three required separate signals for R–Y, B–Y, and Y components. As a result, you can input a far superior picture through the Mojo and gain uncompressed resolution.

So which method of capture should you use? Start with Component. If the deck doesn't offer Component output (or if you don't own the optional component cable), try S-Video (Y/C). If the deck doesn't have that kind of output, you're stuck with Composite.

DV-25 (4:1:1) or DV-25 4:2:0 (PAL Only) This compression uses standard DV codecs. DV video is compressed 5:1 in its native form. No additional compression is added when coming from a DV-25 source directly through FireWire. You can also use DV-25 as a compression scheme on any input source, including sources that originate as analog signals coming in through Mojo or a transcoder.

DV-50 This compression uses DVC Pro (DV-50) codecs. DV-50 provides twice the information of the standard DV codec and is used on DVCPRO-50 machines.

15:1s Compression Although the ratio for this compression sounds bad, it isn't. 15:1s compression is a great offline resolution and usually is clear enough to detect fine focus. Thus, it can be used for any offline cutting. It is especially great because it uses far less drive space than DV-25 or 1:1 does. For those used to higher-end Avids, 15:1s gives almost twice the space as 20:1. 15:1s shines when it comes to cutting documentaries, especially DV-based documentaries in which the shooting ratios can be extremely high. The only problem is that the DV Scene extraction feature doesn't work at this compression, which is really handy for a documentary. Although one might figure that the compression ratio runs at about one-third the storage of DV-25, 15: 1s doesn't use the same compression scheme. The "s" in 15:1s stands for "single field," meaning that only the first field of the video frame is captured. As a result, the storage is closer to one-eighth that of DV-25. So for a 100 GB disk, which can store as much as 9.5 hours of DV-25 footage, one could get as much as 75 hours or more at 15:1s.

You can choose your Capture resolutions directly in the Capture tool or select them under Settings > Media Creation Dialog Box.

Selecting Target Drives

The Capture tool will display the available drives on your system that can be used for storing media. To see what media drives are available or to switch between them, click the drive name in the Bin section of the Capture tool (see Figure 2.28). (If you have only one drive for capturing, you need not use this selector.) The drive with the most storage space available is in bold type.

Figure 2.28 Selecting a drive

To the right of the Drive Selection tool is a time register, which gives an estimate of how much time is left for digitizing at the chosen resolution using the chosen tracks on a specific drive. Alt-clicking/Opt-clicking the Single/Dual Drive icon at the left (it looks like this in FDV ⬚ and like this in Xpress Pro ⬚) will allow you to see the total time left for a chosen drive at the selected resolution.

Please note that the time-remaining estimate is always slightly conservative. As you capture materials, it's important to remember that there will always be a need for space on the drives for your media database information. Media database information is contained in two files on each drive that catalog all the media in the folder. Be sure not to overfill your drives, because the media databases will continually need to rebuild as you edit

Which drive(s) should you select for capturing media? If you have a set of striped or RAID drives, you can choose it. If you have a spare drive for media, choose that one. It's not a particularly good idea to choose your system drive, but if you're on a laptop and it's all you have, try using it. Most system drives are too slow for capture at high resolution. If the selection is grayed-out, there's a Drive Filtering Setting that needs to be changed. Here's how to do it: Go to your Settings tab in the Project window and select Media Creation, or optionally press Ctrl+5/⌘+5. The Media Creation box appears. Deselect Drive Filtering Based Upon Resolution. This will allow all available drives (except the operating system and launch drive) to be selected. If you want your system drive to be available, deselect these drives as well. When you return to the Capture tool and click the drive selection button, the drive names will appear in black, indicating that they can be selected.

Digitizing Tracks to Separate Drives

On the left side of the Drive Selection register is a single drive icon (or). Click it, and two drive icons appear. Cool, huh? The two icons represent the capability to place video and audio on separate drives, assuming that you actually have more than one drive.

There are number of reasons to split the video and audio capture to separate drives. For example, if the video files need to go out for special effects processing, or if the audio files are needed for mixing or creating a premix of your sequence, it makes the file organization easier if you use separate drives. If you have two drives, and one is running at a slower rpm or cannot cache data as quickly as the other, digitize the audio files to the slower drive and the video to the faster one. Audio files are smaller and can be processed using lower drive speeds, but video—particularly at lossless resolutions—is more demanding for speed and data rates. Splitting audio and video can also help throughput and prevent dropped frames or underrun errors.

DV Capture Offset

Although FireWire is a fairly reliable protocol for capturing, you might encounter some unexpected turbulence. For example, when processing pictures with any type of device through FireWire protocol, there is a chance that audio can precede video when going into your Avid. This usually occurs when using a transcoder while capturing from a non-DV source through FireWire. As the images go through processing to convert to a FireWire signal in the transcoder, the resulting picture and sound arrive through FireWire, but are captured out of sync.

Another possibility is that timecode information might arrive earlier than picture and sound. When using RS-422 for deck control and digitizing picture and sound through DV, there will possibly be a mismatch of the timecode versus picture information. The problem is that the two signals are not transmitting in sync.

How can you detect these latencies? For video, it's fairly simple. If you are capturing, and the audio and video look out of sync while processing through a transcoder, try adjusting the Delay Audio setting; available values are from 0 to 5 frames (see Figure 2.29). If the latency is more than five frames, you have a bigger issue than a simple processing delay. Check your original to see that picture and sound are in sync.

Figure 2.29 Adjusting for DV delay

Timecode latency is very simple to inspect. Find a videotape with a timecode burn-in. A timecode with "burn-in" has timecode numbers superimposed on it that should match the actual timecode on the tape. Or in some decks, there is a switch that turns on the feature of the deck that displays timecode (on many Sony decks, this switch is called "Character") and uses the video output of the deck that includes the timecode characters. Digitize it. Look at the tracking menu above the source monitor and see whether the numbers match. If it doesn't, the timecode needs to be delayed using the DV Capture Offset window. If you're not digitizing pictures through FireWire and using an RS-422 controller, you shouldn't have this problem.

The Capture Tool: Deck, Camera, and Timecode Controls

Let's take a look at the deck controls and configurations in the Capture tool (shown in Figure 2.30). We'll also look at the Tape Name button and discuss some methods used to name your source tapes.

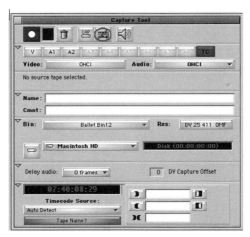

Figure 2.30 The Capture tool

Selecting a Deck or Camera for Capture

As I mentioned earlier, there are two standards of control for decks and cameras. The first is IEEE 1394, more popularly known as FireWire. The second standard is known as RS-422. The manner in which the deck is controlled by the system depends largely upon the format of deck or camera that you use. FireWire is always better and requires fewer connections and configurations.

 If your deck has neither an RS-422 serial interface nor a FireWire control, you will have to control the deck manually during capture. Manual control of a deck works fine with Xpress Pro, but keep in mind that no timecode information from the tape will be stored. Once again, this practice is not recommended.

Identifying the Source Tape

When you begin to capture material, it is extremely important that you correctly identify the source tape name. If you fail to do this accurately, you could find yourself in several quandaries, not the least of which is, "Where is that shot?" If you are offlining material that is to be finished on another Avid or online system, tape identification could mean the difference between a smooth online session and a disaster.

If the deck is controlled by Xpress Pro and is put in Remote mode, every time that you insert a new tape, the Select Tape dialog box will appear (see Figure 2.31). If you are controlling the deck manually, you can still change tape names by clicking the Tape Name button at the bottom of the Capture tool.

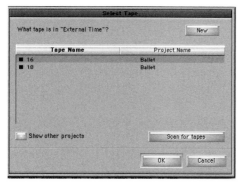

Figure 2.31 Selecting a tape

In the Select Tape Dialog box, you will find the names of all tapes associated with the current project. If the project is new, the tape list will be empty. If your tape name isn't in the list, click the New button, or press Ctrl+N/⌘+N. A new tape entry appears at the bottom of the list. Type in the name of the new tape and press Return. The tape name appears in the list and can now be selected.

If tapes were created in another project (if they were logged on another system, for example), you need to use the Show Other Projects option. This option will let you see the tape names that were assigned previously. From there, you can select the tape without typing it in again.

Configuring Your Deck or Camera

Xpress Pro allows you to establish deck configurations for every camera or deck that you own. The proper configuration of cameras and decks means total control of peripherals through the software interface. Therefore, it is essential that your decks and cameras be correctly identified and adjusted when capturing.

Free DV and Xpress Pro can poll the deck or camera to determine its model and make automatically. There are times, however, when the Avid does not properly identify the deck or camera. Keep in mind that there are now many decks and cameras on the market, and although the protocols are common, the controls are not.

The best thing to do is to go to your deck configuration settings and do it yourself. To do that, first go to the Project window and click the Settings tab. Locate the Deck Configuration Settings and double-click.

It might take a moment or two for the deck templates to load. The deck templates contain information about how to control the most commonly used decks. If your deck is not among the templates, you can still use a generic template and configure it for your deck.

If this is your first time using Deck Configuration (see Figure 2.32), click the Add Channel button; the Channel Options appear. You can choose between Direct (RS-422) and OHCI (IEEE 1394 or FireWire), which we mentioned before.

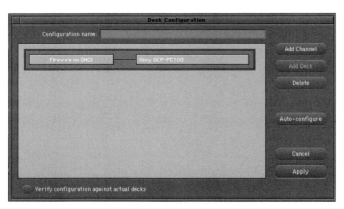

Figure 2.32 Deck Configurations box

On Windows machines, usually an RS-422–to–RS-232C adapter, such as Addenda's Rosetta Stone, is used for controlling the deck. The deck is therefore connected to one of the two RS-232C serial ports built into your system. On Windows systems, you must choose between the Com 1 and Com 2 RS-232C ports on the computer.

On Mac systems, RS-422 control can be established, but it requires either a third-party card (such as Gee Three's Stealth card) or an adapter from USB to serial (such as those made by Keyspan). A Mac serial–to–9-pin cable will also be required. The Stealth card and many others like it will allow direct connection between the RS-422 connector on the deck and the card on your Mac. The Keyspan adapter, which is a less-expensive option, connects to any USB port and will control the deck directly through your Mac without dealing with any card installation. In Deck Configuration, it is shown as the Direct choice. If you are using a hardware codec or a Mojo and you want RS-422 control, you should choose either the Com 1/Com 2 selection (Windows) or the Direct selection (Mac).

If your deck has neither RS-422 nor OHCI capability, you'll need to control the deck manually. In such cases, there is no need to configure a deck because the deck cannot be controlled by the Avid system.

After you add your channel, it's time to add a deck. Click the Add Deck button, and the deck selection window appears. To properly select a deck, you must choose the manufacturer first. For example, if your deck is a Sony DSR-11, choose Sony. When the list of Sony configured decks appears, scroll down the list and select DSR-11.

If your deck is not listed under the manufacturer's name, you might be able to find the template on Avid's website. Avid frequently adds or creates new templates because new decks and cameras are manufactured frequently. Another option is to select a generic deck, which follows standard protocols for controls of OHCI and RS-422 controllers. It is not particularly sensitive to the full capabilities of a specific deck, but it usually works well.

Deleting Deck Configurations

To delete a previous deck configuration, do the following:

1. Go to your Project window and click the Settings tab.
2. Select Deck Configurations.
3. Click the deck and Shift-click the channel. Or lasso them both in the Deck Configuration tool.
4. Press Delete.

Selecting Decks through the Capture Tool

An easier method of selecting a deck is to automatically configure it through the Capture tool (although this doesn't always work, particularly with FireWire decks). At the bottom of the tool underneath the deck shuttle slider is a window that identifies the type of deck that the system believes is being used. If this is not the correct deck, click it. A pull-down menu appears (see Figure 2.33). From the pull-down menu, select Autodetect. The system polls the deck to determine which template best fits it. In many cases, the Autoconfigure might not present the best selection because some DV devices do not respond to the Autodetect command. In other words, some decks and cameras will not reveal their make and model when polled by the system. If you know that a template for your deck exists but Autoconfigure did not select it, configure it manually as previously described.

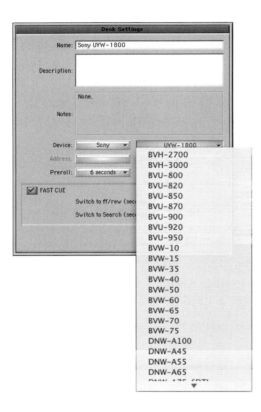

Figure 2.33 Selecting a deck template

Note: When Autoconfigure does not select the correct deck model, but you are sure that there is a template for it in your system, open Deck Configuration in your Settings menu. Click the incorrect deck setting and hit the Delete button. Then click Add Deck, which will open up the deck selection tool. Find the model name of your deck, select it, and click Apply Settings. Changing the template to the correct deck always ensures proper control of the deck.

Using Timecode

The Xpress Pro capture system works like any other good nonlinear editing system. With specific information, it functions flawlessly. Without that information, however, your capture session can be tedious and laden with issues. Timecode is a tool that is used for numbering video frames—nothing more and nothing less. Without timecode, reference to any specific frames is lost. Most modern DV devices use timecode, including those that are generally classified as consumer or prosumer decks and cameras. For DV cameras and decks, the timecode usually begins at zero hours (00:00:00:00) and cannot be changed to a specific hour. This is unfortunate, in the sense that it would be good to have the hour of timecode match the number of the tape (for example, Tape 1 timecode begins at 1:00:00:00, Tape 2 timecode begins at 2:00:00: 00, and so forth). Nonetheless, *any* timecode is better than none because it refers to a specific frame on the specific tape.

> **Note:** Editors who are new to nonlinear systems frequently make the error of forgetting to change the tape number when capturing. It is much easier to change names when capturing than trying to discern which pictures came from which tape later! Try to maintain an accurate database as you capture your materials. This is especially important if using source materials from mini-DV cameras with 1:00:00:00 timecode. Otherwise, you could have two very different clips with the same timecode and the same tape name in the same bin, which would undoubtedly cause problems with media management.

Although Avid systems are very reliable, there is nothing better than a feeling of security. If for some reason you lose media, you still have accurate timecode and tape names. Most of the time spent during capture is getting the numbers. As long as your bins still exist, recapturing takes little time and is very simple to do.

The Marks Registers

The Marks registers are located on the right of the Deck Control tools (see Figure 2.34). They allow you to Mark In and Mark Out, enter timecode numbers directly, jump to specific points, and store a timecode number temporarily in a register.

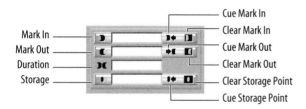

Figure 2.34 The Marks registers allow you to enter or cue to particular points in your footage.

Mark In This button allows you to mark the beginning of the clip that you want to capture. With the tape rolling, click it, and the timecode that occurred when you clicked the button will appear in the register to the right.

You can also use this register for direct timecode entry. To do this, first clear any existing timecode (by clicking the Clear button at the right or by highlighting the number and pressing Delete). Then type the correct timecode number and press Return.

To the right of this register is a Mark In button with an arrow. This button allows you to cue the tape to that specific point, or "go to" the Mark In. Each of the marks registers, with the exception of the duration register, has this capability.

Mark Out This register denotes the last frame of capture. To use it, follow the same procedures mentioned above in the Mark In description.

Duration The Duration icon has both a Mark In and Mark Out icon together. Actually, it isn't a button at all. This is Xpress Pro's calculation of the duration of your clip based upon the Mark In and Mark Out. If you adjust either Mark In or Mark Out, the number in this register will change. You can also do direct entry of timecode in the Duration register. For example, if you have a Mark In and you want the clip to be 20 seconds long, type **20:00**. The Mark Out will be calculated based upon your duration. You can also do this inversely to back-time a clip with Mark Out already entered; enter the desired duration in the register, and the Mark In will be calculated based upon the Mark Out minus the duration.

Storage Register The last entry on the Marks register is a temporary storage place for a timecode number to be used later. You can mark this timecode using the adjacent Locator button to the left of the register or manually enter the timecode by clicking in the register and typing in the number.

Go To (Cue) On the Mark In, Mark Out, and Storage registers, there is a button just to the right of the register with an arrow. Clicking this button will cue your tape to the timecode that is entered into that register.

Clear Marks Clicking one of the buttons at the far right will clear the timecode from the relevant register.

Capturing Using Mark In and Mark Out Points

Capturing using marked points offers the convenience of doing two things at once: log and capture. Although this once was prohibitive on more-expensive nonlinear editing systems (because of the cost per hour of renting or maintaining the system), it's pretty common on less-expensive systems such as Free DV or Xpress Pro.

To capture using Mark In and Mark Out:

1. Find the first frame of the footage to be digitized and click the Mark In button on the Capture tool.

2. Find the last frame of the footage to be digitized and click the Mark Out button.

3. Press the Capture button at the top-left of the dialog.

The system prerolls the tape to a specified point a few seconds before the in point, rolls it forward, and begins capturing. After the capture is completed, the system sends a message that the media has been digitized.

You can also digitize footage with no set out point. Simply click Mark In and press Record. When you're sure you've captured enough for that clip, press the Capture button a second time to stop capturing. Similarly, you can set an out point for your capture (for example, before a timecode break or the tape end) and not mark an in point by using the Capture button to capture on the fly wherever the tape is cued.

Another similar method is to capture from a handwritten log, using specific times from that log. When I do this, I try to find a *barker*, someone working nearby who needs some time away from regular work. This person can call out the numbers while you type them in. To enter the times, type the number for the in point next to the Mark In button and tab to the Mark Out entry and type that number in. Then you can either log it by clicking the Log/Digitize button (on Xpress Pro only) at the top of the Capture tool or immediately digitize it and talk to your new friend, the barker.

Note: About barking and barkers: Old-time editors like me prefer the number read in two-digit cadences. Why? For some reason, a cadence helps you remember the numbers more easily (it's a short number, after all), and it also appeals to an editor's sense of rhythm. Why two digits only? I haven't the foggiest recollection. So, for timecode 1:03:04:08, it would be read "01 … 03 … 04 … 08." Now that you've learned the black art of barking, you have something to fall back on.

On-the-Fly Capture

Capturing from timecode sources doesn't require typing or marking in and out points. You can also capture on the fly, as the tape rolls forward. To do this

1. Play the tape and find the footage that needs to be captured.

2. Roll it back so that you have plenty of preroll or footage adjacent to the beginning of the needed footage.

3. Play the tape forward, giving the deck plenty of time to get to speed.

4. Press the red Record button. You're capturing.

5. Press the red Record button again to end the capture.

Capture Keyboard Shortcuts

The Capture tool has plenty of buttons, but if you prefer to use the keyboard, the following shortcuts can be used:

Tab Jumps from one timecode entry to the next

I Marks in

O Marks out

Spacebar Plays the source tape

F4 Begins capture

J and L Moves the source forward (L) or backward (J) in speed increments, with each press increasing the speed of shuttle

Naming and Commenting Clips During Capture

As you are capturing the source material to your drives, you may have noticed that the Clip Name space has an active cursor. During capture, you can type in a name for your clip. This speeds up the capturing process by not having to go back later to do data entry. There is also an entry for a clip description. To switch between the two, press Tab and begin typing.

DV Scene Extraction

Perhaps the best thing about nonlinear editing is its random access capabilities. However, the randomness of access becomes glaringly apparent when you have long clips containing varying subject matter. In fact, if the project is not carefully constructed, you could find yourself shuttling through long clips, much as you would though linear videotape. To solve this issue, there is DV Scene Extraction.

The concept behind DV Scene Extraction is simple: divide and conquer. In a world where too much information is the order of the day, DV Scene Extraction allows you to choose smaller sections of a clip and create subsections (or subclips) and then categorize them more specifically. Let's say, for example, you shot footage at your local zoo. On a single recorded clip, you captured the penguins, an aviary, some alligators, a lion, and two tigers. If you want to go straight to the alligators, how can you do it? Isn't it simpler to create a subclip for each?

When DV footage is shot, time of day (TOD) information is recorded. DV Scene Extraction allows you to capture from the entire tape, but will create subclips and/or locators from each individual shot in a clip. This is distinguished through TOD information.

 Note: DV Scene Extraction works only when you capture at DV-25 resolution.

Whenever the TOD changes between shots, DV Scene Extraction recognizes it and creates a locator on the master clip (or it can create a subclip of each shot, depending on how you've set it up).

To set up DV Scene Extraction *before* digitizing footage:

1. Go to the Project window and select Settings.

2. Choose Capture Settings.

3. Click the DV Options tab (see Figure 2.35).

4. Select Create Subclips, Add Locators, or Both.

Figure 2.35 The DV Scene Extraction window

The system will automatically extract each scene digitized as a subclip. Add a locator to the beginning of each scene, or both as selected.

To set up DV Scene Extraction *after* digitizing footage:

1. Click the source clip or clips.

2. Select Bin > DV Scene Extraction.

3. Choose Create Subclips, Add Locators, or Both.

4. Choose a source bin for your subclips.

The system extracts individual scenes from the master clips, based on TOD information.

Capturing Directly to the Timeline (Xpress Pro Only)

In some cases, your project might require that you capture footage straight into the Timeline. Xpress Pro can do this, even allowing you to patch tracks when necessary. There are several reasons for you to want to do this. If your sequence is only a few shots long and relatively simple in nature, capturing to the Timeline directly prevents the need to load footage, mark it, and edit it across to a sequence. News organizations often do this when receiving satellite feeds.

Capturing directly to the Timeline also saves you time. No need to re-mark in and out points; just do it while capturing. If you're pretty confident about what you want and if the job doesn't require a lot of tape changes, this is a fast way to get it done. This capability was acquired from Avid's Newscutter because in news editing, getting material into a sequence quickly is very important.

To capture directly to the Timeline:

1. Go to the Project window and select Settings.

2. Open your Capture Settings.

3. Select the Edit tab.

4. Select the Enable Edit to Timeline button.

5. Choose the number of frames that you want captured as a handle to each clip. A *handle* is a number of frames digitized before and after the in and out timecodes specified for the clip.

   Why use handles? If you decide to nudge an edit or use a transition, you'll need some extra media. Without handles, that media might not be present. Better to be safe than sorry, especially on a tight deadline.

6. Select OK.

Before you begin digitizing, create a new sequence in which the footage will be captured if you don't have one open already.

Patching Directly When Capturing to the Timeline

You can patch your tracks before you capture to the Timeline. There are several reasons to do this. If, for example, you need a voiceover on audio Track 2, but the voiceover exists on Track 1 of your source, you can patch the track before capture.

To patch tracks before capturing to the Timeline:

1. Click the track selector for the source track in the Capture tool.

2. Click and hold on the track selected. A pop-up menu of destination tracks appears.

3. Choose the destination track in the sequence for this source track.

After you begin capturing footage, the track is patched directly to its proper destination in the sequence.

Capturing Across Timecode Breaks

One of the Capture Settings that is very useful is Capture Across Timecode Breaks. Created originally during the development of Avid MultiCam, Capture Across Timecode Breaks is used to capture entire tapes that have frequent start/stops where the camera stops rolling and the timecode is not continuous. When selected, Capture Across Timecode Breaks will enable the system to stop when the timecode stops, create a clip, and then roll forward to find the next piece of timecode and sync. When the next piece is found, the system rolls forward to a point where sync is stable, prerolls, and begins recording again. There are only three caveats when using this option:

• You must have plenty of preroll on your shots. If not, the system may go past the desired in point and begin capturing later than anticipated. When shooting, it is a good idea to count to ten after the tape is recording and before beginning your shot. Without enough preroll, you will have to capture manually.

- There must be very little space between start/stops. The system understands that there is no sync between shots and will roll forward. But if you have shots with, say, five minutes of blank tape in between, the system might not be able to find the next sync piece.

- The system will capture *everything* that is timecoded with sync and on the tape. If you have need for disk space and there are plenty of outtakes on the tape, this might not be your best option.

Logging (Xpress Pro Only)

Logging with the Capture Tool

The Capture tool can be used as a logging station. To the right of the Capture button is a small disk icon with the letters DIG (for *digitize*). Click this icon and it changes to a pencil icon with the word LOG. You have now successfully switched to Logging mode.

In Logging mode, you can still shuttle the machine and enter timecode just as you do during Capture. The difference is that the actual Capture function is disabled. When you log, the timecode and clip information go into a bin, but the media itself are not captured on your hard drives.

There are plenty of reasons to use the Logging mode:

- If you are awaiting more drive space, but want to get all of your clips ready for capture.

- If a client is doing the logging, but is not familiar enough with setting up for capture and wants you to control the actual process of setting resolution, checking capture settings and doing the media management for the project.

- If the tapes are not present, but a handwritten or typed paper log has been created.

Understanding Frame Code Mode

It is important when logging to know whether your source tape was recorded in drop frame or non–drop frame timecode. Normally, most NTSC DV tapes are recorded using drop frame timecode.

> **Note:** This discussion applies only to NTSC video, so PAL users can skip this section.

Drop frame timecode is a system of counting frames so that the actual playback time of the recording matches real clock time. That may sound repetitive, but it isn't. Here's why.

Video does not really record at a rate of 30 frames per second. It's slightly off that number; it's actually 29.97 frames per second. This difference might seem insignificant, but in these days of automated broadcast equipment, it *is* significant. For example, if we were to measure the duration of a television program that is supposed to last 28 minutes and 38 seconds using non–drop frame (30fps) timecode, the duration would read 28:36:08 because although the clock duration needs to be 28:38:00, the 30fps count would read 28:36:08 when it reached that point in real time. To solve this inconsistency, engineers developed drop frame timecode, a system of counting frames in which recorded time is the equivalent of clock time, so that video timecode remains the same as actual clock time, and the two numbers match.

This is achieved by skipping two timecode numbers every minute except on the tens. So at minutes 1 through 9, you will see the timecode jump like this: 00;01;59;29 to 00;02;00;02. The same holds true for minutes 11 through 19. On minutes 0, 10, 20, and so on there are no skipped numbers. Here, the timecode will count 00;09;59;29 to 00;10;00;00. Don't worry about your picture and sound, though; even though this frame code mode is called drop frame, there are no missing frames! Only the counting method is skipping numbers, and your media is all present and accounted for.

Which frame code mode should you use? Common sense might tell you that drop frame timecode should always be the choice, because it always keeps up with real time. But there are occasions where non–drop frame timecode would be better. Here are some examples:

- Anyone using animated frames knows that precise frame counts are necessary. For every frame of animation used, there should be a corresponding timecode number. Drop frame timecode "skips" some numbers in counting frames so that the code keeps up with clock time rather than corresponding to actual frame counts. Thus, non-drop frame code is necessary to avoid an incorrect frame count.

- Thirty-second commercials rarely use drop frame code because the frame count does not change until a minute duration has passed. Thus advertisers usually prefer using non-drop frame code so that the beginning and end of each 30-second spot land on an even-numbered minute. For example, if we used drop frame timecode, the first commercial on a reel could begin at one hour even (1:00:00:00), but the second commercial would begin at the top of the next minute at 1;00;00;02 because drop frame code skips two frames in the count at the beginning of each minute (except every tenth minute in the count).

It's not as important to remember the actual counting scheme of drop frame video as it is to understand what it does:

- Frame code modes are only methods of *counting* frames. In other words, all the pictures will appear regardless of whether the frame count uses drop frame or non-drop frame coding.

- You do not add or subtract actual frames of video when using either drop or non-drop frame timecode.

- When you are logging a videotape without the actual tape in the machine, how do you do it? If you are copying numbers from a paper log, you will need to know whether it is recorded with drop or non-drop frame timecode. Here's how you can check:

On most modern video decks and cameras, the timecode display will indicate drop or non-drop frame timecode by using a semicolon or a colon between the numbers, respectively. For example, if your timecode display reads 01;00;00;00, the number is drop frame timecode. If it reads 01:00:00:00, it is non-drop frame timecode.

Note: A good way to remember this is that the symbol for a semicolon has a descender that "drops" down (indicating drop frame), whereas a colon has no such descender (indicating non-drop frame).

Another way to determine frame code mode is to look at timecode on your tape at the beginning of every minute (except the tens). If the code jumps two frames, it is drop frame. If it doesn't, it's non-drop frame. Be sure to check the code on several different minutes to determine this correctly.

Unfortunately, some tapes will contain *both* drop and non–drop frame code, which is unfortunate and should always be avoided. But if this problem does occur, you have to log using the actual tape—otherwise, the log will not match the tape. If this occurs, the system will prompt you that the timecode on the clips and the timecode on the tape are in different frame code modes; therefore, there is a problem. This is easily avoidable if you know the frame code mode of the tape when entering timecode information.

Because Avid will not allow for mixed frame code on the same tape, it will force a new tape name for the section with a different frame code type. So tape F1, which started as drop frame, will be forced to carry a second tape name by Avid when it encounters non-drop code. Avid will warn you and then add the name F1NDF to the tape registry.

Importing Logs

If the logs were created using a database and they are in an Avid-readable format, they can be imported into a bin as follows:

1. Create or open a bin for the logged clips.

2. Under File, select Import. The Import menu appears.

3. Select Shot Log under the type of import.

4. Navigate to your log and select it. The log is imported.

Converting Log Formats with Avid Log Exchange

Avid Log Exchange (ALE) is a conversion program that allows you to read from the most common log-creation tools to an Avid-readable log, which can then be imported into a bin. The ALE program comes with the other installers (such as EDL Manager) on your Xpress Pro CD.

Avid Log Exchange can convert the following log types:

- Avid Log Exchange
- ATN (Aaton)
- Apple Cinema Tools
- CMX EDL
- Final Cut Pro
- FLX (Flex files, from telecine)
- Keyscope
- Log Producer
- OSC/R
- Tab-delimited databases such as those from Filemaker Pro and Excel

ALE outputs ALE, ATN (Aaton), or FLX (flex) files.

You can drop a shortcut or alias of ALE on your desktop and automate input. ALE will read your log files and convert them to Avid Log Exchange files.

Batch Capturing Using Previously Logged Bins (Xpress Pro Only)

If you already have logged bins and simply need to capture the media, all you have to do is set the resolutions, assign the correct drives, and tell Xpress Pro what to capture by selecting the clips in their bin. The system goes into an automatic capturing mode that can be monitored or, in the case of offline editing, simply set and left to do its own work.

Before we begin this batch capture, let's take a look at some of the Batch Capture settings. To access these settings, click the Settings tab in your Projects window and select Capture; then select the Batch tab (see Figure 2.36). You can optimize the batch capture process for speed and for disk space. The first two selections in the Batch settings allow you to do this. If you choose Optimize For Speed, the system will determine the fastest way to digitize your footage and proceed accordingly.

For example, if two clips are relatively close to each other on the tape, the system can choose to continue capturing between the clips without stopping. Doing this does waste a little disk space, but it also allows you to finish capturing more quickly. If you prefer to save disk space and are not in a big hurry, you can choose to optimize for disk space. Even if two clips are close to each other, the system digitizes only what is needed.

Figure 2.36 Batch Capture settings

The next setting is Switch To Emptiest Drive If Current Drive Is Full. When selected, this option allows the system to switch between drives rather than stop and inform you that the current drive has run out of space. This setting is a great way to prevent unexpected stops in your batch-digitizing session. If you choose to use this setting, be sure to switch to the Media Creation Settings tab in the Settings window and choose the amount of drive space that is to be left before the system switches. Xpress Pro will not switch drives in the middle of capturing a clip. It is "smart" enough to recognize whether or not a clip will be able to be captured on a drive before capturing it, as long as this option is selected. You can choose between 1 and 10 minutes of drive space left when the switch occurs.

If you're using the optional Mojo and digitizing uncompressed footage, one minute of drive space is plenty. For offline or DV resolutions, consider switching at 5 or 10 minutes to ensure plenty of room on the drives for the media database.

The next two batch settings are intended for convenience. First is the Eject Tape option. Rewinding the tape after digitizing is useful—it returns the tape to the front in case you need to view it again and prevents you from having to do it later. Ejecting the tape prevents wear on the tape and the heads on your deck. Although most modern decks are smart enough to pull the tape off of the heads after a specific amount of time, the drum continues to spin and wastes drum hours. Ejecting the tape prevents this from happening.

Underneath the Eject Tape option is Log Errors to Console and Continue Digitizing. This option is very useful, particularly when you are not monitoring the batch closely. When Xpress Pro encounters an error and it cannot cue up a tape, it will log it as an error and continue with the next clip. If you have multiple clips from the same reel, this feature can save you from returning to the edit suite only to find that the system got stuck after only capturing a few clips. However, if you use this feature, you'll need to remember to check the console. Once you've quit Xpress Pro, that information goes away.

Other Batch Settings

The final four Batch Capture settings allow you to either use the compression settings as logged in the bin or change them to your current settings for media creation. Let's take an example of why you might want to adjust these settings. A director comes to you with what appears to be a very simple documentary and only 10 tapes. You log the 10 tapes and intend to digitize at DV resolution. No worries, you have plenty of space on the drives. Then the other shoe drops. The director comes in with 40 more tapes, explaining, "Here's the bulk of what we'll use."

Has it happened to you? It has to me. This usually occurs when either the director is less organized and "forgets" or when he or she chooses not to disclose enough information to you. As a result, you will have logged all your footage as DV compression and when you're going to need to do it at 15:1s in order to fit it on your drives (your actual mileage will vary).

Go to your Batch Capture Settings and deselect Use Video Compression Logged For Each Clip. Set your Capture tool for 15:1s and delete all the media from your original clips. Batch capture them again at 15:1s and you can finish the project without worrying about drive space. You can also use these settings to adjust for audio sample rate, for sample size, and for the tracks selected. Capturing Tracks Logged is extremely useful. The logger often has no clue about what should be captured and so will log all the tracks available for the clip. As you begin to familiarize yourself with the footage for the project, you might notice that some tapes have no sound and capturing sound will waste space. By deselecting this option and picking tracks in the Capture tool, you can save a lot of disk space.

To batch capture using logged bins:

1. Choose your Batch Capture Settings, as described previously.
2. Open the bin with the logged clips.
3. Select the clips to be batch captured. Make sure that you have selected the correct drive(s), video resolution, and audio sources.
4. Ready for some automated fun? Under the Bin menu, select Batch Capture.
5. The system instructs you to load a tape and begins to capture material automatically. From there, follow the system prompts. When complete, it will tell you "Batch Capture Complete."

Note: If you are using XpressPro and you want to make sure that you have enough space on the drives to capture all your logged shots, you can select them all in the bin (Ctrl+A/⌘+A) and then press Ctrl+I/⌘+I ("I" stands for "info"). This will open up the Console and display the total length of shots that were selected. Make sure that no titles or sequences were selected, or it will add in those lengths for the totals.

Tutorial: Capturing to Your Avid

For many editors, the process of capturing is overlooked because although we edit almost every day, capturing is a prelude to that process. I've even heard from new editors who claim that they cannot capture—it's too technical. Actually, you get used to all the bells and whistles of the Capture tool. Over time, you recognize all the settings and the problems that they cause. As a result, proficiency on the Capture tool will be gained through time and experience. If you can use the Capture functions efficiently, you will have more time to edit. Isn't that the whole idea of modern day nonlinear tools? Try out some of the options and see which best fits your workflow.

Now that you've learned how to capture, we'll begin a short tutorial and go over it again. This particular tutorial is a little difficult to follow because Free DV and Xpress Pro do not have the exact same capture options. At any rate, I'll point them out as we go, so that you can learn to capture most efficiently.

Connecting the Peripherals

To start, you need to turn off your computer and connect all your peripherals.

Capturing with Mojo

If you have Mojo (Xpress Pro only), connect it directly to the FireWire port on your computer using a cable with duplicate six-pin connectors. One end goes to the "Host" connection on the back of the Mojo. The other end goes to your FireWire six-pin connector on the computer. Next, you need to connect a four-pin FireWire cable to your camera or deck and the "DV" connector on the Mojo.

If your drives are also FireWire, be sure that you connect them to a separate FireWire card. If you try to connect both the Mojo and your drives to the same FireWire bus, they will not work correctly.

What is a FireWire *bus*? When your computer has one or more internal FireWire connections, they are said to be on the same bus. Adding an additional PCI FireWire card adds a separate bus. Thus, you can connect Mojo to the computer bus and any external drives to the FireWire card.

> **Note:** When using Mojo, always connect it to the computer's built-in FireWire. This way, the computer will recognize the Mojo first, and no additional issues will occur when using both Mojo and external FireWire drives.

Next, turn on the deck and insert your first tape. Then boot up the computer and start the Xpress Pro application. Jump ahead to the "Configuring the Deck or Camera" section that follows.

Capturing Directly with FireWire

If you intend to capture directly from a DV deck to Free DV or Xpress Pro, it's a lot simpler to set up:

1. First, turn off the computer.

2. Attach a four-pin FireWire connector to the DV out connection on your deck or camera.

3. Connect a six-pin FireWire connector directly to the FireWire input on your computer.

4. Turn on your camera or deck and insert your first tape.

5. Boot the computer and then launch Free DV or Xpress Pro.
   Now you can jump ahead to the "Configuring the Deck or Camera" section.

Capturing with a DV Transcoder

If you do not have a DV deck and are using a transcoder, such as those manufactured by Canopus and other companies, follow these instructions.

First, turn off your computer. Connect your deck or camera to the transcoder. Each transcoder has a variety of different connection options. Remember that the options are dependent on which types of outputs are available on your camera or deck, and which types of inputs are available on your transcoder. The order of preferences is as follows:

1. Component (R-Y, B-Y, Y)

2. S-Video

3. Composite

To make the transcoder work, you must have duplicate connections on *both* the deck or camera and the transcoder.

Connect the DV out directly to your FireWire input on your computer. Next, turn on the deck and insert your first tape. Boot up the computer and start the Free DV or Xpress Pro application.

Configuring the Deck or Camera

The next step is to configure your camera or deck so that it works correctly with the Free DV or Xpress Pro software:

1. After you launch the application, create a new project named "Capturing Exercise." Be sure the frame rate is 30i if you are working with NTSC video. If you are working with PAL video, select 25i.

2. Add the project and select it. The interface should appear on your screen.

3. Before going to the Capture tool, configure the deck. Go to the Project Window and select Settings. Choose the Deck Configuration setting by double-clicking it. The Deck Configuration menu appears.

4. Note that there are two things to select here: the channel (see Figure 2.37), which is the way the deck will be controlled, and the deck itself. Before you can configure the deck, you have to choose a channel for it to communicate to Free DV/Xpress Pro. If you are using FireWire, choose FireWire on OHCI. If you are using RS-422 nine-pin connectors, choose Direct.

Figure 2.37 Selecting a channel

5. Now you need to choose a deck. Click Add Deck in the Deck Configuration window. A new menu appears. When you choose a new deck, first select the maker of the deck on the left column of deck listings; then choose between the different model numbers available. If you don't find your particular camera or deck in these listings, choose Generic as the device and select one of the Generic options in the right column as the model. Remember that not every deck is included in the templates.

6. After you're finished, click Apply and OK. The deck is now configured.

Opening the Capture Tool

Now that our deck has been configured and our project is created, we'll set up to do a little capturing.

First, go to the Bin tab in the project window and select New Bin. We'll call this bin Capture Practice. After the bin is open, click it, and go to Tools > Capture. The Capture tool appears.

Adjusting Video Levels (Mojo Only)

If you're using Mojo, click the Vectorscope icon at the top of the Capture tool 🖼 . In the next window, open both the Waveform and Vectorscope. If you have SMPTE bars on your tape, cue the tape to that point and you can adjust the video levels.

If there are no bars on the tape, you can still adjust levels for a proper picture, but you have to depend somewhat on the monitors to adjust levels. This is not particularly easy to do. Find a section of the tape that is the most common composition used in the picture content. If the picture content of the tape varies significantly, you might want to adjust levels every time it changes.

Now you can begin to adjust the video levels, starting with the contrast. Adjust the contrast so that the darkest element of the picture, where it should be black, appears at 7.5 percent on the Waveform.

Next, adjust the brightness (the brightest parts of the picture should not exceed 100 percent on the Waveform). If you do not have any elements in the image that are actually white, shuttle ahead on your tape until you find one. Examine the Waveform carefully. There should not be any part of the picture, no matter how small, that exceeds 110 percent on the Waveform.

Take a look at the color. If you do not have SMPTE color bars on your tape, this is difficult at best. If you do, adjust all of vectors so that they fit into the appropriate color box in the Vectorscope. If the vectors are off to the right or left of the box, adjust the hue. If they are smaller than the boxes or go beyond them, adjust the saturation until they fit correctly into each color vector.

If you have no color bars and the colors in your image look okay, don't adjust the saturation or hue. If the color tends to appear more green or red/magenta, try adjusting the hue until it looks like the color is more balanced. If the picture appears washed out, try adding color with the Saturation adjustment. Remember, too much saturation causes noise, so don't overdo it. If the image appears too colorful and the video looks noisy, try pulling the saturation down until the noise goes away and the image looks best.

Adjusting Audio Levels

Now you can adjust the audio levels. First, you should adjust audio levels coming from your deck or camera. If your deck or camera has an audio adjustment tool, adjust the audio to proper levels using the meters on the deck or camera.

Most DV decks do not have an adjustment on them because the audio is recorded digitally and will reproduce the same way. If you are using Mojo, there is no way to adjust the incoming audio, because Mojo keeps the audio in the digital domain.

If you have a tone recorded on the tape, it makes adjusting the audio easier. If you don't have a tone, try to find a place in the tape where the audio is loudest. Remember that you are adjusting the sound level to prevent distortion, so you want to make sure that the loudest point of the tape does not overmodulate and cause the resulting clip to be distorted.

Open the Audio tool on the Capture tool 🔊 . Your meters should appear. Next, play back the tape and open up the Audio settings (see Figure 2.38). Choose Input and move the audio slider up or down while looking at the audio meters. Be sure not to exceed +0 on the digital scale and +14 on the VU scale. After you've made the adjustments, your audio setup is complete. Close the Audio settings.

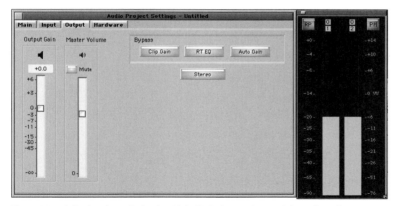

Figure 2.38 Adjusting the audio levels with Audio Project settings and the audio tool

Naming the Tape

Name this tape by clicking the Tape Name button under the deck controls. From the menu that appears, select New Tape. When you do this, a new tape entry will appear; type the new tape name.

Some caveats that we have already discussed: Use the same name on the videotape as you use here. Consider the option of naming the project and the tape number together to avoid confusion. Thus, Tape 1 would be called Capture Exercise 1. After you figure out the name that best fits your tape, select the tape icon next to the tape name in the Tape Name box and click OK.

Setting Points

Now it's time to play back the tape and create a clip. Because I have no idea what is on your tape, it's up to you to select the item to be captured here. One word of warning: You need to have as much preroll time as possible. In other words, the contents of your clip need a few seconds or more before the tape begins. This section of tape is known as the preroll. Having more preroll makes it easier for the deck or camera to cue up to the edit point.

Go ahead and play back the tape. Click the Mark In button where you want to start and the Mark Out button where you want the clip to end. There should be no camera starts or stops in the middle of this clip. In other words, it has to be one continuous recording without interruption.

Choosing a Drive

Next, choose where to store the media for your clip: Click the Drive Selection icon ⊂▭ The Bison ▾ , which should show you a list of available drives to choose from.

If you are capturing to a system drive or have drive filtering turned on, you might not see any highlighted drives in the list. In that case, here's what to do:

1. Click the Settings tab in your Project Window.

2. Open the Media Creation settings. Choose the Drive Filtering tab.

3. If you are capturing onto your system drive, deselect Filter Out System Drive. If you are capturing on the same drive where your Free DV or Xpress Pro application exists, deselect Filter Out Launch Drive.

4. Click OK and return to the Capture tool. The drives should all be available.

Choosing a Resolution

Here's a good tip. If you are using Free DV, you have only one resolution choice: DV 25 411 OMF. Choose it and you're done. If you are using Xpress Pro with Mojo, you can choose (see Figure 2.39) between 1:1 uncompressed, DV 25, DV 50 (DVC Pro), or 14:1. For Xpress Pro without Mojo, you have the same choices, except there is no 1:1 uncompressed option. For these purposes, go ahead and choose DV 25.

Figure 2.39 Selecting a resolution

Choosing Video and Audio Channels

Finally, select the audio and video channels to be digitized. Play back your tape and look at the audio meters. If you have audio present in both Tracks 1 and 2, select them. If there is only audio in one track, select it.

Now select the V track for video and the TC track for timecode. You're all ready to go!

Recording

You made all the selections, so you can capture. Click the red Capture button. Here is what is *supposed* to happen:

1. The videotape cues up a few seconds before your Mark In point.

2. It begins playing back.

3. The light next to the Capture button flashes on and off.

4. The Capture stops after it reaches your Mark Out point.

5. A new clip appears in your bin.

If everything happened the way it is supposed to, you did it! Congratulations. Here are some things that can go wrong:

- If the deck failed to find a cue point, try giving it a longer or shorter preroll time under Custom Preroll at the bottom of the Capture tool. If this does not work, try setting your Mark In point later in the clip.

- If a message appears, telling you that your tape is supposed to be non–drop frame timecode but appears to be drop frame (or vice versa), try re-marking the clip, giving it plenty of play before marking in and out.

Now that you have captured a clip, continue this process, but with some variations:

- Capture on the fly by clearing out all the marks and pressing the Record button as the tape plays back. To end capture, press the Record button again.

- Capture using a single in mark by marking an in point but leaving the out point blank. The machine will cue and capture at the in point, continuing until you click the red Capture button.

- Capture using a single out mark by marking an out point but leaving the in point blank. To do this, after you find the out point, rewind the tape a little and click the Capture button while playing. The tape will begin capture and end on the preset out point.

Basic Editing

Let's take a look at the basic editing functions of Free DV and Xpress Pro. We'll start by exploring the Avid graphical user interface (GUI), including the preset toolset that is stored on your system for each type of editing. We'll take a complete tour of the interface, examining the Project window, the Source and Record windows, the bins and their various display methods, and the Timeline. And you will learn how to load clips, mark them, navigate comfortably through media to find edit points, make edits, and—perhaps most importantly—how to change those edits.

3

Chapter Contents

How to Make Editing Fun

Everywhere you go, from post house to corporations, homes, and small businesses, you will see people in front of editing systems. They are grimacing, focusing, gnashing their teeth, pulling their hair. They say they will someday blow up their computers, burn their software, shave their cats. How is it that so many people are so unhappy about a remarkable invention that was intended to make life simpler?

In Chapter 1, I mentioned that editing is fun. If it's so much fun, why do people maintain a face of death while doing it? Not everyone does this, of course, but I can always tell when an editor needs help.

The reason for so much misery and despair is that many editors don't take the time to learn the interface. And learning the interface is the key to editing, especially Avid editing.

Let me give you an example. If you need a new shirt, there are two ways to get it. The first is to go to a department store and buy one. The second is to buy a loom and make one. One is much easier than the other, but both are ways of getting a shirt.

The problem with most editors, both professional and amateur, is that they have not figured out the best and most efficient ways of doing things with their editing systems. They don't take the time to sit down and learn what the system can actually do. As a result, they have only a few methods of doing everything that needs to be done when editing. Something that could take two mouse clicks becomes eight mouse clicks and a pull-down menu.

In addition to using the wrong methods, many editors have not gained enough experience to know what to use and when to use it. It's human nature to find a method and stick with it (see Figure 3.1). It's easier to use old ways than to have to learn something new. But when we act this way, we don't progress. Editing becomes difficult. We become one of the teeth gnashers, struggling to do something that requires only a few morsels of education.

One of my favorite tricks when consulting is to tell an editor about a solution to a problem. Usually their eyes glaze over, they begin to quiver, and then the famous words come: "And … how … would … you … do … that?" What is even more amazing is what they *don't* know. (Those of you who have worked for me, don't worry—no names mentioned here.)

When I was consulting with Avid, a member of my consulting team had no idea about J-K-L navigation. "That's cool!" she said. Not so cool. Actually rudimentary. There is no excuse not to know this interface.

Reading this chapter is not easy; it requires your full attention. *Please* do not "skim" it. If you get tired of reading, put the book down, step away, and pick it up when you're ready to focus again. I know, I've made a living off of consulting with editors, but I would rather focus on workflow rather than inexcusable lapses in education. It's time to expand your horizons. The time it takes to read this simple little chapter will save you many hundreds of hours of frustration. Turn down the stereo, send the cat to bed, and focus. Ready?

Figure 3.1 A happy, educated editor

The Avid Graphical User Interface

First, we'll go over the Avid graphical user interface, also known as the GUI (pronounced "goo-ey"). So just what is a GUI? It is the windows that appear on the screen when you have opened up your project. The Avid GUI, shown in Figure 3.2, is where all the tools of common use are stored, where the source clips and sequences are displayed, and where a chronological Timeline is displayed. The GUI also shows you bins and the Project window.

The keyboard can be used (in addition to the mouse interaction) with the GUI. Together, they coexist for easy recall of specific functions.

Using the mouse is usually more time-consuming than using a keyboard. To click a button on the interface, you have to move the mouse and click. To do the same thing with the keyboard, you press a button. Most experienced editors will tell you to configure and learn the keyboard functions to save time. But if you are more of a clicker type, the mouse works fine. Trackballs, digital tablets, and other devices also work well with Avid.

The buttons on both the interface and the keyboard can be specifically configured for your style of editing. If you don't use the Play In To Out key but want the Trim key in its place, you can configure it. The system was designed with the understanding that not all editors work the same way, and many experienced (read grumpier) editors like myself demand that the system work specifically the way we want it to.

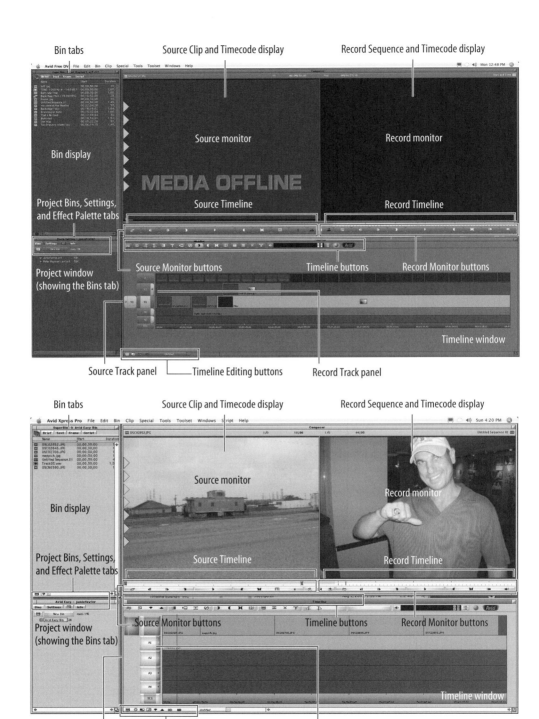

Figure 3.2 The Avid graphic user interface: top, in Free DV; bottom, in Xpress Pro

The Avid GUI is remarkable. Like any good GUI, it displays the most commonly used functions on the screen at all times. Lesser-used functions are found in the menus at the top of the screen. Functions that are rarely used are stored in places like the settings list, from which they must be recalled through a few mouse clicks.

A Quick Walk Around the GUI

Now that you've seen the GUI, let's take a quick walk around it. Lace up your tennis shoes, turn off your iPod, and we'll stroll quickly through.

Project Window This is a display for whatever tab is selected from the Project Bins, Settings, and Effect Palette tabs. Here is where the list of Bins, Settings, or Effects is presented. Clicking a bin in this window opens it. Same for Settings. If you drag one of those effects over to your Timeline, it applies it immediately. (Note to the uninitiated: This is known in the business, and when I say business, I mean The Industry, as "drag and drop." </comedy>)

Bin Display The Bin display is exactly what it says it is—it displays the bin. Using this display, you can view a single bin, or if you want, you can open more bin windows on the interface. I like to keep things tidy. The location of this bin, called the *Super Bin*, keeps everything neat and in place. Speaking of neat and tidy, you might want to tie your shoelace as we continue our walk.

Bin Tabs These tabs, which are located above the bin display, determine how you want your bin displayed. Click a tab, and it shows you a different type of view. The choices are Brief, Text, Frame, and Script. Remember, it's all about different strokes for different folks. Me? I prefer brief because it fits very nicely on the page. Text is the preference of most assistant editors because it gives you more info.

Project Bins, Settings and Effect Palette Tabs Within the Project window are the Project Bins, Settings, and Effect Palette tabs. The Bins tab shows you a list of every bin in your current Project. The Settings tab shows you a list of all of your current settings. You can click on these and change the settings to customize the system to your desires. The Settings list is a bit longer in Xpress Pro than it is in Free DV. We'll explore the settings later in the chapter.

The Effect Palette tab reveals ... guess what? All the effects in the Effect palette. The Effect palette is pretty neat; it's divided into two columns when you click on it. The first column lists the types of effects in your palette; the second column lists the individual effects. You can probably guess that that list of effects is mighty small in Free DV. In Xpress Pro, you get more than 100.

Oh, you may have noticed that I didn't really mention the Info tab, because it really isn't too pertinent to the interface. In fact, it is a very boring place. Let's not even walk there.

Source Clip and Timecode Display Now here are some handy tools. The Source Clip Name menu reveals the name of the clip currently in the Source monitor. The Timecode display gives you all kinds of different timecode information—anything from the actual timecode of the thing to duration, time remaining, and so on. If you're doing a film project, it will show your key numbers (also known as *edge numbers* to some film editors)

Record Sequence and Timecode Display This place on the interface is much like the Source Clip and Timecode display that we just visited, except that it shows the Sequence Name and Sequence Timecode feature. Another cool difference is that it can show the timecode of the source that is currently displayed in the Record monitor below it.

Source Monitor Your source video is displayed here. You can change the interface where your sources are those cute little pop-up monitors. Most editors don't like cute little pop-up monitors. Let's move on.

Record Monitor This is the place where the video of your edited sequence is displayed.

Source Timeline This is a cool little mini-timeline underneath the Source monitor in which you can click, drag, or otherwise move to different points in the clip that is loaded into the Timeline.

Record Timeline This is another one of those mini-timelines in which you can click and navigate through the sequence that is currently displayed in the Record monitor. It is not to be confused with the big Timeline below.

Source Monitor Buttons These are specialized buttons under the Source monitor. An interesting th—ACK! Watch out for that banana! *Remember*, you have to read *every word* of this chapter. Every word. Just seeing if you were skimming. As I was saying, an interesting thing about the Source Monitor and the Record Monitor buttons is that when selected, they apply only to what is in that particular monitor. In other words, if I press a command in the Record Monitor buttons, it doesn't affect anything going on in the Source Monitor. We call that being *condition-dependent*.

Record Monitor Buttons Like the Source Monitor buttons, these buttons affect only what is in the Source monitor.

Timeline Buttons The Timeline buttons, unlike the other two button sets, are sort of function-independent. In other words, they have functions that could affect Source, Record, or both. Not very specific, but this is just a casual walk.

Source Track Panel Here's an interesting place. The Source Track panel reveals whatever tracks were recorded in the clip that is currently loaded in the Source monitor. These track panels are interesting because each little square can be moved around and patched. For example, if I want to patch Source Audio track 2 to Record track 1, I can drag it over to the Record Track panel and voilà! Patched.

Record Track Panel The Record Track panel is where you show all the tracks that are recorded in the sequence. It can also display additional tracks if you create them.

Timeline Window This big place at the bottom of the GUI is where the Timeline is displayed. When you have a Timeline, you can display your cut sequence graphically. We also use this window for Timeline editing.

Timeline Editing Buttons These buttons enact a timeline-editing mode, in which you can grab a hunk of your Timeline and move it to different places in the chronological graph, which in turn changes your sequence. We also use this for deleting chunks of material, juxtaposing them, even cutting and pasting.

Note: If you're uncertain about the function of a button, check box, or other interface element, hover your cursor over it and you'll likely get a tooltip that provides some explanation.

The Toolsets

When you open a project, the GUI is displayed. Avid Free DV and Xpress Pro have different ways of configuring the GUI for more efficient operation. You could say that the GUI is function-specific. When editing, you can set it up one way; when creating effects, it can be configured another way, and so on.

These toolsets come preset to appear on-screen in a specific configuration, but you can change them somewhat to make that configuration better for your monitor and the way you like to work. The toolsets also initialize some functions that are specific to the type of work associated with the toolset.

The toolsets available on Free DV (shown in Figure 3.3) are as follows:

- Basic
- Source/Record
- Effects Edit
- Audio Edit
- Capture

Figure 3.3 Toolsets on Free DV

Xpress Pro has the same five toolsets available plus one more: Color Correction.

Let's take a look at these toolsets and explore how they function to make editing simpler.

Basic Toolset

Avid refers to the standard Xpress layout as Basic (see Figure 3.4). Although its name might imply its popularity, it is not the most commonly used toolset (the Source/Record Editing toolset is most used). The Basic interface has a single monitor named Composer, which plays back your edited sequences. When you double-click a clip in one of your bins, a pop-up monitor appears with the clip loaded inside. You can open as many pop-up monitors as you like on the interface using this toolset.

Figure 3.4 Basic toolset

This Basic display was not created by Avid until it created the first Xpress system: the MC Xpress. The idea is that you can access multiple clips easily, play them back at the click of a mouse, and move from clip to clip without having to open and reopen them. At that time, this display was what the industry referred to as "truncated functionality." The MC Xpress was less expensive than the other model of the day: the Media Composer. So Avid made it so that pop-ups popped, but you could not do a Source Record display.

Try using the Basic toolset. It's not for everyone, but some editors actually like it, despite the original intentions of Avid.

Color Correction Toolset (Xpress Pro Only)

The Color Correction toolset (shown in Figure 3.5) is intended for use when working with the Color Correction effect. The interface expands into three monitors: The center monitor is intended to view the current clip that is being corrected; the other two monitors can be used to display before and after clips for comparison while correcting colors or for viewing a scene with elements similar to the corrected clip for comparison.

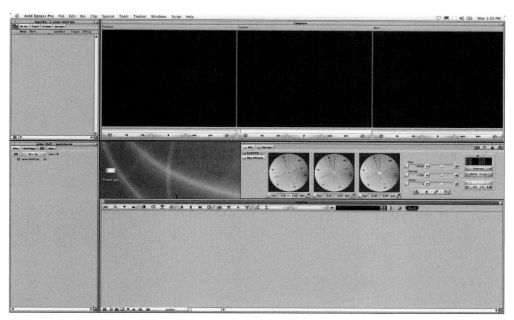

Figure 3.5 Color Correction toolset

Below the three monitors is the correction control panel, which has a tab so that you can correct using color wheels or sliding parameters. It's all pretty intricate stuff to have an entire toolset created for one effect, but color correction can get pretty elaborate.

Source/Record Editing Toolset

The Source/Record Editing toolset (shown in Figure 3.6) is my favorite one and is by far the most commonly used. The display is set up so that it resembles a typical interface, with a Source monitor on the left and a Record monitor on the right. You can load your clips from bins and display them in the Source monitor. The clips can then be marked and spliced or overwritten to the sequence in the Record monitor. Simple, huh?

I personally prefer Source/Record over Basic because it allows me to focus on one source and one sequence. Although Basic lets me instantly view and manipulate multiple sources, I find this method a bit overwhelming and occasionally lose track of which clip I am accessing—especially when some of the clips look similar. Besides, it's the toolset that I learned on, and it emulates every other type of major editing system.

Effects Editing Toolset

The Effects Editing toolset is (of course!) the toolset used when editing effects (see Figure 3.7). When selecting this toolset, the GUI switches to a one-monitor configuration that shows the current sequence. The monitor and Timeline expand so that they are each covering 50 percent of the screen. The reason for an expanded Timeline is that many effects are stacked vertically, and a larger view of the Timeline is required.

Figure 3.6 Source/Record Editing toolset

Figure 3.7 Effects Editing toolset

The Project window will switch tabs to reveal the Effect palette using this toolset. (You can alternately reveal a floating Effect palette by pressing Ctrl+8/⌘+8.) The Effect Editor also is displayed, which shows all the parameters for the selected effect. We'll discuss the Effect Editor in detail in Chapter 7.

Audio Editing Toolset

Like Effects Editing, the Audio Editing toolset (shown in Figure 3.8) optimizes the interface so that you can adjust and control the audio levels during a mix. The interface is similar to the setup for Effects Editing, except the Audio Mix tool opens instead of the Effect Editor. On Xpress Pro, the Audio Automation Gain tool opens (Audio Automation is not enabled on Free DV). Using Automation Gain, you can adjust levels on the fly while your sequence is playing back.

Figure 3.8 Audio Editing toolset

Capture Toolset

The Capture toolset (shown in Figure 3.9) allows you to get ready for capturing new media instantly by selecting it. The Capture tool is displayed, and a single monitor for viewing captured media is shown, as it is with the Effect Editing, Audio Editing, and Basic toolsets.

Figure 3.9 Capture toolset

Saving Toolsets

If the current toolset doesn't quite meet your needs, you can open other windows, move windows around, and configure them to your liking. After you've adjusted the GUI the way you like it, you can save it as one of the toolsets by using the Toolset > Save Current command.

For example, you might want to change the Capture toolset so the Audio tool is displayed alongside. Follow these steps:

1.   Open the Audio tool (Ctrl+1/⌘+1 or Tools > Audio Tool).

2.   Adjust the Audio tool so it is next to the Capture tool.

3.   Choose Toolset > Save Current.

If you decide you do not like the new toolset configuration and want to go back to the previous toolset display, just choose Toolset > Restore Current to Default.

A Tour of the Interface

Now that we've examined the toolsets available on Xpress Pro and Free DV, let's take a look at the functions available on the editing interface. The editing interface on Xpress Pro is completely customizable. Unfortunately, being able to move buttons on the interface is limited only to Xpress Pro. With Free DV, you can customize the interface window displays, but not the individual buttons on each component of the interface,

Let's take a few moments and go over each component and its functions.

The Project Window

The Project window is something of a master key for each project created. When you close the Project window, it closes everything else associated with the project. From that point, you can either open another project or quit the program.

The Project window contains four tabs: Bins, Settings, Effects, and Info.

Bins Tab

The Bins tab (see Figure 3.10) contains a Fast menu to perform bin functions, a New Bin button, a memory display, and a list of bins that also displays the bin status (open or closed),

Figure 3.10 Bins tab

The Fast menu has long been a main staple of the Avid interface. This icon , also known as the hamburger (although it looks nothing like a hamburger), is used to display a multiple-selection pull-down menu. Click it, and a number of functions will appear.

On the Bins tab, the hamburger displays Open Bin, New Bin, New Folder, Close Project, Delete, Empty Trash, Reveal File, and Flat View. The first two functions are self-explanatory. The third, New Folder, allows you to subcategorize bins.

Bin management is just like database management. Some editors use very little of it and do not take advantage of the advanced functions of bin management; others use all the capabilities of bins, including subcategorization, customized displays, column entries (Xpress Pro only), and so on.

I'm somewhere in-between those two extremes. Although I like the advantages of using multiple bins, I am hesitant to create folders with subcategories.

When working with projects in Free DV and Xpress Pro, I like to create two different types of bins. The first bin, a tape bin, contains everything captured from a single tape. The second type of bin, a subject bin, categorizes clips by their subject matter.

For example, let's say that you interviewed a subject for a documentary. The recording was made on Tape 8. So all your clips from Tape 8 are in a bin called Tape 8. Now you want to distinguish the contents of your tapes, so you create a bin with the subject's name: **Mrs. Gould**. Now you can Alt- or Option-drag all the clips from the Tape 8 bin into the Mrs. Gould bin. This process copies the clips so that they exist in both bins.

A brief moment to explain just why you would want to use this method. When referring to a clip, you, your director, or your producer will refer to either the tape where it is located or the subject of a clip. Copying clips from a tape bin to a subject bin allows access to specific clips using either method. I have found this to be the easiest method of access.

Let's expand this basic idea. Suppose that new information has come to light, so you interview Mrs. Gould again. This second interview exists on Tape 18, along with a portion of an interview with Mrs. Gonzales. How do you subcategorize the tape? First, create a new bin titled Mrs. Gonzales. Alt- or Option-drag all clips with Mrs. Gonzales from Tape 18 into your new bin. Then, take the clips from the second Mrs. Gould interview and Alt- or Option-drag them into the Mrs. Gould bin.

Alternatively, you might want to distinguish between the two interviews with Mrs. Gould. Here, it might be wise to create a new folder titled **Mrs. Gould**. You could create a new bin entitled **Mrs. Gould Second Interview**. Drag all the second interview clips from the Mrs. Gould interview into that bin. Retitle the first bin **Mrs. Gould First Interview**. Place both bins inside the folder, and you now you have a way of accessing all the Mrs. Gould bins instantly.

Of course, you could just use the two bins without creating a folder. Different strokes for different folks. I personally don't use the New Folder option, simply because I tend to think of my bins in a flat way and I avoid multiple levels of access. But you might find that folders keep things tidier.

The Flat View option in the Fast menu allows you to see all the bins in a flat list. Deselecting it will show the list with the folders displayed. I think that if I had learned Avid when this function was first created, I'd use it. But for most of my projects, this added function is unnecessary.

Settings Tab in Free DV and Xpress Pro

The Settings tab is a list of all the settings available on Avid. Settings can be saved, deleted, duplicated, and modified—and you might even have several different settings for the same thing. For example, you can have settings for exporting graphic files and another completely different export setting for QuickTime files.

Clicking the Fast menu or hamburger gives you several display options (see Figure 3.11), which are listed in Table 3.1.

Figure 3.11 Hamburger menu in the Settings tab on Free DV

▶ **Table 3.1** Categories on the Settings Fast Menu

Category	Contents
Active Settings	Displays Active settings used by your system
All Settings	Displays all Settings for your system
Base Settings	Displays User, Site and Project settings only. No Bin or Timeline Views are displayed
Bin Views	Displays saved or preset Bin Views
Export Settings	Displays all preset and saved Export settings
Import Settings	Displays all preset and saved Import settings
Timeline Views	Displays all preset and saved Timeline views
Title Styles	Displays all user-created Timeline style templates
Workspaces	Displays all workspaces
Workspaces Linked	Displays linked workspaces

The settings for Free DV (shown in Figure 3.12) are limited when compared with the settings that can be manipulated in Xpress Pro (I suppose that's one of the reasons that Free DV is free). With Free DV, you can adjust the following:

Figure 3.12 Settings tab on Free DV

Audio The Audio settings (see Figure 3.13) control scrubbing length when searching for audio cues, audio playback buffers (to ensure playing of longer streams of audio), panning controls of audio channels, and audio hardware selection.

Figure 3.13 Audio Settings window

Audio Project Audio Project settings (see Figure 3.14) control audio sample rates, rate conversions, audio input settings, audio output settings, and audio hardware selection.

Bin The Bin settings (see Figure 3.15) determine the time interval between automatic saving of bins (bins are automatically saved at regular intervals), as well as enabling the Super Bin, which confines bin display to a single window. There is also a preference selection for the way an object in the bins will load for editing in either a Source or Record monitor or in a new pop-up monitor.

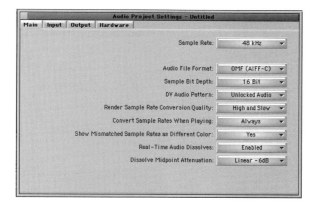

Figure 3.14 Audio Project Settings window

Figure 3.15 Bin Settings window

Capture The Capture settings (see Figure 3.16) include some capture methods, a master preroll method, some deck controls used when capturing, batch settings, media file configuring, and DV scene extractions (available on Xpress Pro only).

Figure 3.16 Capture Settings menu

Deck Configuration Discussed fully in Chapter 2, Deck Configuration settings (see Figure 3.17) allow you to select a supported deck and a controlling protocol such as FireWire (OHCI) or Serial Direct (RS-422).

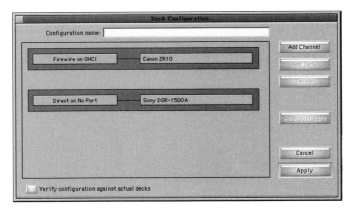

Figure 3.17 Deck Configuration Settings window

Deck Preferences Deck Preference settings (see Figure 3.18) determine how your deck will operate, both during capture and output (also known as digital cut).

Figure 3.18 Deck Preferences Settings window

Desktop Play Delay Desktop Play Delay settings (see Figure 3.19) are intended for FireWire operation, in which the picture can sometimes appear on the desktop sooner than it does in an external monitor. This adjustment allows for DV material to play in sync on your desktop as well as your video monitor.

Figure 3.19 Desktop Play
Delay Settings window

Export Export settings (see Figure 3.20) determine the default settings for exporting either graphic files or QuickTime movies.

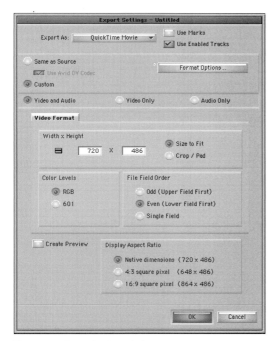

Figure 3.20 Export Settings window

General General settings (see Figure 3.21) include the default start times for digital cut, the naming conventions for files, and the default directory for storing project files.

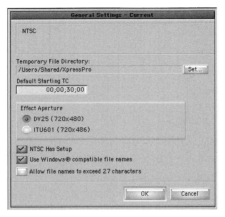

Figure 3.21 General Settings window

Import Like the Export settings, Import settings (see Figure 3.22) determine default settings for input. These file types include image, OMFI (Avid Media Files) Shot Logs, and Audio Files.

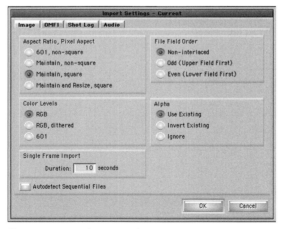

Figure 3.22 Import Settings window

Keyboard Keyboard settings (see Figure 3.23) work differently on Free DV and Xpress Pro. On Free DV, these settings show you the keyboard configuration as it is. With Xpress Pro, it allows you to reconfigure the buttons on the keyboard.

Figure 3.23 Keyboard Settings window

Media Creation The settings for Media Creation (see Figure 3.24) allow you to predetermine a set resolution for different types of files, including captured files, imported files, titles, mixed-down files, motion effects files, and rendered files. Why would you need different resolutions? These are not important on Free DV, but in Xpress Pro if your original media is DV-25, you might want to do a title in uncompressed video to improve the overall image quality. By allowing different resolutions of media streams, you can improve the overall quality of images and save drive space.

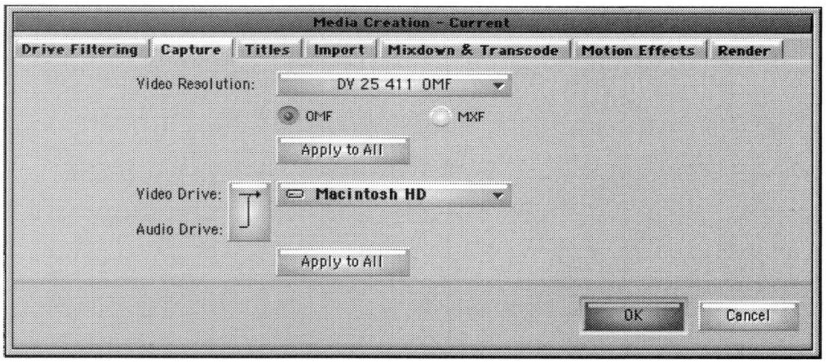

Figure 3.24 Media Creation Settings window

Render The Render settings (see Figure 3.25) allow you to activate a sound when rendering, determine how motion effects are rendered, and further determine the quality of rendered effects (high-quality, low-quality, or rendered as set in each effect. More about that in Chapter 7.)

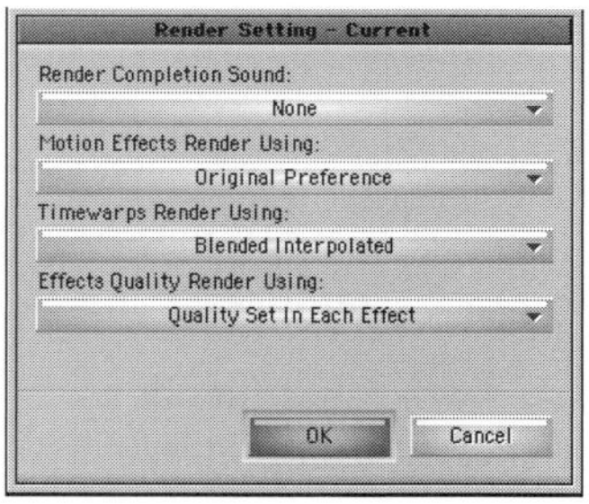

Figure 3.25 Render Settings window

Timeline Settings for the Timeline (see Figure 3.26) include different controls for the Timeline display as well as settings for Timeline editing.

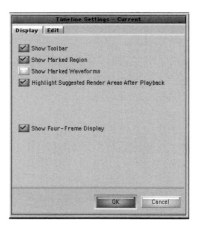

Figure 3.26 Timeline Settings window

Trim The Trim settings (see Figure 3.27) determine the preroll and postroll times when playing back a trim preview. When trimming and analyzing each edit, you have a pre-roll, which is the time in which footage is played before the edit point, and a postroll, which is the footage played after an edit. When playing a trim loop, it repeats itself until you tell it to stop. You will often want an "intermission," in which the loop actually stops before replaying itself. The Intermission settings are here. The Features portion of the Trim settings is used for enabling J-K-L controls. J-K-L controls are enabled only on Xpress Pro, and they are worth the cost of upgrading to Xpress Pro all by themselves. They are one of the best navigation controls invented by Avid.

Figure 3.27 Trim Settings window

Video Display The Video Display settings (Figure 3.28) determine how many streams of video that you want to play at one time, as well as buffer settings for playback. Just a word of caution here: I tend to stick with the defaults because if you try to increase these numbers for maximum playback power, it tends to slow down other functions. On some occasions, it can cause video underruns, in which the system will not be able to play the capacity requested—usually when too many streams of video and unren-dered effects are on the Timeline.

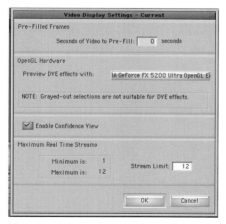

Figure 3.28 Video Display Settings window

Note: The Video Display menu has some new features used in Xpress Pro HD. See the appendix for all the details.

Additional Settings in Xpress Pro

The Settings tab in Xpress Pro (see Figure 3.29) has more controls than in Free DV, plus advanced functions for some of the settings already described. The features unique to Xpress Pro are as follows:

Figure 3.29 Settings tab in Xpress Pro

Controller These settings are for a DigiDesign Control 8 (see Figure 3.30), used for controlling audio playback and missing with Audio Automation. The Control 8 needs a control port (such as RS-422) and is an amazing interface for mixing and fading audio without accessing the GUI.

Figure 3.30 Controller Settings window

Correction The Correction settings (see Figure 3.31) are used for determining color sampling amounts and for the Autocorrection feature, which is a simple tool for color match and color correction.

Figure 3.31 Color Correction Settings window

Interface Interface controls (see Figure 3.32) in Xpress Pro are fairly extensive and fun to use. These settings allow you to change the color scheme for the interface, show tooltips, use tool icons, change the shading of buttons, tweak shading patterns, alter button styles, and do other fun stuff. These settings (obviously) don't affect performance of the system, although they can affect how well you can see and work on the interface. Be sure to try out some of the color schemes. It really makes the system look and feel like your own.

Keyboard In Xpress Pro, the keyboard settings (see Figure 3.33) allow you to remap the keyboard to a custom configuration when used with the Command palette (Ctrl+3/⌘+3). After you're up to speed on Xpress Pro, you can map the most-used keys to the keyboard for more efficient operation of the system.

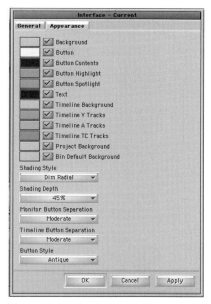

Figure 3.32 Interface Settings window

Figure 3.33 Keyboard Settings window

Safe Colors Xpress Pro will warn you if your output to NTSC goes beyond standard color and brightness signal levels (see Figure 3.34). Because Xpress Pro has the capability to go beyond the limits of NTSC color and brightness, you can adjust these settings to limit output of the system.

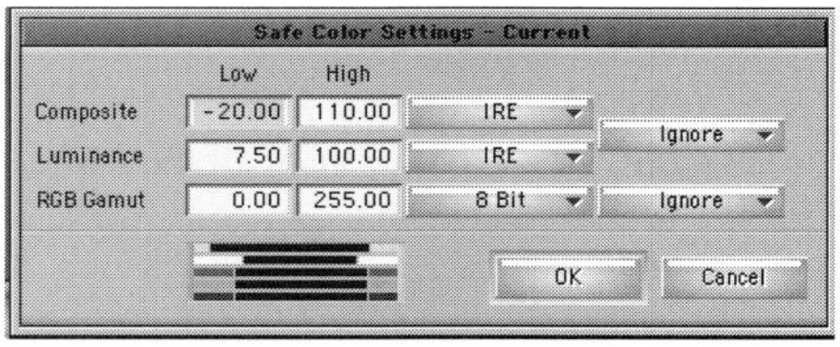

Figure 3.34 Safe Colors Settings window

Script The Script settings (see Figure 3.35) determine how a script will look (font, colors, and so on) when using the Script function of Xpress Pro. The Script function allows you to import a script and use it visually as a bin when editing, much as you would mark a script on paper.

Figure 3.35 Script Settings window

Workspace You can configure your workspace (see Figure 3.36) so that the windows in the interface appear exactly as you like. Workspace settings allow you to continually save your workspace as you edit, activate settings linked by name, or manually update the workspace.

Figure 3.36 Workspace Settings window

Effects Tab

Clicking the Effects tab in the Project window (shown in Figure 3.37) reveals the Effect palette, which displays all the effects available on your system. The Effect palette is composed of two columns. The left column displays the various categories of effects; the right column shows all of the effects available in the selected category. With Free DV, only a few effects are available. Xpress Pro has more than 100 effects, as well as AVX third-party effects that can also be used.

Figure 3.37 Effects tab on Xpress Pro

Info Tab

The Info tab (shown in Figure 3.38) displays system, hardware, and memory availability. There is nothing to set here except information, just as the tab says.

 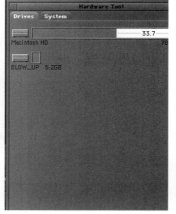

Figure 3.38 The Info tab

Source and Record Windows

Finally, we get to the meat of the subject. The Record and Source windows are key elements when doing basic editing. Notice that the windows have all kinds of information, Timelines, and buttons around them. Let's start at the top and work our way down.

Clip Menu

The Clip menu is a versatile tool (see Figure 3.39). Although it doesn't exactly look like a menu, it is. First, let's make sure that the selected toolset is Source/Record Editing. Now you should see two monitors displayed: the Record and Source monitors. Look above each monitor. The name of the sequence (Record monitor) and clip (Source monitor) should be displayed. Because you probably have not built a sequence yet, we'll focus on the Source monitor. Load a clip in the Source monitor so you can see the name above it. Now click the name, and voilà! You have additional functions: Clear Monitor, Clear Menu, and Duplicate.

Figure 3.39 Clip menu

The Clear Monitor function allows you to clear the display monitor for Source and Record screens. The Clip menu will display the last 20 clips or sequences loaded into each monitor. To clear out the list of clips and sequences, choose Clear Menu. Duplicate will duplicate the clip or sequence currently displayed. This function places the duplicated clip or sequence in the same bin as its original.

Mini-Timeline

Just below the Source and Record monitors is a mini-timeline (see Figure 3.40). This timeline allows you to skip through material instantly or quickly. For example, you can place your cursor on the mini-timeline and drag it to quickly scan through footage, or you can click the Timeline to go to a specific place instantly.

Figure 3.40 Mini-timeline

A word about the mini-timeline. Nonlinear editing allows not only for random editing but also for random access. Many times I see editors who are new to nonlinear dragging through Timelines to find a specific point. This is usually unnecessary, especially if you know approximately where the point exists. Just click the mouse on that section of Timeline and you're instantly there!

Source and Record Buttons

With both Xpress Pro and Free DV, a single row of buttons is displayed underneath both monitors (Figure 3.41). This row of buttons contains some of the most commonly used functions, as we discussed earlier in the chapter. With Xpress Pro, you can customize these interface buttons. Free DV cannot do this, but there is a "hamburger" (Fast menu) button in the middle of the row ▬ that displays other functions.

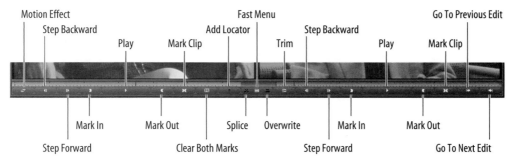

Figure 3.41 The Source and Record buttons

Let's take a look at this row of button icons and describe the function of each button. As we go from left to right, remember that some buttons are duplicated: Those under the Source monitor refer to functions that affect that side, and those under the Record monitor refer to functions that affect that side. But I'll describe each button type only once. Right now, we're just touring the buttons and discussing functions, but don't worry, we'll actually use them in the tutorial at the end of this chapter.

Note: Avid icons are pretty easy to remember, but if you find yourself lost amid the hieroglyphics, hover your mouse over the button and wait. A tooltip will appear that shows the name of the function.

Motion Effect The Motion Effect button, located under the Source monitor, allows you to create different types of slow or fast motion from original clips. Avid does this by using the original source and then creating a new clip with the motion control applied. For example, if you want to have a certain portion of a clip played back at 50 percent speed, you can mark the original clip and click the Motion Effect button to bring up the dialog box shown in Figure 3.42. There, you can tell the program to create the media playback at 50 percent, resulting in a new separate clip that has the marked portion playing back at 50 percent speed.

Figure 3.42 Motion Effect dialog box

Step Backward 1 Frame Clicking this navigation button will move the playback media backward one frame. Clicking and holding the mouse will move it backward slowly. Be careful when clicking and holding, however, because the system might get behind and try to "catch up," continuing to move the media backward after you release the mouse.

Step Forward 1 Frame This button does exactly the same as the Step Backward 1 Frame button, except that it moves forward.

Mark In This button marks an in point on the Source side. When playing back media, you can update Mark In by clicking the button again.

> **Note:** If you play back media and click the Mark In button using the mouse, the playback will stop. If you like to continuously mark during playback without stopping the media from playing, use the Mark In and Mark Out buttons on the keyboard.

Play Plays back the media in the Source monitor.

Mark Out Same as Mark In, but marks an out point.

> **Note:** When you have marked your in point and out point correctly, the icons will appear to be shaped like two faces looking at each other [ ]. If the round "faces" are not "looking" at each other, the clip is marked incorrectly [ ].

Mark Clip Marks an in point at the first frame and an out point at last frame of the clip in the Source monitor.

Clear Both Marks Clear Both Marks will erase the in and out marks on the Source side.

Add Locator The Add Locator button allows you to add a mark to help you locate a particular section of a clip that might be used later or for reference, as shown in Figure 3.43.

When you add a locator, a little red dot will appear under your Source monitor. (This dot will not appear when you play back the clip.) If you click the dot underneath the picture, a box will open up (see Figure 3.44), which will allow you type information, such as why you added the locator in the first place.

Let's take a moment to describe why locators are used. Some of your clips might contain lots of different subject matter. For example, let's say you shot a lot of footage at the zoo and digitized it in one clip. From there, you can add a locator for monkeys, another for alligators, a third for elephants, and so on. Using the locators when you edit will make it easier for you to access the right information without shuttling through the entire clip.

Splice The yellow Splice button is one of two record buttons on the interface. When splicing, you are doing what is called "nondestructive" recording. In other words, anything that appears after your current edit will be moved downward in your sequence versus erasing whatever exists after your edit. This is the major difference between the Splice button and the red Overwrite button.

Figure 3.43 Locator in the Source window

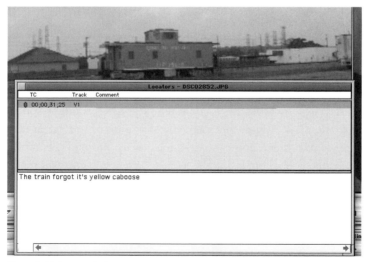

Figure 3.44 Locator window

Fast Menu The Fast menu contains additional functions, as we described before. The Fast menu below the monitors offers the same as the Fast menu on the button bar located at the top of the Timeline. Some of these functions do not work with Free DV. Table 3.2 is a list of those functions.

▶ **Table 3.2** Fast Menu Button Icons

Icon	Action
	Quick Transition allows you to perform certain types of transitions, such as a dissolve or fade, without entering Effects mode.
	Render Effects allows you to render a single effect where the blue position indicator is located.
	Fade Effect will fade the current effect where the blue position indicator is located.
	Remove Effect will remove the effect where the blue position indicator is located.
	Rewind allows you to step backward in the Timeline to the first frame of the previous edit. When you hold down the Alt/Opt key and click this button, it will move backward to the previous locator.
	Fast Forward works like Rewind. When you click it, it will move to the first frame of the next edit in the Timeline. Holding down the Alt/Opt key while clicking it will move forward to the next locator.
	Clear marks will remove the marks in whichever monitor (Source or Record) has been made active at that time.
	Trim Mode activates Trim mode.
	Clipboard pastes whatever is in your Clipboard to the Source monitor. You can press Ctrl + C/Cmd + C to copy clips or marked clips to the Clipboard.
	Match Frame finds the source of wherever you are parked on the Timeline. It finds the source and matches the exact frame where the blue position locator currently resides. You can match the audio or video source, depending on what is selected using the Track Panel selectors.
	You can create a subclip of a clip by marking a section of a clip and clicking the Create Subclip button. The subclip will appear in the bin with the suffix .sub, which indicates that it is a subclip.

Continues

Icon	Action
T	Title Tool activates the Title tool (discussed in Chapter 7).
	Effects Mode activates Effects mode (discussed in Chapter 7).
	Add Keyframes adds keyframes in the Effects or Audio Automation modes.
	Collapse Tracks allows you to collapse multiple video tracks into one single embedded track, which works well when adding a transition effect from a multiple video track section to a single track of video instead of having to add transitions to each layer of the track.
	Grid adds a title-safe and action-safe grid to whichever monitor is selected.
	Go To In Point goes to the in point on the active monitor (Source or Record).
	Go To Out Point goes to the out point on the active monitor (Source or Record).
	Splice splices an edit.
	Overwrite overwrites an edit.
EQ	EQ activates the audio equalizer menu (Xpress Pro only).
	Activates Automation Gain does not work in Free DV, but you can select Auto Gain through the hamburger at the bottom left of the Timeline and add keyframes to adjust levels.
	Audio Punch In Tool activates audio punch in, where you can record from an external source (e.g., a microphone) and record directly to the Timeline (Xpress Pro only).
	Audio Suite enables the Digidesign Audio Suite menu, in which you can add Digidesign audio effects such as reverb and echo (not available on Free DV).

Note: All the icons for Audio Suite, Audio Punch In, Automation Gain, and EQ are on the Fast menu button palette for Free DV. When you click them, however, the system will beep at you and do nothing more. I believe these buttons were left over from building Xpress applications, but they might entice you.

Note: Click the Fast Menu button, and move your mouse over it to the right bottom icon [image]. If you jerk the mouse a little, the Fast menu detaches itself. You can move this icon box onto the desktop and use it to give yourself more functions.

Overwrite The Overwrite button creates a destructive edit. When using Overwrite, the edit will destroy anything after it on the Timeline for the duration of that edit. If you want to keep everything beyond your current edit intact, use the Splice button (with sync locks turned on).

Trim Clicking this button enables Trim mode, which we will discuss later.

Go To Previous Edit This button moves to the previous edit in the sequence.

Go to Next Edit This button moves to the next edit in the sequence.

Timecode Registers

The Timecode registers on the Source and Record monitors are located at the top center of the interface (see Figure 3.45). The registers allow you to display a variety of different timecodes, including the master timecode, original timecode from the source tape, the duration from the marked in point to the marked out point, the absolute location of the media from the beginning of the clip, and the remaining time of the clip from where it is currently parked. The Record monitor register (see Figure 3.46) also allows for showing footage and code from the original film.

Figure 3.45 Timecode registers on the Source monitor

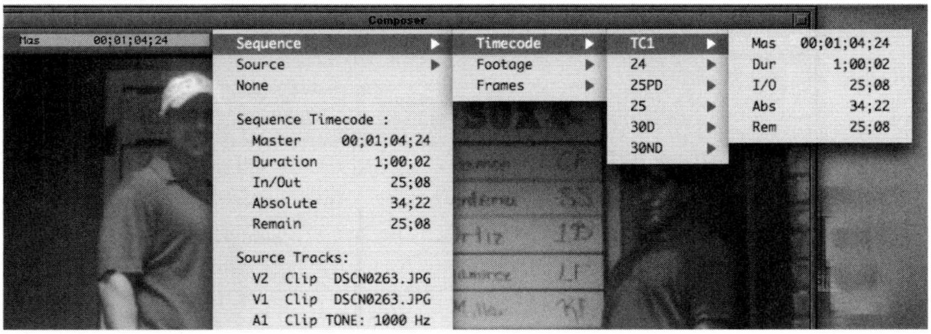

Figure 3.46 Timecode registers on the Record monitor

Bin Views

The bins are, of course, the places in which you store clips, sequences, effects, and so forth. But different editors have different ways they would like to see this information displayed. For example, you might want to see a thumbnail icon for each clip instead of a line of information. Or you might want to see a brief line of information. A single line of information with just the name of the clip usually takes up far less screen space than icons. Some editors (myself included) tend to prefer that method of display. Still others, especially assistant editors, need every bit of information necessary about all the clips, which tends to take up a lot of space. Fortunately, with Free DV and Xpress Pro, you have the ability to display your bins in any of these manners.

Brief View

The Brief bin view (shown in Figure 3.47) allows you more screen "real estate" than the other views. With the Brief display, headings for clip name, start timecode, duration, tracks, and offline media are displayed. You can also resize the bin window so that only the name of the clips appears. I do this frequently on projects with which I am familiar with the material in each clip.

Figure 3.47 Brief bin view

Text View

The Text view (shown in Figure 3.48) is similar to the Brief Bin view, except that more criteria are added. Additional default headings in Text mode include Mark In, Mark Out, In-Out, Video (resolution, such as DV-25), Audio (sampling rate such as 48 kHz), Drive (the drive in which the media for the clip is located), Creation Date of the clip, and the Tape ID name.

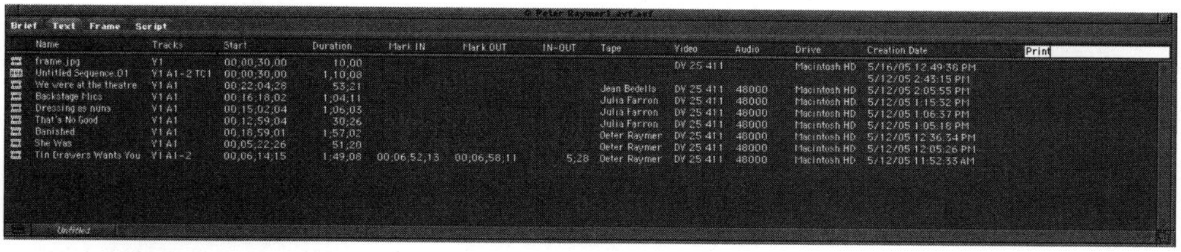

Figure 3.48 Adding a heading in Text view

You can also customize your bins in Free DV or Xpress Pro by adding new headings. For example, you could add a heading called **Print** to the bin, which could be used to determine which clips should be captured. On each clip, we will type a **Y** or **N** for Yes or No. To create this custom heading, do the following:

1. Click the Brief tab above your bin.
2. Click in the empty space beyond all the other columns. A cursor should appear.
3. Type the word **Print**.
4. Click Return.
5. Your custom heading will appear. From here, you can enter data underneath this heading for each clip.

> **Note:** Once you have entered your Y and N, Alt/Option-clicking in that custom column will reveal a choice of the text you have entered on other rows.

Cool, huh? You can create custom headings for just about any criteria that you can think of. They can be sorted, sifted, amended, and saved. Also, note that custom headings can be viewed only in the Text view of Free DV, but they can be displayed in Brief or Text view on Xpress Pro.

There are also other preset bin headings that can be displayed in both Xpress Pro and Free DV. To access these, use the Text view and then choose Bins > Headings. A menu will allow you to select bin headings (columns), including custom headings that you have already created.

Frame View

The Frame view (shown in Figure 3.49) allows you to view a single thumbnail frame of each clip inside the bin. The idea is to have a picture that will help you identify the clip. The default display shows the first frame of the clip.

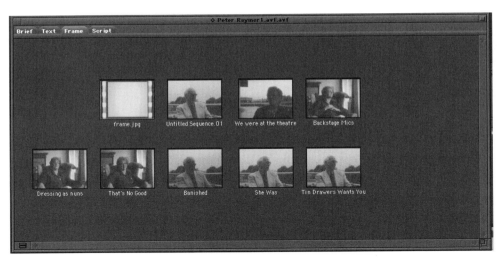

Figure 3.49 Frame view

However, that frame may not be the one that you need. You can change the default frame by doing the following:

1. Click the thumbnail icon that you want to change. You might need to enlarge the thumbnail; to do this, press Ctrl+L/⌘+L on the keyboard. (You can shrink them down again by pressing Ctrl+K/⌘+K.)

2. Use the 1, 2, 3, and 4 buttons on your alphanumeric keyboard as follows:

Key	Action
1	Moves the picture 10 frames backward
2	Moves the picture 10 frames forward
3	Moves the picture 1 frame backward
4	Moves the picture 1 frame forward

3. After you choose the correct frame, the bin saves it as the default icon for that clip.

Underneath each thumbnail icon is the name of the clip. You can arrange the thumbnails in any order you want. Another method is to press Play or use the J, K, and L key combinations to get to the proper frame quickly.

Script View

The Script view (shown in Figure 3.50) allows you to combine text, thumbnails, and notes for each clip. The thumbnail is displayed on the left, the text information is displayed on top, and there is a large space to type or cut and paste information about the clip.

The Script view isn't used often, but for some situations it allows you to attach information inside a bin for clips that may need it for some specialized purpose.

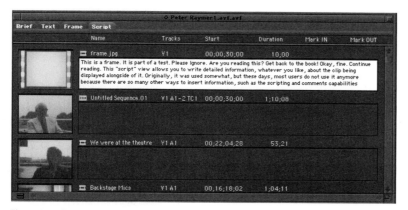

Figure 3.50 Script view

Note: This view was created before Avid created the Script function, in which you can actually import a text script and use it as a bin (available only on Xpress Pro).

The Timeline

If you've looked ahead in this book, you probably already know that the next chapter is all about the Timeline. Nonetheless, in our tour of the interface, we must take a look at the basic functions of the Timeline because it is a very powerful tool.

In some ways, it's funny. When Avid first developed the Timeline, it did very little. In fact, it did nothing more than graphically represent a chronology of edits made in your current sequence, which it still does. But as the industry continued to explore the possibilities of using the Timeline, Avid made it much more powerful than in the early days. Now you can digitize in the Timeline, move clips, juxtapose shots, monitor audio, and so much more. Let's take a look at a typical Timeline and examine the components that you expect to see.

Source and Record Track Indicators

The Source and Record track indicators to the left of the Timeline tell you what tracks are available on the Source side and what tracks have been created on the Record side. You can add more tracks on the Record side as needed. The track indicators are also used for patching Source tracks to the Record tracks (see Figure 3.51). In other words, you can patch a Source from audio track 2 to the Record track of audio track 1, and so forth. I'll show you how to do it in the next chapter.

Figure 3.51 Patching tracks using track indicators

On Free DV, you can have two video tracks and two audio tracks. It might not seem like much, but you can do a lot with it. Most documentaries need little more. Xpress Pro will allow 24 tracks of audio and 24 tracks of video. Why so many tracks? It depends upon the complexity of the sequence. For films, I use a maximum of four video tracks and rarely more than eight tracks of audio. But I have to admit that it's nice to know that I have more than I need. If you're doing an effects-laden sequence, you need all the video tracks you can get.

When the track indicators are active, they light up. In Free DV, they change from gray to silver. Try clicking one of the indicators and you'll see. In Xpress Pro, the tracks normally change from silver to purple when active. The track indicators have even more have more capabilities that we'll discuss in the next chapter.

Buttons

The buttons in the Timeline (shown in Figure 3.52) offer more functions at the click of a mouse. There are 16 buttons at the top of the Timeline. Let's take a moment to examine these functions.

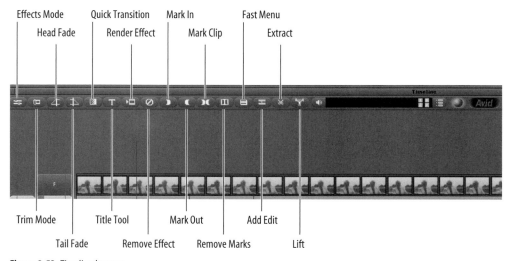

Figure 3.52 Timeline buttons

Effects Mode The Effects Mode button changes the interface so that you are in Effects mode. This might seem similar to the Effects Editing toolset, and in some ways it is. The difference is that the Effects Editing toolset changes the entire interface.

Note: Instead of seeing Source and Record monitors, the Effects Editing toolset displays a single monitor where the effects are displayed. Clicking the Effects Mode button puts you into the Effects mode, where you can change effects, but both Source and Record monitors remain on-screen. I tend to prefer using the Effects Editing toolset because it focuses on one specific effect and eliminates the clutter of Source/Record mode.

Trim Mode Like the Effects Mode button, the Trim Mode button changes the functionality of the interface so that you can work on transitions rather than edit additional material. When we use the Trim mode, we are adjusting each edit so that more or less material is shown in the transitions between edits. You might say that in Trim mode we are fine-tuning the cut. You can also use the Trim mode for adding simple transition effects such as dissolves and fades.

Note: We'll be trimming like crazy in Chapter 5.

Head Fade The Head Fade button allows you to add a video and/or audio fade to the beginning or incoming part of a sequence. Park your Timeline where you want the transition to end, select the tracks to be faded on the track indicators, and click the button. That's all there is to it. The head fade begins the transition at the edit point before the blue position indicator and continues it to wherever you have parked it. When you bring up the Effect Editor, you can change the duration of the effect at the bottom right of the screen by clicking the number and entering a new number of frames for the transition.

Tail Fade The Tail Fade button acts exactly like the Head Fade button, but it applies the fade at the end of a sequence in the Timeline. The procedure to create a tail fade is exactly like creating a head fade, except that the position of the Timeline is on the end of a sequence rather than the beginning.

Quick Transition The Quick Transition button enables you to add a limited number of transition types, including dissolve, fade to color, fade from color, or dip to color. For most purposes, this button (shown in Figure 3.53) is used as a method of transitioning quickly between clips on the Timeline. For example, if you want to dissolve between two scenes, there's no need to go into Effects mode and adjust the effect—you can do it much more quickly by clicking the Quick Transition button.

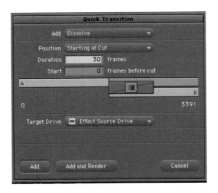

Figure 3.53 Quick Transition window

The Quick Transition button also allows you to adjust the duration of the transition, select a drive for rendering the effect, render the effect to the drive, and determine the position of the effect between segments.

Title Tool Clicking the Title Tool button activates the titling interface for your system. This is a shortcut to the menu command Clip > New Title. The Title Tool button creates titles for your sequence using the fonts available on your computer as well as some basic geometric figures; controls for varying opacity, shadow, and color; and adjustments for varying opacity or "washing" elements onto the screen.

Note: I talk more about the Title Tool button in Chapter 7.

Render Effect When you create an effect such as a dissolve, the system can frequently reproduce the effect during playback. Effects such as these are called *real-time effects*. When you add an effect to the Timeline, you will notice that an effect icon appears. There is also a dot next to the effect, which is either green or blue. To the far right of the top of your Timeline is a green or blue button. If that button is blue, click it. It should turn green. After the green dot appears at the top of your Timeline, real-time effects are enabled on your system.

Note: If you are using a Mojo, the effects are all real time, and no dots appear.

After the real-time effects are enabled, you can see if you can play back an effect. If the effect on your Timeline is blue, it is not a real-time effect and needs to be rendered. If the effect is green, you probably won't need to render it until you're finished with your sequence.

So just what is rendering? Rendering is the creation of an effect or effects so that they can play back on your system without causing the system to be overloaded. When we render, Free DV or Xpress Pro looks at the media and creates a new piece of media containing the effect. This is necessary because the computation required to reproduce an effect using just computer power is too extensive. It's much easier for your system to just read a media file than to have to create it on the fly. So rendering is necessary. It can also be time-consuming.

To render an effect, place the blue position cursor on the effect in the Timeline and click the Render Effect button. Choose a source drive (the drive where the rendered effect will reside) and choose Render. The effect will render. Once rendered, an effect in the Timeline will have no dot next to it. It is ready to play in real time.

Note: Rendering is discussed in more detail in Chapter 7.

Remove Effect If you've decided that you would prefer to remove an effect that already exists in your Timeline, move the blue position indicator so that it rests on the effect, select the track where the effect exists on the track indicator, and click the Remove Effect button. The effect icon will disappear from your Timeline.

Mark In This Mark In button works exactly the same as the Mark In button underneath the Source and Record monitors, with one exception: The mark will be placed on whichever monitor is selected. Note that when a monitor is selected, its mini-timeline is silver—slightly brighter than the usual gray. So if you want to mark in on the Source monitor, click the Source monitor first to activate it and then use this key.

Mark Out The Mark Out button works the same as the Mark In button, as explained previously. The Mark Out key will apply only to the selected monitor.

Mark Clip The Mark Clip button is the same as described previously. It affects only the selected monitor.

Remove Marks The Remove Marks button clears the Mark In and Mark Out of the selected monitor.

Fast Menu The Fast Menu button displays additional function buttons. This is redundant to the Fast Menu button underneath the Source and Record monitors.

Add Edit The Add Edit button has so many uses that it is somewhat difficult to describe. Basically, all it does is create an edit in the middle of a clip, splitting it into two clips. At the outset, adding an edit does nothing. But in the hands of a skillful and creative editor (i.e., *you*) Add Edit can create interesting transitions.

Here's an example. Let's say that you have a picture of a woman walking down the street. Not a particularly interesting shot, mind you. You can spiff it up with some fun color effects! By using the Add Edit button every five frames or so, you created several separate edits. Now you can apply the color effect to each and adjust the colors so that the image changes colors every five frames as the woman walks. Wow! Boffo spiffo whammo effects!

All right, maybe not the most creative thing, but you get the idea. Add Edit can isolate parts of a continuous clip in which you can add effects or audio adjustments so that the continuous clip no longer appears to be continuous.

Extract We already know that the Splice button makes an edit so that any edits after your current edits are moved down in the Timeline. What if you want to remove an edit and move everything on the Timeline backward? Enter the Extract button, indicated by an icon with scissors.

Clicking the Extract button removes any marked part of the sequence and pulls any material after it back to the first frame after the extracted material.

Lift The Lift button works like Extract, except that any material removed from the Timeline will be replaced by a black (empty) gap, rather than having the material after the extraction pulled up. Lift is pretty much the opposite of Overwrite.

Audio Meters

The Audio Meters on the Timeline are new features—and good ones, too. Using these meters allows you to monitor audio at any time without having to pull out the Audio tool and take up more desktop space.

The Audio Meter enables you to adjust the monitor level (not output levels) of your audio (as shown in Figure 3.54); switch from input to output monitoring; adjust, create, and play back tone; hide the meters; and adjust peaks.

Figure 3.54 Adjusting audio monitor level

 Note: Audio monitoring will be discussed more in Chapter 4.

Toggle Digital Video Out (Non-Mojo Systems)

Toggling the Digital Video Out button allows you to switch between enabling real-time effects and disabling them. At first glance, you might wonder why in the world you would ever want to disable real-time effects. Here's why: The only way that you can monitor your video on an NTSC screen is by disabling real-time effects. When the real-time function is on, this button is bright green. When real-time effects are disabled, this button is blue.

Wouldn't it be great if you could both enable real-time effects *and* play back on an external monitor? Yes, it would, but the problem is that when you play back on your Xpress Pro or Free DV with real-time effects and have to also create a true video signal that can play back on a monitor, it's a little too much for the system to take. Every system has limitations. Is there is a solution? Yes, there is. Disable real-time effects, mark your sequence from beginning to end, and hit the Render button. After all your effects are rendered, they will play back in real time on an external monitor.

Shortcuts for Navigation and Editing

In the following tutorial, I'll point out at appropriate places the ways that you can speed up your work using keyboard shortcuts. But to get you started, Table 3.3 provides a preview of the most common time-savers.

▶ **Table 3.3** Keyboard Shortcuts for Navigation and Editing

Key	Action
Caps Lock	Toggle digital scrub on or off
3 or right arrow	Advance one frame
4 or left arrow	Go back one frame
5 or spacebar	Play the current clip
J	Fast backward; press repeatedly to increase speed
L	Fast forward; press repeatedly to increase speed
J and K	Scrub backward at $\frac{1}{4}$ speed
K and L	Scrub forward at $\frac{1}{4}$ speed
I	Mark In
O	Mark Out
Q	Go to the marked in point ("cue")
W	Go to the marked out point
A	Go to the previous edit in the Timeline
S	Go to the next edit in the Timeline
Home	Go to the start of the current clip

Tutorial: Making the First Edit

Well, you've learned a lot about the interface. Time to put it to use. Before we begin the next several tutorials, you have a little file-shuffling to do.

Prepping the Project

First, if the Avid application is open, close it. Find the folder on your system named Avid Projects. You're going to copy some projects from the companion DVD to your system so that you can complete the tutorial. Open the Avid Projects folder and you will see your username. Open that folder and any projects that you have created should be displayed in folders.

On the DVD, you will find two folders: One is named Xpress_Pro, and the other is named Free_DV. Be sure to use *only* the projects for your system. Free DV projects and bins cannot be read on Xpress Pro systems, and vice versa.

1. After you've found the right spots, copy those project folders from the correct named DVD folder (Xpress Pro or Free DV) to the hard disk folder with your username. The correct path on your computer should be should be one of these:

    \Xpress Pro\Avid_Projects*your_username*
    \Free DV\Avid_Projects*your_username*

2. The next step is to copy the media files. If you've already done the exercise in Chapter 2, you will note that there is a folder on your computer named OMFI MediaFiles. There is a folder by the same name on the DVD. Copy the files from the DVD to the OMFI MediaFiles folder. Do not copy the folder, just the files.

3. Eject the DVD, and start the Avid application.

4. Open the project named Avid Made Easy. In this tutorial, we're going to do some editing and a little media navigation, and we'll play around with some of the functions to get you familiar. To begin, open the bin named Tin Drawers.

Before we begin editing, let me give you a little background on the subject matter here. The clips are from the film *When We Were Queens*, a documentary about the founding of the Royal Ballet in England. (The film is copyrighted by Nunaka Valley Films. These clips have been licensed for educational use only with this book.) What we're going to do in the tutorials is edit a couple of pieces from interviews with some of the dancers and crew that were with the ballet before World War II.

Interviews can be very tough and exacting, particularly when subjects add parenthetical information that is unnecessary to a story being told. Are you ready? Let's start cutting!

Loading Clips

Let's take a look at the first and only clip in the bin: Tin Drawers. Double-click the clip; it should load in the left (Source) monitor. If the source appears in a pop-up monitor, choose Toolset > Source/Record Editing so the two monitors appear side by side.

Click the Play button underneath the Source monitor and listen to the story. As you can see, there's some work that can be done to move the story along a little faster. The duration of the story is one minute and 49 seconds, but we don't have that much time for this anecdote. So we're going to go through this story bit by bit and clean it up by editing in the parts that comprise the story and leaving out those that don't.

Marking Clips

Now that you've heard the Tin Drawers story, do you understand it? I purposely used subjects from the U.K. for these tutorials because their accents can be challenging to decipher. Also, the story is drawn out way too much, with a lot of parenthetical detail that we can do without. So let's start by going back to the beginning of the clip. Click the Source monitor, and press the Home key on your keyboard. This should bring the clip back to the beginning.

Now we want to mark the beginning of the story. Just where *does* this story begin? Play it back again until you hear "She came to one...." We'll need to mark an in point (see Figure 3.55) right before the word "she." First, try marking the clip when playing it back at normal speed. Try to mark an in point before he says, "She came to one." If you don't think you came close enough, try it again until you get the rhythm or cadence of his voice.

Figure 3.55 Marking the Tin Drawers clip

Now you might be wondering, "How well did I mark it?" Let's find out. Go to your Settings tab in the Project window and double-click the Keyboard settings. A keyboard should appear. Leave the keyboard up on the interface so that you can see all the functions available.

Press the Q key, which cues the clip up to your marked in point. Now press Play. What you will hear is the clip played from your marked in point. Does it sound right? Probably not. This is a tough point to mark, so you have to try some other tools to locate the correct point. Go back to the in point (press Q) and you'll do a little scrubbing.

First, try digital scrub. To digitally scrub the audio, do the following:

1. Press the Caps Lock key.

2. Scrub back and forth around the area of your in point by pressing the 3 key (on the alphanumeric keyboard, not the numeric keyboard). The 3 key moves a single frame backward every time you press it. Or you can hold the 3 key down and it will progress backward frame by frame. Notice that you can hear each single frame of audio as it moves backward.

3. You can use the 4 key on the alphanumeric keyboard to move forward frame by frame.

4. When you've found the right point, click the Mark In icon underneath the Source monitor.

5. Now press Q on the keyboard to return to the marked frame and press 5 to play it back.

Does it sound better this time? You might do better by trying analog scrub. Analog scrubbing is achieved through the letter keys. Here's how to do it:

1. First, turn off digital scrub (press the Caps Lock key again) and cue up to your marked in point (Q).

2. Now you use the J, K, and L keys on the keyboard. To scrub backward on the clip, hold down the J and K keys together, which should cause the clip to play backward at about ¼ speed (approximately 8 frames per second [fps]).

3. To move forward, hold down the K and L keys again, pressing them at the same time, which moves the clip forward at ¼ speed. With analog scrub, you can hear as the clip rolls, not one frame at a time, but continuously.

You can also "rock and roll" through the piece by holding your fingers on J, K, and L. Rock backward by holding J and K and then roll forward by holding K and L. This is a great way to find your points. Every time you attempt to find and mark a new point, press Q followed by Play until you're satisfied with the in point.

Now you need to find an out point. The best out point that I found is when he says, "and she suddenly called for the stage manager." So let's mark it.

First, try marking it as it plays. Here, you use the O key on the keyboard. Notice that on the keyboard, you can mark in using the I key and mark out using the O key. It's an intuitive way to remember where the marks buttons are on the keyboard. Further, in order to "cue" the edit to the first marked frame, you are using the Q button on the keyboard. Clever, huh?

Note that when you make a mark on the GUI using your mouse, the clip stops playing. This isn't true with the keyboard. When I mark a clip, I like to click the mark button on the keyboard continuously until the correct point occurs. You can achieve this only by using the keyboard.

All right, away you go. Find the mark out point that you designated and then overwrite audio track 1 and video into your sequence by activating those tracks on the Timeline. Click and make the A1 and V1 track selectors active on both sides. Remember, Overwrite is the Red record button on the interface, or you can use the B button on the keyboard.

By doing this, you should have created a brand new sequence. Take a look at the upper right of your screen. Above the Record monitor should be the words Untitled Sequence.01. Look in the bin for a sequence with the same name. Click the name and retitle it **Basic Editing Sequence**.

Huzzah! You've made your first Avid edit ... okay, party over, let's move on.

Navigating through Media

We're going to continue to edit our way through this story, but first let me show you some more navigation tools.

The most important navigation tool is the mouse. Remember, there is no rewinding and fast-forwarding necessary. You can move to any point in the interview *instantaneously* by clicking your mouse in the mini-timeline underneath the Source monitor. You can also do this on the Record side, either clicking on the mini-timeline underneath the Record monitor or clicking the Timeline at the bottom of the screen.

Another great navigation tool are the J, K, and L buttons. In the last section, we talked about using the slow motion analog scrubbing with the JKLs. Now let's try some faster navigation.

1. Go to the beginning of the clip (press Q).

2. Press the L key. The clip should play normally.

3. Now, press the L key again. It will play back the clip at double speed (60 fps) Clicking it again plays at 90 fps and then at 150 fps. At 150 fps, the analog sound scrub goes away.

4. Click it yet again, and the clip will play at 240 fps, which is top speed.

The J key does the exact same thing, only backward. Press it once for –30 fps, again for –60 fps, –90 fps, –150 fps, and –240 fps.

I use both J and L to find points without listening in slow motion as we did earlier. To do this "rocking and rolling" technique, place your fingers on the J and L keys and then move the clip backward and forward until you find the right point.

Here are some other ways to navigate through your media:

- The W button takes you to the marked out point.
- The 5 and spacebar keys play back the clip.
- The A key takes you to the previous edit in the Timeline.
- The S key takes you to the next edit in the Timeline.
- The left and right arrows on your keyboard jog one frame backward and one frame forward, respectively.

Making the Edit

We've already made our first Avid edit. Yay! Now we'll continue. When we make the first cut of a piece, we try not to focus too much on precision. That will come later. So leave the Record side alone. That may seem strange at first. After all, don't we need to see if it plays correctly as we originally marked it?

Well, no.

We'll look for precision later, when we study the Trim mode. Right now, we're just trying to get the material into the sequence. So again, I advise you not to play back the Record side.

There's another reason for this. If we lay down each cut from the clip while ignoring what's there on the Record side, we don't have to make a new marked in point on the Record side; it automatically places the new clip where the last clip ended.

Playing back after each cut is germane to the video editor because video editors have been taught from the beginning to check each edit after it's done. That's because the edits were linear, so they were "permanent." Nowadays, you can lay it all down and clean up later.

Now we'll do the second edit. Make a mark in where the subject says, "Send for Alastair James up here." Let it continue for approximately 53 seconds. The out cue is "leave them … alone." After marking, use the yellow Splice button or the V key on the keyboard to record audio track 1 and video to the sequence.

The Two Methods of Editing: Splice and Overwrite

The second edit is too long. I did that on purpose to show you specifically how the two methods of recording work. First, we'll try splicing, which opens up the sequence and adds new material, but does not erase anything that existed where the new material is recorded. Splicing expands the sequence to include newly recorded material as well as any material that was recorded before it.

1. First, we need to find a mark on the Record side, where we will add our new edit. Play back the second edit. You can cue up to the second edit by pressing the Ctrl or Command key while clicking the mouse in the Timeline near that edit. Play back the edit and mark a new in point after "tell him to come up here."

2. Go back to the Source side. We'll pick it up on the source where he says, "off I scuttled." Make an out point where he says, "tin drawers wants you." Be sure to lose the big laugh at the end.

3. Press the yellow Splice button. You will see that we've made another edit on the Timeline. Let's play it back from the beginning.

The first edit is there, followed by your third edit, and the second edit follows. Note that the second edit is intact with nothing missing. That's because we spliced, which moves the edit down on the Timeline.

Now we'll overwrite:

1. First, we'll use our Undo keys. You're probably familiar with the Undo function from other applications. The Undo command is ⌘+Z on Mac OS, Ctrl+Z on Windows. Doing this will erase or undo the third edit that you made. Go ahead and do this, noting that the edit disappears from the Timeline. Avid has a maximum of 32 undos available, so you can go backward quite a bit. Keep in mind that once the application is closed, the Undo buffer disappears. In other words, if you quit and restart the system, there is nothing to undo. The Undo buffer also disappears when you switch sequences in your Record monitor.

2. Now we'll go ahead and make the previous edit again, this time using Overwrite. With Overwrite, the edit covers whatever existed underneath it, thus "erasing" some of that long second edit that we made.

> **Note:** A better analogy is to say that Overwrite works like videotape. Make an edit on videotape, and whatever used to be there is erased. Splice works like film. When you make a splice, you open up the film, add the new material, and then splice the other existing material after it.

3. Okay, overwrite the third edit, much as you did with the Splice function. All the previous marks still exist, so just press the red button.

Take a look at what was done. The Timeline doesn't expand because you replaced the old material with new material. The last segment of the Timeline is garbage. In the next part of the tutorial, we'll get rid of it.

Changing Your Edits: Lift and Extract

Once again, I remind you that anything in your Timeline is not set in stone. You can always go back and replace, move delete, add, and otherwise change any existing edits that have been made.

Note: In fact, there is a dark side to all of this. If you can change your edits, so can anyone else! Be sure to make copies of your projects on an external drive, thumb drive, CD, or other device. Just find the Project folder, copy it, and you're done. If something happens to your project, you can always replace it with your backup copy.

Now, let's take a look at two ways of changing your edit.

The Lift key works like videotape. If you were to remove an edit using the Lift key, it would remove the edit and leave a black hole where it existed. Let's try using Lift.

The Lift icon ![lift icon] is the last button at the top of your Timeline. It resembles a muscular person lifting weights. Get it? He's LIFT-ing. Oh, never mind.

1. Find the second edit in your sequence and put your blue position indicator there on the Timeline. You can put the blue position indicator anywhere in the edit; it doesn't have to be at any one given point.

2. Now, click the Mark Clip button below the Record monitor. Remember, this is the first button to the right of Mark Out. This button marks the second edit in the Timeline. Now take a deep breath. If you're nervous, take another.

3. Click the Lift key.

Note that the second edit disappeared, leaving a blank space in the Timeline. If you play the sequence back, black will appear where the edit previously existed. You've lifted out an edit.

Now we'll try extracting. Extract works much like Lift, except that instead of leaving a blank hole in the Timeline, it pulls up all the edits that exist after it. Rather than explaining it in detail, let's use this function and see it in action.

1. If you just did the Lift edit, undo that action (Ctrl+Z/⌘+Z).

2. Click that second edit in the Timeline and press Mark Clip. This time, instead of using Lift, we'll use the Extract key. The icon for Extract is a pair of scissors ![scissors icon] . The icon is just to the left of the Lift key on the top of the Timeline.

3. Click the Extract key.

Note that this time, instead of leaving a black hole, you've extracted the edit and moved the remaining material up to the point of your extraction. This also has shortened the sequence. So we can say that extracting will remove unwanted material and pull up the material after it.

You can use Splice and Extract to do subtractive editing as well. If you laid down the entire clip, marked an in and out point on each section to be removed, and then used Extract, it would pull out unwanted pieces and pull together the elements that remained. Using this method, you mark the edits to be pulled *out*, not the edits to place *in* the sequence.

Undo and Redo

The Undo/Redo buffer (see Figure 3.56) allows for 32 different actions, as mentioned before. You can undo (Ctrl+Z/⌘+Z) or redo (Ctrl+R/⌘+R) any actions that you've done that alter either the Source or Record sides of your sequence.

Figure 3.56 The Undo/Redo buffer

This buffer works only in a linear way. For example, let's say you did the following:

1. Mark In Source
2. Mark Out Source
3. Mark In Record
4. Splice

So the Splice was the last thing that you did. And now, you want to undo the Mark In on the Record side. If you Undo it, you will have to also undo the Splice, which was done after it. In other words, you cannot selectively undo or redo. These functions work in the buffer chronologically, or as they occurred.

Finishing the Editing Tutorial

Continue the editing on your own, using all the tools learned thus far. I wrote the story line that follows. Edit the story as best you can, leaving out less-important elements. Listen for story content only. Don't worry about the jump cuts—we'll fix them later. If you lost track of how the story should go, take a look in the Finished Sequence bin for Basic Editing Final for my version of the cut.

She came to one performance, so we put her into a box on the front side there, and she suddenly sent for the stage manager, and she said, "Send for Alastair James up here, tell him to come up here."

Off I scuttled and I said, "I hate to say it, but I think Tin Drawers wants you." He said "Oh my God!" and he came up aquake and aquiver and he said, "Yes, Ma'am." And she said, "Can't see … more light I must have more light, more light."

So Alastair James said, "Yes, madame"… I mean, to change the light in a conventional theatre is like asking for rain in the Sahara! I said, "What are you going to do?" He said, "Leave them alone." So up it came, one of the ballets and she said, "Get Alastair James up here …," she said. "Much better. Much better dear boy!"

The Timeline

The Timeline, once an almost insignificant window that graphically displayed a chronology of your sequence, has now become a fully interactive tool. With the Timeline, you can now edit, juxtapose, move segments, trim, and delete. In this chapter, we'll review the various segments of the Timeline and explore in depth how each works.

Chapter Contents

Working with Tracks: Track Panel Selectors
Audio Tool
Audio Settings
Tutorial: Building a Timeline

Working with Tracks: Track Panel Selectors

As mentioned in the last chapter during the walkaround of the GUI, the track panel selectors of the Timeline (see Figure 4.1) appear on the left side of the space where your sequence is represented. These selectors are indicators of which tracks are available on both source and record media. These selectors appear in two columns: the left side indicators are for the Source clip, and the right column of track selectors are for the record sequence.

Figure 4.1 Track panel selectors

Source Track Panel

In the track panel selectors, the Source track panel represents the tracks that have been created when you captured or imported your source. These track names cannot be changed, because they were created when the source was created. So when you've captured a clip containing video and channel 1 of an audio source (see Figure 4.2), the Source track panel selectors appear, indicating video and audio channel 1. When you import a visual file with no audio whatsoever, the Source track panel selectors will indicate that only a video track is available as source.

Figure 4.2 (left) Video and audio 1 source;
(right) video-only source

Of course, there is no possible method of capturing to video track 2, so your Source panel indicators will never show a second video track. Furthermore, you cannot add additional tracks once the source has been created (either through the Capture tool or by importing sources.)

Record Track Panel

The Record track panel selectors work a little differently from the Source track panel selectors that were already described. The Record track panel indicates those tracks that have been added to the sequence at any time. However, there are a few rules of the game.

USING FREE DV

When you create a brand new sequence using Free DV, the Record track panel indicators show filmstrip, video, audio track 1, audio track 2, and a timecode track for the sequence (see Figure 4.3). It does not matter what the source is; they will always be present on the Record track panel selector.

Figure 4.3 Record track panel selector (right) when a new sequence is created using Free DV

> **Note:** The filmstrip track is a visual representation of what is inside the sequence. It cannot be edited except by adding or subtracting footage from the video track. Other than being a visual representation, there isn't much you can do with it, but you can print out your Timeline by clicking on the Timeline and pressing Ctrl+P/⌘+P to see thumbnails of your sequence in this track.

USING XPRESS PRO

When you create a brand new sequence using Xpress Pro, the Record track panel selectors appear differently. In this case, video, audio 1, audio 2, audio 3, audio 4, and a timecode track appear (see Figure 4.4). The filmstrip track is not present.

Figure 4.4 Record track panel selector (right) when a new sequence is created using Xpress Pro

I Want My Filmstrip!

If you want the filmstrip track to appear in a Timeline using Xpress Pro, click the Timeline Fast menu at the bottom of the Timeline window and choose Show Track > Film. The filmstrip track appears on-screen. Using this feature, you can show whatever tracks you prefer in Xpress Pro. (Unfortunately, you cannot choose the tracks to display using Free DV.)

Track Panel Selector Characteristics

Each track panel selector has specific characteristics relating to activating, monitoring, soloing, and—in the case of audio—scrubbing.

ACTIVATING

When a track panel selector is activated, it changes color. In Free DV, it changes from charcoal to silver. In Xpress Pro, it changes from silver to purple. But what does "activation" do?

When you activate a track panel selector, you are indicating that it is active for an edit. If the Source selector has no horizontally corresponding Record track panel selector activated (see Figure 4.5), nothing is edited. However, if the Source track panel selector has a horizontally corresponding Record track panel selector activated, an edit will be possible.

Figure 4.5 (left) The activated tracks do not horizontally line up = no edit. (right) The activated tracks horizontally line up = edit.

If you've had any experience with patch bays, you probably follow this fairly easily. If not, pretend you're using one of those old phone line patch bays. You have two active lines, but unless they are "patched" side by side, they do not connect.

Another way to activate or deactivate tracks is to hold the Alt/Option key and click and hold the mouse. Notice the little rectangle at the tip of the cursor? Drag the cursor either up or down across the tracks you want to activate or deactivate. This process works with both the Source and Record tracks.

To activate all tracks at once, select your Source composer monitor for Source tracks or the Record composer monitor for your Timeline tracks. Press Ctrl/⌘+A on the keyboard. Voilà! All your tracks are activated. To deactivate all tracks, follow the same procedure, but press Shift+Ctrl+A/Shift+⌘+A.

MONITORING

Here's an interesting thought: If panel selectors allow you to activate them, can you still turn on and off the ability to monitor them? The answer is yes.

With Source track panel selectors, the on/off switch for monitoring is the little adjacent minipanel on the left. With Record track panel selectors, the switch is on the right. To toggle between on and off (see Figure 4.6), click the minipanel. In Xpress Pro, you can monitor a maximum of 16 out of a possible 24 audio tracks.

Figure 4.6 Note that some of the adjacent minipanels are on (Monitored) and some are not (Not Monitored).

The one anomaly here is how video is monitored. Video can be monitored only one track at a time. But it reads from the top down. In other words, the top monitored track takes priority. If the top track is a key, it reads both the key and whatever is underneath it. But we'll cover keys later. The important thing is to understand that the top monitored track takes priority, then the track underneath, and then the track underneath that one. So if you are using Xpress Pro, have four video tracks, and turn monitoring on the fourth track, the fourth track will be read first, then the third, then the second, and then the first.

If the top monitored track covers anything on the tracks below, they will not be seen. If you select a lower track, it will be seen, but the higher track will not.

SOLOING

There may be times when you need to see or hear a track independently and alone. Okay, I'm talking like a lawyer now. What I mean is, in a multitrack sequence, it becomes kind of like a jungle out there, and it can be difficult to distinguish certain elements. In cases such as these, you need to be able to see or hear those tracks by themselves without the outside interference of other existing tracks.

That's what soloing does.

To solo a track, video or audio, hold down ⌘/Ctrl and click the track's monitoring panel. Note that the minipanel turns hideously jungle green. Electric Jungle. Remember, it's a jungle out there. Well, I don't know the exact name of the color, but you'll definitely see it when it happens! If you solo video tracks, the soloed track will play, but you will not see any other tracks. If you solo an audio track, the soloed track can be monitored, but you won't hear any other tracks.

SCRUBBING AUDIO

When you want to intensely scrutinize audio tracks, you can turn the Caps Lock key on for scrubbing. But with four audio tracks in Free DV (24 tracks in Xpress Pro) and a two-track scrubbing capability, how do you choose which tracks are scrubbed? You'll see it in the minipanel next to the track panel selector. If the minipanel has a gold speaker icon, it is one of the two chosen tracks that is scrub-capable. If the speaker icon is black, it is not chosen for scrub.

How do you change it? First, the hard but common way. Let's say that we want to change scrubbing capability from audio 1 and audio 2 to audio 2 and audio 3 (see Figure 4.7). The first thing to do is to completely turn off audio 1 monitoring, which switches scrubbing to the next available track, which is audio 3. Now, when you turn audio 1 back on, its speaker icon is black (thus, not scrubbable). You'll get the hang of it.

Figure 4.7 (a) By default, audio tracks 1 and 2 are the scrubbed tracks. (b) When we click the speaker icon on track 1, track 3 is automatically selected for scrubbing. (c) When we click the blank space next to track 1, tracks 2 and 3 remain scrubbed.

But if you don't get it, you can always Alt/Option+click a minipanel to make the track scrubbable. That's the easy way.

Now why did I go through the trouble of showing you the first method? I did it because I see the first method all the time, but I rarely come across the second one. This is an example of how you can choose between something simple, like remembering to Alt/Option+click, or spin your wheels clicking on monitor icons.

Patching Tracks

Sometimes, you will want to patch tracks. For example, if you have music on Source track 1 and want your music to be on Record track 2, you'll need to patch it. The individual track selectors line up by default. That is, normally the Source track panel selector for audio 1 is always next to the Record track panel selector for audio 1, which simplifies the process in case you want to patch directly, track to track.

In many cases, however, you're not going to want to go from a source to its corresponding track on the record side, so you'll have to patch. To patch tracks, do the following:

1. On the Source track panel selector, click the track in the track selectors that you want to patch *from*.

2. Drag it to the track on the Record track panel selector that you want to patch *to* (see Figure 4.8).

Figure 4.8 Patching tracks: Method 1

Obviously, you cannot patch an audio track to a video track. If you don't believe me, try it.

3. The tracks will line up alongside each other. The patch is complete.

An alternate way to patch is achieved by clicking the Source track panel selector and holding down the mouse. A list of available tracks appears. Pick the track that you want to patch to (see Figure 4.9). Once selected, the Source track panel selector that you chose lines up with the Record track panel selector that you chose. Your patch is complete.

Figure 4.9 Patching tracks: Method 2

The Rules of Patching Tracks

There are certain rules that apply when using the track selector panels. Each rule is simple and might even seem to be common sense, but just in case, let's look at them:

- First, you cannot edit deselected tracks from your Source side to the Record side. Although this may seem obvious, it's a common error. Select the Source tracks so that they are highlighted and horizontally lined up.

- The second rule is complementary to the first one. You cannot edit on deselected tracks on the Record side to from selected tracks on the Source side.

Sync Locks

On the left side of each Record track panel indicator is another minipanel. Using this box will engage sync locks and will also allow you to lock tracks, as we will see later.

Using this tool and the Sync Locks function has advantages and disadvantages. Sync locks will allow you to keep things in sync, no matter what you do. (The exception here is Timeline editing, which we'll discuss later.)

The advantage is that after you engage sync locks, it's a kind of worry-free editing. If your edits are simple and basic—just building a nonintricate audio and video track—you'll probably find sync locks indisposable. When I say "simple and basic," I mean you're just laying down chunks of synchronous audio and video together, and then going back and adding some cutaways as video-only over the basic track.

But if you have to move bits of audio here and bits of video there, and you're dealing with multiple video tracks and outside nonsynchronous audio, using sync locks might not be as desirable. You might even find yourself mired in situations in which the sync locks took over to "protect" you, and you didn't want that kind of protection.

When you create a new sequence, the Timeline will default to sync locks being on. Sync lock settings are saved with your Timeline.

Note: A word of caution: Older versions of Avid software, from the not-too-distant past, do not save sync lock settings with the Timeline and always default to off when you reopen the Timeline.

Although I personally don't use the Sync Locks option, that decision is given to you. To apply sync locks, click the left minipanel of the Record track panel indicator. A slash mark appears. The selected track has locked sync (see Figure 4.10).

To turn sync locks off, click the minipanel on the left of the Record track panel indicator again. The Sync Locks indicator will disappear.

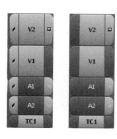

Figure 4.10 (left) Sync locks are on; (right) they're off.

Note: Here's a shortcut for sync track lovers: You can quickly turn sync locks on or off for all tracks by mouse-clicking the Sync Locks panel next to the timecode track.

Locking Tracks

You can also use that same left minipanel as an indicator that tracks are locked.

Locking tracks is something you may want to do once you're pretty well satisfied with your sequence. There are a lot of things that can happen when the tracks are not locked:

- A meddling assistant editor unknowingly uses your cut sequence as "edit practice."
- Timeline editing is turned on and you accidentally have grabbed clips and moved them, only to discover this *after* restarting the computer.
- Audio keyframes get moved by scraping the mouse across the Timeline (that one's for the Xpress Pro users!).
- A snoopy editor (not Snoopy editor—he's a dog and cannot edit) takes a look at what you're doing and accidentally "improves" it. Multiple editors on a single system make for all kinds of interesting cases, and although Avid has tried hard to ensure that some of these things do not happen, they somehow still do.

For instances like these, and oh so many more, Avid made sure that locking tracks is simple and allows for a little peace of mind.

To lock a track, do the following:

1. Click the track to be locked.
2. Next, select Clip > Lock Track.
3. The track is locked (see Figure 4.11).

Figure 4.11 (left) Track locking is on; (right) it's off.

Unlocking works much the same way:

1. Click the track to be unlocked.
2. Select Clip > Unlock Track.
3. The track is unlocked.

These choices to lock and unlock tracks are also available in a contextual menu: Park your cursor over the Timeline and (Windows) right-click or (Mac) Ctrl+Shift-click to reveal commands for adding tracks.

Adding Video Tracks

With Free DV, you can create one or two video tracks. Xpress Pro allows for the creation of up to 24 tracks. To add a video track, do the following:

1. Click the Record monitor, making the sequence active.
2. Press Ctrl+Y / ⌘+Y or select Clip > New Video track from the menu (see Figure 4.12).

Figure 4.12 Adding a new video track

If the New Video Track is grayed-out, you either are out of video tracks or a sequence has not been loaded into the monitor, so no tracks can be added. If you try to create a new video track and none is available, you will receive a message that the maximum number of tracks has been reached (see Figure 4.13).

Figure 4.13 No more video tracks can be created.

The Audio Tool

There are some settings that can be made using the audio metering right on the Timeline. Let's go over each of them. To access these tools, click the menu box to the right of the audio meters. The menu will appear (see Figure 4.17). You can use the audio tool on the Timeline or optionally select a vertical version of the same thing by selecting Tools > Audio Tool.

Figure 4.17 Audio Tool menu

Peak Hold

Selecting Peak Hold allows you to see the loudness of peaks easily. The entire purpose of holding peaks is that the meter can be very responsive and our eyes might not notice an occasional burst in audio levels. Peak Hold will display a peak of audio and hold it for a second while continuing to monitor at the same time. I personally recommend that you use it when monitoring audio. This is the default setting.

Infinite Peak

It might not seem necessary to use the Infinite Hold setting. After all, why on earth would you want to see the top peak for an infinite amount of time?

The most common use of Infinite Hold is for capturing. When capturing long segments, you might not be giving your complete attention to the audio levels. If you select Infinite Peak while capturing, you can see what happened to the levels while you were away. If the infinite peak is too loud, you can reset levels and start again.

You can also use Infinite Peak when you do an output of your cut, just in case you are not monitoring it carefully. (I am *not* recommending that you not monitor your outputs! If you don't, you're on your own, pal.)

Reset Peaks

Reset Peaks allows you to view new peak holds and ignore the past ones. If we use the previous example of using Infinite Peak while capturing, you could reset the peaks and recapture the bad audio after adjusting it.

Set Reference Level

Setting reference and calibration tone levels is a bit tricky. If you refer to the Xpress Pro manual, you'll see that the reference level for digital is –14dB. But the reference levels really depend on what destination deck that you are outputting to.

To confuse things even more, take a look at the Audio tool (refer to Figure 4.17). There are two scales that vertically measure the audio. The left scale is for digital audio—note that the maximum level for digital audio is 0dB. Anything beyond that level is distorted. On the right, analog levels are measured. The levels are measured in VU (volume units) as indicated on the scale. The maximum level for this is +14.

Here's what you should do. When outputting to an analog deck (nondigital, non-FireWire) use the analog scale. The reference level is set to +0 VU, *but* when setting this level, we use the digital scale. If you look from the analog scale on the right to the digital scale on the left, you'll see that +0 VU equals –14 dB in the digital world. So when setting levels for output to an analog deck such as Betacam, VHS, and any non-FireWire source, set the level to –14dB.

Are ya with me?

Now let's look at that scale once again. If we are outputting via FireWire to a digital deck (DV cam, DV camera, DV deck, etc.), we set our reference on the digital scale at –20dB.

Now you want to know why on earth you would do this when the manual says –14dB, don't you? Well, the original level for digital decks wasn't set in stone when Xpress Pro and even Free DV were created. As a matter of fact, it still isn't today.

What we're dealing with here is a thing called *headroom*. Headroom is the amount of additional volume that the source can go beyond the reference volume without reaching a point of distortion. If you go beyond the headroom, the audio will be distorted.

But when the first digital machines were created, everyone had a different idea of how much headroom should be allowed. Some said 18 dB, some said 14 dB, and others said 16 dB. Analog had long been standardized to +14 VU as the highest peak. But digital levels were not standardized.

As a result, Avid now uses –20 dB as the accepted reference level, with 0dB as the peak level. This gives us 20dB of headroom, which is a lot, but for quality and purity of the digital signal, it's a very good standard.

So when setting reference level for output to an analog deck, set it at –14 dB. For a digital source (such as DV cam, DVC Pro, DV decks and cameras, and any FireWire destination), use –20 dB.

Setting Calibration Tone

Your Calibration Tone should be set to match your reference level, giving you true reference of the content. So analog destinations should be set to –14 dB. Digital destinations for output should be set to –20 dB.

Creating Tone Media and Color Bars

You should always use bars and tone on your sequences. Let me repeat: You should always use bars and tone on your sequences.

If you don't, you might be setting yourself for a disastrous series of consequences because your master might be copied in several different places by several different dubbing facilities. Someone could end up complaining, and what do they have to complain about? You, that's who. When you put bars and tone on every output, it covers your, er, umm ... rear end.

Think of it: Your audio goes to a dubbing house, in which the operator calibrates it incorrectly. Then it goes to an ad agency, in which the agency's dubbing facility calibrates it worse. That tape goes to the client, who listens to a tape with really bad audio. Then someone at the agency gets blamed, the account is canceled, the agency sues the post-production facility, and you end up going home for good.

On the other hand, there might be occasions when the client does not want audio tone at the beginning of the tape. If this is true, put audio on the beginning of your sequence, but create the output *after* the tone media in the sequence. That way, you'll have all your bases covered. Even if you output without bars and tone, make sure that it is on your sequence in the edit, just to be safe.

Tone Media

To create tone media, click the menu box to the right of the audio meter (see Figure 4.18) and choose Create Tone Media. A window appears (see Figure 4.19); let's take a look at what we can do to create tone.

Tone Media Level In dB This setting determines the level of tone. Before you switch it to 0 dB, realize that we're talking digital levels here, not analog. With Free DV and Xpress Pro, the standard digital level is –20 dB. Unless you have some reason for diverting from standard, keep it that way.

Tone Media Frequency In Hz Standard tone frequency is 1000 Hz. Again, this is standard and shouldn't be changed unless the audio house recommends it.

Tone Media Length In Seconds Sixty (60) seconds is standard. If you need more, you can always loop it. If you need less, then at least you'll have plenty. Remember, we're just creating media here, not editing.

Figure 4.18 Selecting Create Tone Media

Figure 4.19 The Create Tone Media window

Number of Tracks I recommend making it for as many audio tracks as you have in your sequence. Otherwise, you have to do a lot of editing later, just to put tone on your sequence. It's a waste of time, and that time is better spent editing the meat of your sequence. The reason for this is, if the tracks are being sent to a sound mixing facility, they will want reference tone on every track. However, if you are going to mix the audio to stereo, you can put tone on only two tracks.

Target Bin I like to use a bin for audio bits and pieces. It could go there, or you could create a new separate bin for bars and tone.

Target Drive This one is pretty self-explanatory. Just be sure that your drive has room on it.

After you click OK, Avid creates a clip with your tone media that you can edit at the beginning before the sequence.

Bars and Tone Standards

Every production house has some kind of schematic for creating bars and tone, so you should check to ensure that you follow it. Often, production house staff will say something like "Just do it the standard way," even if there isn't one. This is how I do it:

1. First, create tone media for 60 seconds at the standard –14 level for analog output or –20 for digital.

2. Select all tracks (including video) or activate all sync locks, and splice the tone media at the beginning of your sequence. By selecting Splice, we have moved everything in the sequence beyond the first minute, thus it remains in sync. If you didn't select Splice or forgot to select all tracks in the sequence, you messed up. Undo it and then do it again.

3. Next, in the Clip menu at the top of the interface, select Load Filler, which will load filler in the source monitor. Mark 30 seconds of filler. It does not matter where you make the marks as long as it is exactly 30 seconds long.

4. Select all tracks and mark in on the first frame after tone on the sequence side. Make sure that you have no out point marked on the sequence side.

5. Splice in the filler. Everything in the sequence should have moved down another 30 seconds, and it remains in sync.

Now let's talk about how you can create bars. To begin, you will need to import a graphic file of SMPTE bars into a bin:

1. Click a bin of your choice, preferably the same bin where you created tone media.

2. Choose File > Import. Make sure that the File Type at the top of the menu is set to Graphic Files. Be sure to set your import to the following options:

Option	Set To
Aspect	601 non-square
Color levels	601
Field order	Non-interlaced
Alpha	Ignore (although there is no alpha channel, so you could skip this one)

3. Navigate to the Avid Free DV or Xpress Pro folder. Inside is a subfolder called `Supporting Files`, which has a subfolder named `Test Patterns`. You will find a `SMPTE_Bars.pct` file there. Select and import it. The navigational path is `Free DV` or `Xpress\Supporting Files\Test Patterns\SMPTE_Bars.pct`. If you're doing a PAL project, go to the PAL folder and select `colorbars.pct`; if you want 100% brightness bars, select `colorbars_100pct.pct`.

4. Import this .pct file into the bin by selecting it and choosing OK.

5. From there, you can load the color bars into the Source side and edit it in at the beginning of the tone media. The length should be the same as the tone media: one minute.

Figure 4.20 shows a Timeline of how I edit color bars into my sequences, with the beginning timecode noted.

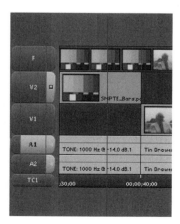

Figure 4.20 Bars and tone in the Timeline

Audio Settings

The Audio Settings selection in the Project window allows you to adjust your scrubbing as well as the panning of audio on Xpress Pro and Free DV. Let's take a look at these controls.

Audio Project Settings

Audio Project settings are settings that you create for a single project (as opposed to the Audio settings, which are created globally in your system).

Input Settings

As discussed in Chapter 2, you can adjust input settings on your system by going to the Project window, selecting Audio Project, and then choosing Input (see Figure 4.21). A small Input slider appears. The Input should be set to zero, which is its default setting.

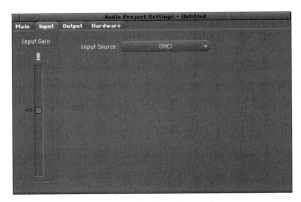

Figure 4.21 Adjusting input with Audio Project settings

Before you adjust this level, take a look at your input deck. If you can control output from your deck, do it before adjusting this parameter. If there are no output controls on your deck, the input to the system can be calibrated here.

Click the slider and move it up and down—this is how the input to the system is controlled. If you want to return the level to zero, click the +0 icon next to the slider.

Output Settings

Another adjustment that can be made is output. When you click the Output tab in the Audio Project Settings menu (see Figure 4.22), two sliders appear. You can adjust output levels just as you did using audio input. Again, you should check your deck first to see whether it has input level controls. Adjusting both input and output levels should be your last solution.

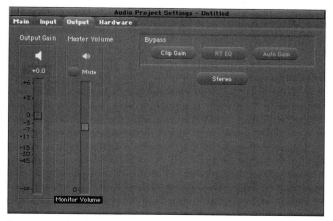

Figure 4.22 Adjusting output in the Audio Project Settings menu

Sampling Rates

The sampling rate of audio on your system is very important. You can select a sampling rate before digitizing audio (on the Main tab of the Audio Project Settings menu; see Figure 4.23). The highest sampling produces the best quality. Sampling rates available are 32 kHz, 44.1 kHz, and 48 kHz.

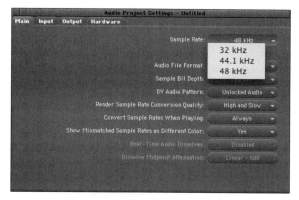

Figure 4.23 Selecting a project sample rate

Obviously, 48 kHz is the best quality, so it should be selected. On the other hand, if all four audio tracks are used on a DV camera, the audio is sampled at 32 kHz. You can select lower sampling rates, but they will apply globally to all the audio in your system. Changing the sampling rate does not minimize the file size, so you should normally go with the best quality.

Another parameter in the Audio Project Settings menu is Convert Sample Rates During Playing. I always use this parameter, but it is especially important when capturing from a variety of sources.

After the sample rate is established, you might encounter a tape that has a lower sample of audio recorded. In these cases, it is essential that you select Always for sample conversion. If you select Never, the system will inform you that the tape has the wrong audio sampling rate, and it cannot be played. This selection has to be done if any sample rates differ from the one that you have established. If you always select sample rate conversion, you will be asked to upsample the lower rates when you do your output.

Timeline Editing

When Avid first introduced the Timeline editing functions, I thought it was a waste of time and a kid's toy. All that silly clicking and dragging! A *real* editor wouldn't need anything more than a Source/Record interface.

Once again, I was wrong. The Timeline editing functions do a lot more than clicking and dragging. With Timeline tools, you can move, adjust, juxtapose, and delete portions of your Timeline. In fact, I now find it indispensable.

Let's start off by looking at the Timeline editing tools. There are only two of them, but each does a lot.

Lift/Overwrite Mode

The Lift/Override button does two things: It lifts the selected segment on the Timeline, leaving a "black hole" or filler where the segment was previously positioned, and it overwrites the video at the exact point in the Timeline where it is moved. The consequence of overwriting here should be noted—it's severe. It's sorta like that movie where they overwrote a house on the Wicked Witch of the East.

Here's an example of how that process can work. We're editing a montage. So far, we have edited shots A, B, and C. Now the director says that you should move shot B so that it is located *after* shot C. He wants to put something else in the place where shot B was located. Here's how to do it:

1. Click the red Lift/Overwrite button at the bottom of the Timeline (see Figure 4.24).

Figure 4.24 Lift/Overwrite button

2. Click the B shot.

3. Press Ctrl/⌘ and drag it so that it will be placed after shot C. Using Ctrl/⌘ moves the selection to the beginning of each segment on the Timeline. Otherwise, you have to approximate where the segment would go, which can result in flash frames.

The result is that the previous location of shot B is opened up, and now the clip formerly known as shot B has become shot D. If you chose to move your selection to where shot C begins, shot B would replace shot C.

Note: Be sure to turn off segment-editing tools before continuing to edit in a standard way. Otherwise, when you click and drag on the Timeline, it could damage your sequence. The Timeline editing tools are toggle on/off. Click a selected button and it turns segment editing off.

Extract/Splice Mode

The Extract/Splice button (see Figure 4.25) is located to the left of the Lift/Overwrite button and is colored yellow. The Extract/Splice button works much like Lift/Overwrite, but it handles both the Timeline source and destination differently, extracting selected media from its current location and splicing it to a selected location.

Figure 4.25 Extract/Splice button

Juxtaposing Clips

You can juxtapose clips quickly on the Timeline using the Extract/Splice button. For example, let's say you have a sequence with animals: a brown bear, a penguin, and a panda. The director likes the sequence so far, but requests that the brown bear and panda go first and second, leaving the penguin as the third shot in the sequence. To do this, follow these steps:

1. Select Extract/Splice.

2. Ctrl-click/⌘-click the penguin.

3. Drag the penguin clip so that it snaps to the first frame of video beyond the panda clip (see Figure 4.26). Notice that there is no space opened up where the penguin shot used to be, but rather the brown bear and the panda shots are now adjacent to each other, edited together.

Figure 4.26 Juxtaposing clips using Extract/Splice

You can move a single clip or multiple consecutive clips by using this process.

You can also move multiple tracks such as video and two audio tracks by Shift-clicking the desired tracks or clips or by lassoing them. To lasso the desired clips or tracks, move the Extract/Splice cursor above the top track and drag from left to right down over the desired clips and tracks on the Timeline. Your selection will be highlighted, and now you can move your selection to a new location in the Timeline.

Audio and video elements of a clip do not automatically follow each other. They must be selected by one of the preceding methods.

If you undo and instead move the brown bear to the beginning of the panda clip, the panda clip is moved forward and is not replaced by the brown bear as it would be using the Lift/Overwrite tool.

It is important to understand that there is a setting that will affect the Extract/Splice tool in the Timeline settings in the Project window. If you open this and click on the Edit tab, you will see a check box for Segment Drag Sync Locks with this checked, dragging and dropping a clip with the Extract/Splice tool will open space for the clip on all tracks and close up the gap where the clip was previously. With Segment Drag Sync Locks unchecked, you will be moving only clips that you select on that track. There is a potential to throw sync sound off by using the tool in this manner.

Moving Sections of the Timeline

On occasion, you might encounter a situation where you want to move entire segments of video and audio on the Timeline. As long as these segments are contiguous (a fancy word meaning that there are no segments between them), you can do this.

Let me give you yet another example. You've created a little sequence with some in-studio shots of interviews. In the middle of your section is a segment in which a music video appears, followed by more in-studio shots. Now the director has requested that the movie video be moved to the very end of the program. How would you do it?

1. Select the Extract/Splice button.

2. Move in the Timeline so that the entire music video appears.

3. To select multiple contiguous clips, hold down the Shift key and click above the top track, drag down over your tracks, lassoing the clips from left to right. When the lasso is finished, let go of the mouse (see Figure 4.27).

Figure 4.27 Moving contiguous clips

Hey! My Contiguous Clips Won't Move!

One of my first bad experiences with Timeline editing was when I was editing a commercial for a soft drink company and we had everyone there in the room watching the spot—I mean everyone. The client decided to move a few contiguous shots, so I turned on the ol' Timeline editing button, Shift-clicked all the segments, and ... nothing. It wouldn't budge. So I tried again—nothing. There were some giggles from the back. The animation director gave me that "What the heck?" look. I tried again—still nothing. After everyone decided to take a quick break, the creative director came up to me and whispered some harsh words very quickly in a restrained tone.

Eventually, I found out what was wrong. A single flash frame between two segments was not Shift-clicked. I still had my job, but from that point on, all I heard was "Check it for flash frames."

Video Quality Previewing

Xpress Pro and Free DV have the capability to display different qualities of video in the interface. That is to say, the quality differences that you control will show in the interface but not in an NTSC or PAL display. The quality there is measured by the capture resolution. Please make note that video previewing is used so that you can get the best quality of video displayed while not slowing down your system, particularly with regard to real-time effects.

Video quality is used in conjunction with the green Toggle Digital Video Out button that was discussed previously. If the blue dot is displayed, the Video Quality Preview button will not appear at the bottom of your Timeline. That's because when the toggle is set to not show real-time effects, there is no need to reduce the video quality on your display. The preview quality button is located to the right of the Fast menu on your Timeline. It consists of a box with a diagonal slash in the middle. Here are some of the options available with Realtime (green dot) video selected.

Best Performance When the color of the box is yellow on yellow, you are in Best Performance mode. To help you to remember, the diagonal divider between the colors is stair-stepped or jaggy to indicate poor quality. The best performance mode reduces the quality of the display to about $1/16$ of its original quality. Why would we ever want to do this? Strictly for better overall performance of the system. For example, if you captured media on your system drive, it could possibly cause some errors. With Best Performance, those errors are minimized.

Best Quality Best Quality (yellow on green) displays the video at $1/4$ of its original quality. This is the optimum quality that can be achieved without the Mojo while you use Real Time Effects mode.

Full Resolution You can monitor video in full resolution by either attaching a Mojo or by turning the digital toggle button to real-time preview off (displayed by a blue indicator). This allows you to monitor in full resolution, but all the effects in your sequence must be rendered.

Without a Mojo, output to NTSC/PAL cannot be achieved unless all effects are rendered and the Digital Video out is toggled to the Non Real Time position. If you have a Mojo attached, there is no need to render real-time effects. Non-real–time effects, such as third-party AVX effects, will have to be rendered.

Navigating through the Timeline

As you navigate your way through the Timeline, you may find it frustrating. All of your cuts may appear to be tiny, the system might update or redraw the Timeline slowly, or you might find it difficult to expand the Timeline to see a small section. Here are some tools to help reduce your frustration

Focus Button (Xpress Pro Only)

The Focus button will enlarge the Timeline so that 60 frames appear before and after wherever you've placed the cursor on your Timeline. To focus, select the round target-like button at the bottom of your Timeline. Your sequence will expand so that only 60 frames are displayed before and after the Timeline (blue position indicator) cursor.

To adjust the Timeline back to where it was before you pressed the button, click the Focus button again. Your Timeline will be restored.

Timeline Scroll

The Timeline scroll bar at the bottom right is like any other scroll bar. Scrolling forward will move the expanded Timeline forward in the sequence. Moving it backward will move it to previous portions of the sequence. Although the scroll bar may seem redundant to the Timeline, it can be especially useful when skipping over large portions of your sequence, especially when the Timeline is expanded and only a small portion of the sequence is visible.

Timeline Movement Controls

Certain modifiers can be used when dragging through the Timeline to advance in specific increments. These modifiers can also be used for moving clips using Timeline editing.

Snap to Head Frames To snap to the head frame of the next transition, Ctrl-click/⌘-click and drag the mouse. The position indicator snaps to each first frame of each edit on the selected track(s).

Snap to Tail Frames To snap to the last frame of each segment, press Ctrl+Alt/⌘+Opt, click and drag the mouse. The position indicator will snap to the tail frame of each edit on the selected track(s). This is useful if you want to mark an edit that includes the last frame of a segment but doesn't include the first frame of the next segment.

Frame by Frame To move in single-frame increments, hold down the Alt/Opt key and drag through the Timeline. The system will slowly jog in increments as small as a single frame.

Expanding the Timeline If your Timeline is short (see Figure 4.28) and you want to expand it to show more detail, click the Timeline and press the Ctrl/⌘ and] keys. Another way to do this is to select the Fast menu at the bottom left of the Timeline and select More Detail. (see Figure 4.29). You can do this in increments until the Timeline stops expanding.

Note: Using this tool is great for checking for flash frames and viewing tiny edits that you wouldn't normally see in the Timeline.

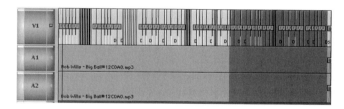

Figure 4.28 The Timeline is compressed and it's difficult to see the video edits.

Contracting the Timeline If the Timeline has been expanded too far and you want to see more detail, press the Ctrl/⌘ and [keys to reduce it. You can also select this from the Timeline Fast Edit menu by clicking and selecting Less Detail.

Figure 4.29 Here the Timeline is a little too stretched out.

Showing the Entire Sequence To display your entire sequence, press Ctrl+/ or ⌘+/. Again, you can alternately do this by selecting the Fast menu and selecting Show Entire Sequence.

Alternatively, you can also use the arrow up and down keys on the keyboard to show more or less Timeline detail. This is the fastest and most convenient way to use this tool. This is a trick that Media Composer and Symphony users don't have!

Other Options

While selecting the Fast menu at the bottom left of the Timeline window, you might have noticed quite a few other enticing options. These options include items that can be displayed in the Timeline as well as the selection of display colors. Let's take a moment to look at these options.

Clip Frames Clip frames show a single first frame of all of the video segments in your Timeline (see Figure 4.30). The clip frame appears at the left of each video segment. Using the Clip Frames option will create a slower redraw of the Timeline in addition to the others mentioned previously. This option is not available on Free DV, but the Film-strip shows them anyway.

Figure 4.30 Clip Frames are shown in the video track of the Timeline

Clip Names Normally, the clip names are already selected and appear in your Timeline. If you don't want them displayed, select Clip Names, and they will disappear.

Clip Durations Clip durations allow you to see the running time of each individual clip in your sequence, which works great when timing is precise. Select this option, and you will see minutes and seconds (but not the number of frames) displayed on the Timeline for each individual segment.

Source Names The source name refers to the tape name that you gave it when it was captured. If you want to view the name of each tape in the Timeline, select this option.

Media Names The media name displays the actual name of each media file on your media drive (see Figure 4.31). These files are somewhat cryptic, but you might have a need to locate a file for deletion, location, or movement of media files. If that is the case (I cannot honestly think of any other), you can use this display option.

Clip Comments (Xpress Pro Only) Any comments entered during capture can be displayed by selecting the Comments option on the Fast menu.

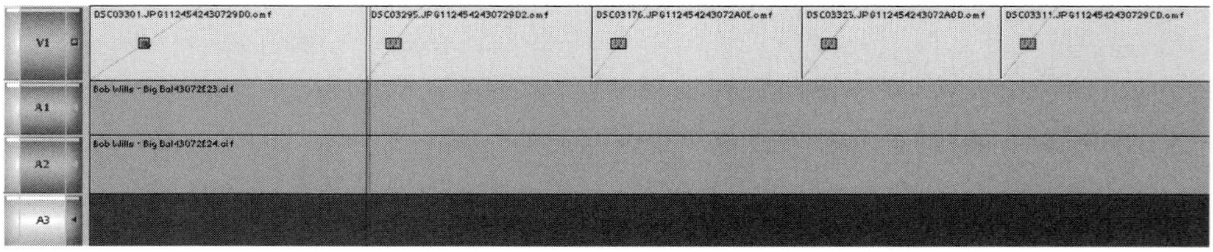

Figure 4.31 Displaying media names on the Timeline

Finding Flash Frames

In some cases, you might have inadvertently placed some stray frames in your sequence. For purposes of definition, a *flash frame* refers to a clip that has an extremely short duration. This is as opposed to, say, a clip that has a camera flash at the end of it—for example, a film clip that has a white flash at the end where an assistant checked the gate or any other longer clip in which something occurred that was not intended as part of the shot. So there can be unwanted flash frames or flash frames intended to stylize a sequence. The Find Flash Frames function is intended for use with unwanted flash frames.

In any case, Find Flash Frames can assist you in locating particular elements that were placed in your sequence but need to be deleted.

To set up Find Flash Frames:

1. Go to the Project window and click the Settings tab.
2. Double-click the current Timeline Settings.
3. In the Timeline Settings menu, click the Edit tab (see Figure 4.32).

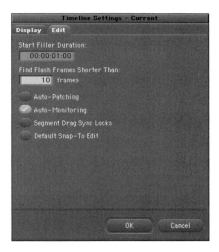

Figure 4.32 Flash frame options in the Timeline Settings menu

In the Find Flash Frames Shorter Than option, enter the maximum number of frames that you are searching for. In other words if you know that you have used edits with 20 frame durations in your sequence, you might type in the number 20 or lower to avoid hitting those edits.

The system will detect flash frames of 19 frames or lower.

To find flash frames, do the following:

1. Click the Timeline.
2. Go to the beginning of the section in which you want to search for flash frames and park your position indicator there.
3. Right-click (Windows) or Shift-Control-click (Mac) the Timeline.
4. From this menu, select Find Flash Frame (see Figure 4.33).

| Default Setup |
| New Sequence |
| New Audio Track |
| New Video Track |
| Render at Position... |
| Add Filler At Start |
| Remove Match Frame Edits |
| Find Flash Frame |
| Timeline Settings... |
| Duplicate |
| Lock Tracks |
| Unlock Tracks |
| What's This? |

Figure 4.33 Finding flash frames

5. The blue position indicator moves to the first flash frames detected.

6. To continue searching for more flash frames, repeat steps 3 and 4.

Adjusting Audio Levels with Key Frames

In some cases, you might need to adjust your audio levels for a better mix.

The first method is fairly simple. Open up the Audio Mix tool by selecting Tools > Audio Mix. Find the point where the audio is to be lowered or gained. Click the tracks that you need to change in the Timeline and click the H button of your Avid. A new edit has been made. From there, move the Timeline to the new edit and adjust the slider on that track with the Audio Mix tool. If the audio needs to be raised or lowered further, add new edits and adjust as needed. The change that you made in the Audio Mix tool applies only to the segment where the audio was lowered. Additional segments will not be adjusted.

A far more intuitive way of adjustment would be by adding keyframes to the audio tracks. To do this, follow these steps:

1. Click the tracks that are to be changed or attenuated.

2. From the fast bin on the Timeline, select Audio Auto Gain.

3. Take a look at the audio in your Timeline. You should see a thin gray line running through each track.

4. Now, click the N button where you want to add a keyframe. Note that a small triangle is added to the Clip Gain. Move this triangle up and down as needed (see Figure 4.34).

If you are adjusting a small section of audio, you may need to add three keyframes: one where the audio starts to rise, the second at its peak, and a third keyframe where the audio will return.

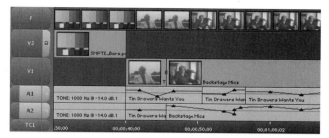

Figure 4.34 Adjusting audio levels through keyframing

Source and Record Timeline Toggling (Xpress Pro Only)

The Source record Timeline toggle switch is located at the bottom left of the Timeline window in Xpress Pro. Using this switch will allow you to switch between the Timeline in the Record monitor to the Timeline in the Source monitor. At first look, it may appear to be absolutely useless. But it's not, as we shall see.

If you are editing using a sequence as the source, the Source record toggle switch is indispensable. For example, if you need to load a previously edited sequence into the Source side and edit it into a new sequence, you can click the Source record toggle and see the edits that were made in the sequence. This makes it easier when using other sequences as source. You can mark at specific points in your source Timeline and reduce any worrying about creating flash frames.

By selecting Sample Plot in the Timeline Fast menu, you are able to see a visual representation of your audio. Using this in combination with toggling your Timeline to the source makes finding audio cues and takes a very fast visual procedure, saving loads of time you may otherwise spend listening for those cues.

Tutorial: Building a Timeline

Now that we've covered all of the aspects of the Timeline, let's take some of the important features and try them out! First, launch Avid Free DV or Avid Xpress Pro and open up the Avid Made Easy Project.

Creating Bars and Tone

In this segment of the tutorial, we will create a brand new sequence and fill it with bars and tone. First, let's create a new bin and, within that, a new sequence:

1. Click the Project Manager window.
2. Select the Bins tab (see Figure 4.35).
3. Click the New Bins button.
4. Name the bin Bars and Tone.

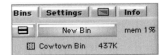

Figure 4.35 Creating a new bin

5. Choose Clip > Create New Sequence in your menus. A new sequence will be created (see Figure 4.33).

6. Name this sequence Bars and Tone.

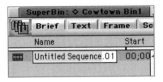

Figure 4.36 Renaming your sequence

Now that we have a sequence, let's put in the media. To do this, follow these steps:

1. Click the menu to the right of the audio meters in your Timeline and choose Create Tone Media (see Figure 4.34).

Figure 4.37 Creating tone media

2. We want Tone Media to be at –20dB, tone frequency at 1000 Hz, and the duration in seconds to be at 60.

3. Below this appears the target bin selection where the tone media will be created. Make sure that Bars and Tone is selected.

4. You also have the option of changing the target drive where the tone media will be placed.

5. After you've made your decisions, click OK. The tone media is then created. If there is not enough room on the selected drive, the system will tell you.

Next, we'll import bars. Follow these steps:

1. Click anywhere on the Bars and Tone bin.

2. Choose File > Import. The Import menu will be opened.

3. Make sure that Graphic Documents is selected as file type. Then set your options for graphics to 601 aspect and 601 color levels.

4. Now find the file using this path:

```
NTSC: Xpress Pro|Free DV\Supporting Files\Test Patterns\SMPTE_Bars.pct
PAL: Xpress Pro|Free DV\Supporting Files\Test Patterns\PAL\ColorBars.pct
```

Select OK; the bars will import in the bin.

Now we can edit the sequence. First, we'll do the tone, as follows:

1. Make sure that your empty Bars and Tone sequence is already loaded on the record side.

2. Open up the Tone clip and press Mark Clip underneath the Source monitor.

3. Press Splice.

The tone has been edited into your sequence.

And finally, edit in the bars, as follows:

1. First, move the blue position indicator to the first frame of the sequence.

2. Mark an in point underneath the Record monitor.

3. Next, load the SMPTE Bars in the source menu and select Mark Clip as you did previously with the audio (see Figure 4.38).

4. Press the Splice button.

The bars will appear on top of the tone in the video track.

Figure 4.38 Selecting SMPTE bars for import

Now, just as an example, toggle the Source record Timeline button (on Xpress Pro only) and take a look at the source media. To return to the edited sequence, press the toggle switch again.

Analog Scrub

Let's take a look at the analog scrub capabilities of the Xpress Pro/Free DV systems (see Figure 4.39 and Table 4.1). Try some of these scrubbing options:

Figure 4.39 Play button indicates speed in frames per second during analog scrub

Action	Shortcut
Play forward at 30 fps.	Press the L key once.
Play forward at 60 fps.	Press the L key twice.
Play forward at 90 fps.	Press the L key three times.
Play forward at 150 fps.	Press the L key four times (note that analog scrub disappears at this point).
Play forward at 240 fps.	Press the L key five times.
Play backward at 30 fps.	Press the K key once.
Play backward at 60 fps.	Press the K key twice.
Play backward at 90 fps.	Press the K key three times.
Play backward at 150 fps.	Press the K key four times (note that analog scrub disappears at this point).
Play backward at 240 fps.	Press the K key five times.
Play forward at 8 fps.	Press the K and L keys together.
Play backward at 8 fps.	Press the J and K keys together.

Moving a Segment

Note that there is a bin titled Timeline. Open this bin and load the sequence titled Moving Segments. Inside the sequence are several still shots numbered from 1 to 7. The first thing that we will do is move a single segment to a desired location. Ready?

1. Turn on the Extract/Splice function by clicking the yellow key on the bottom-left side of your Avid. The key should light up when you click it.

2. While holding down either the ⌘ key (Macintosh) or Ctrl key (Windows) click the second segment in the Timeline and drag it to the right.

   Notice that, as you're dragging, the position indicator is snapping or shifting to the beginning of every segment in the Timeline.

3. Park your segment so that it appears on shot number 7.

4. Release the mouse.

You have successfully moved shot 2 down to the place where shot 7 existed and you've also extracted shot 2, so shot 1 is followed by shot 3.

Now let's try something different:

1. Undo (Ctrl+Z/⌘+Z) until all the shots are in normal order. In this section, we'll do the same thing, except use the Lift/Overwrite key.

2. Click the Lift/Overwrite key (the red button at the bottom left of the Timeline).

3. Click the shot labeled as shot 2. Using the ⌘ or Ctrl key, click it and move it down so that it snaps over shot 7.

4. Release the mouse.

You have now replaced a portion of shot 7 and left a black hole where shot 2 previously existed.

Customizing and Saving Your Timeline View

The Timeline Fast menu provides you with a number of options for customizing and saving your Timeline view. We'll start by coloring the background of the Timeline:

1. Deselect all tracks on the record side of the track selector.

2. Go to the Fast menu and select a background color. The background should change to the color you select.

3. From here, you can select a track or several tracks and follow the same procedure.

Any tracks selected will change to the color you specify. As you select the tracks, the Background Color specification on the Fast menu changes to Track Color.

To save your configuration, go to the bar at the bottom of your Timeline, which should be labeled Untitled. Click it and save it with a unique name (see Figure 4.40). Now, whenever you are working on a project you can recall your color scheme on the Timeline.

Figure 4.40 Saving a Timeline view

Deleting Clips

You can also use Extract/Splice and Lift/Overwrite for quick deletion:

1. Load the Moving Segments sequence and select the Lift Overwrite button.

2. Click Segment 6 and press Delete, which deletes Segment 6 and leaves a black hole where it was located.

Now we'll try the same thing with Extract/Splice:

1. Click the yellow Extract/Splice key and select Segment 3.

2. Press Delete on your keyboard.

Note that instead of leaving a black hole, the other segments pulled up the sequence to cover the area where 3 was located.

Trimming

One of the most challenging yet fun things that an editor does is trimming. In the old days of film editing, trimming meant carrying around a box of tiny trimmed frames and adding or subtracting them to a sequence. The assistant editor, who had to collect just about anything that hit the cutting room floor, usually searched these tiny little "trims." Searching for the trims usually meant having to "eyeball" each small clip and match it to the frames that were already in the sequence.

With Avid editing, there is no box of tiny frames. Today, trimming a digital clip means no trim pieces. The trim remains intact and usable at any time. And you never have to search for tiny bits of film anymore.

5

Chapter Contents

What Is Trimming?

What exactly does an editor do? If you're like me, you've had parents that have been asking that same question for years. And the answer, if you think too hard, is not an easy one.

The scene, for lack of a better term, lives and breathes. The director gives it life, and the editor gives it cadence. Every scene has a rhythm. And it is the editor's job to find that rhythm.

It doesn't matter what kind of program you're editing—be it wedding videos, game shows, sitcoms or drama—the scene always has some sort of cadence to it, and it's your job to find it and refine it.

Here is some food for thought. Take a look at your favorite game show. The contestants are waiting. The announcer announces the host. We cut to a wide shot of our host greeting contestants and audience. We cut to the audience. We cut back to the host at the podium. All choreographed with precision. If you listen carefully, you might note that the cuts come on certain changes in the music underneath the applause of the audience. And from there, it is question-and-answer as the game goes on.

What about your favorite TV sitcom? It has a rhythm, too. When was the last time you saw a character in a sitcom actually hang up a phone? You'll probably never see it for two reasons: any dilly-dallying (such as fumbling with a receiver on the hook) ruins the rhythm of the scene. And if you pay attention, you'll note that events on sitcoms happen faster than real time; that is, faster than they would normally occur in real life. The world of the situation comedy is quick and snappy, just the way the audience wants it.

Note: One of my pet peeves with students is that at times they avoid Trim mode altogether, cutting the sequence and correcting their initial edits by doing the whole cut over again. This is time-consuming and downright inefficient. The true heart of Avid editing is trimming. So read each of these methods carefully and you will quickly pick up all the skills needed to adjust your cuts to perfection.

Commercials are of course obvious. Advertising moves at a quicker-than-life pace to present everything it can to get into your head and make you want to buy product in 29 seconds and 20 frames.

Newscasts, sportscasts, the weather—they all involve precise timing. And without precise timing, they would take forever. If newscasts are covering a tragedy (and they most always are) then you're probably going to see it unfold just as quickly and as precisely as possible—just the right timing to get in a few commercials. Rarely is any event covered in real time.

And that's just the way an audience wants it: timed precisely according to the needs of the program. But timing isn't always intended to make you happy or to feel concise. Witness the scene from *Taxi Driver* in which Travis Bickle is watching his antacid fizzle in the glass. It just fizzles … and fizzles … and fizzles. It's as if his mind is fizzling right along with the antacid. It makes you queasy and uncomfortable. Now *that* is good trimming.

Trimming is a method used to analyze a scene to display it the way it was intended. When we trim, we look for the rhythm of the cut, the way in which it is displayed when taken in context with the adjacent cuts, and the editing errors on each side of the cut. When we are trimming, we are attempting to fine-tune our sequence. All the elements are there, but we must make the visual elements follow a pattern that is pleasing to the eye.

Good trimming requires your focus on two elements: the up-close view, in which we see the actual transition and how the trim occurs, and a macro view, in which we look at the way a trimmed piece looks in context with the entire scene. The ardors of trimming can be exhausting. Eventually, you might need to walk out for a cup of coffee or a soda; then return to look at the scene again.

Many new editors find trimming a little overwhelming. It certainly can be. But after a scene is trimmed properly, there is nothing more rewarding. You get excited about your work and play it back for others with the "I did that" look on your face.

The actual process of trimming can also be a bit tricky at first, as you shall see.

Trim Selection

A transition or cut contains two elements. When trimming, the outgoing clip is referred to as the A side, and the incoming clip is referred to as the B side. By adjusting the length of the A and B sides, we are trimming.

There are a lot of ways to trim the cut. If the A side runs too long, we trim backward, cutting off the excess audio and video. If it is too short, we trim forward, extending the cut before transitioning to the B side. In some cases, we may want to extend the visual of the A side over the audio from the B side (see Figure 5.1). This is known as an L cut because on the Timeline it sort of looks like the letter L lying on its side. Some editors might refer to it as a *split edit* because the audio and video are split into parts.

Figure 5.1 (left) A straight video and audio cut; (right) an L cut or split edit

In other cases, we might trim both sides at the same time. For example, if we roll the A side forward, we roll the B side forward as well. The A side is adding frames as the B side is inversely losing frames.

Are we lost yet? Hopefully not, but don't worry. With a little practice, you'll completely understand trimming.

The Trim mode is one of three modes used in Avid editing:

- Source/Record mode, in which we perform basic editing functions
- Trim mode, in which we analyze and adjust the edit
- Effect mode, in which effects are added to enhance the sequence

Most editors prefer this very simple "modal" type of editing because it reduces the clutter of excess functions and allows you to focus on the work to be done. Other editing systems brag about being *nonmodal*; I never understood why that would ever be considered a feature.

Let's go to Trim mode! (See Figure 5.2.) Here's all you do. Press the button that looks like a little 35mm film can located underneath the Record monitor on the left side. An alternative way to instantly enter Trim mode is to lasso a transition on the Timeline by using your mouse (see Figure 5.3). This procedure switches the GUI from Source/Record mode to Trim mode for that transition, using the tracks that were lassoed. To exit Trim mode, either click the Trim Mode button again, or press Escape on your keyboard.

Figure 5.2 Trim mode

Figure 5.3 Lassoing to enter Trim mode

When you enter Trim mode, the interface changes ever so slightly. Now, instead of a Source monitor, the monitor to the left is the A side of your cut. The monitor to the right is the B side. You might notice that there are pink buttons underneath the A and B monitors, as well as some tiny pink rollers in the Timeline. There's also a button that looks similar to a regular Play button under the Record monitor (see Figure 5.4). Under the monitor windows, the icons change—more under the A or source side than the B or record side. On the Timeline, a pair of pink rollers appears for each track selected.

Figure 5.4 (left) The Trim button; (right) the Trim Loop button

Trim Loop

Take a look at the Play button. Notice that the Play button underneath the record monitor has a straight vertical line running through the center. It is actually not a play button, but a Play Trim Loop button.

The Trim Loop allows you to continuously play back a small section before and after the transition so that you can examine or analyze it. The default trim loop is two seconds of preroll (before the transition) and two seconds of postroll (after the transition), but you can alter this by adjusting your Trim settings. Select your Trim settings in the Project window, and then select the Play Loop tab (see Figure 5.5). From here, you can adjust the Preroll, Postroll and Intermission settings. The Intermission setting is by default set to zero frames so that the trim loop will play continuously, which can be problematic in some situations. For example, when trimming a fast-cut montage, you might be overwhelmed with the number of transitions that take place during the loop. If you set an Intermission time, the loop will play back, switch to black for the intermission duration, and then begin play again. This loop will continue until you tell it to stop.

Figure 5.5 Play Loop tab in the Trim Settings dialog box

Some editors, and even more producers, can't stand the Trim Play loop. Remember that it is only a tool to gauge how well the transition plays. If you'd rather not use it, you can always switch back to Source/Record mode and play it back normally within the context of an entire scene.

Now, let's take a look at the three elements that you can trim: the A side, the B side, and both the A and B sides.

A-Side Source Trimming

When you trim the A or outgoing side of a transition, you monitor the image on the left monitor. When you're in Trim mode, clicking on the A-side monitor tells your system that you're trimming only on the A side. The track selectors on the Timeline below determine which tracks are to be trimmed.

After you begin trimming in this way, you will not affect anything on the B side—all picture and audio segments will be intact. However, keep in mind that when you trim only one track, such as audio channel 1, the location of that element will change so that it comes earlier or later in the sequence, depending on which way you trim. It could make some or all of the sequences go out of sync, which we'll discuss later. If all tracks are being trimmed on the A side (see Figure 5.6), the B side remains intact and in sync, but it will appear either earlier or later in the sequence—again depending on which way you trim.

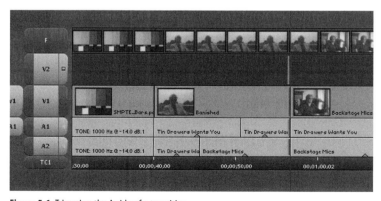

Figure 5.6 Trimming the A side of a transition

I liken this scenario to rolling out carpet. Think of the pink rollers in your Timeline as little rolls of carpet. When you are trimming backward on the A side of a transition, the carpet rolls back *before* the transition, thus subtracting frames that occur before the transition. If you trim forward on the A side, you roll the carpet forward, adding more frames to the transition.

B-Side Source Trimming

Trimming the B side of an edit (see Figure 5.7) adds or reduces the amount of footage in the *incoming* scene. Using the previous analogy, the B-side carpet roll is located at the beginning of the incoming cut, and the tail of the carpet continues in front of it. So if you trim forward on the B side, you are rolling up the carpet and making the B-side clip shorter. If you roll backward on the B side, the carpet is rolling backward, thus adding more frames.

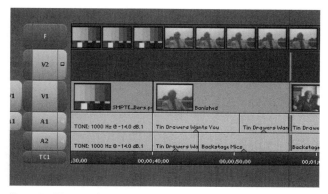

Figure 5.7 Trimming the B side of a transition

Trimming Both Sides

You enter A/B Trim mode by clicking between your Source and Record monitors. There is a scroll icon that appears when you move the mouse. When this icon appears to have two sides, click the mouse and you will be in A/B Trim mode. Notice that the pink rollers appear on both sides of the transition in the Timeline (see Figure 5.8).

Figure 5.8 Rollers appear in the Timeline for an A/B trim

Trimming Mathematics

I so loathe telling people that some mathematics is involved, because it can send many an editor running. But the math is very simple. Let me repeat what I just described: When you trim negative on the A side, you are reducing the number of frames. Conversely, if you trim negative on the B side, you are adding frames. That's because the "roll of carpet" on the B side is at the head of the frames, not the tail, as it is on the A side. On the other hand, when you trim positive on the A side, you add frames. When you trim positive on the B side, you are subtracting frames.

To conclude (and reiterate):

- When you roll forward on the A side, you are extending the outgoing shot.
- When you roll backward on the A side, you are reducing the outgoing shot.
- When you roll forward on the B side, you are reducing the incoming shot.
- When you roll backward on the A side, you are extending the incoming shot.

If you comprehend these simple rules, the rest is a piece of cake. If you still don't get it, experience will teach you, so don't worry.

Trimming Methods

At first sight, the number of trimming methods can be overwhelming. But before you get nervous, I should note that the reason for so many different methods of trimming is that there are so many different reasons that you'll need to trim. Additionally, some editors prefer to trim using only one method. When Avid developers created the Trim tool, they consulted with a lot of different editors who use a lot of different styles.

 Note: When Caps Lock is activated, the system will scrub audio as you trim, so that you can listen for audio cues.

Here are some examples of trim methods you might use: If you're cutting dialogue and need to match eyelines, there is one particularly good way to trim. (For sake of clarity, the *eyeline* is the direction in which an actor is looking in opposition to other actors in a scene.) For cutting music videos, there is another different method for trimming that is very efficient. For compiling a sequence of animation, there is still another. So as you learn each of these methods, keep in mind that you don't have to learn them all at once, and there is no best method.

Adding Rollers

After you enter Trim mode and have selected which side of the transition is to be trimmed, you might have noticed some pink rollers at the transition point in the Timeline. These rollers can be clicked and dragged to adjust the trim interactively on the Timeline with your mouse. Although using this method isn't as accurate as numerical entry or the trim buttons described later, grabbing and dragging the rollers will update the monitors, providing feedback as you trim. You can also add and subtract rollers by Shift-clicking additional tracks.

Using the rollers can be a little hazardous. At first, you might accidentally click on the wrong side of the transition and create a roller on the opposite side of the transition that you intended to trim. When this happens, move the mouse a little more precisely and try clicking again. If you inadvertently moved the mouse and trimmed some frames on the wrong side, release the mouse and undo the trim (Ctrl-Z/⌘-Z). The click-and-drag method with rollers is used primarily for shorter trims, in which only a few frames need to be added or subtracted from the transition.

You can also add rollers at different transitions. For example, if you're trimming a split edit, in which the audio transitions one place and the video transitions in a different place, you can Shift-click to trim both audio and video, even though they transition at different points in the sequence.

You can also add rollers by lassoing a transition.

Button Trimming

The Trim interface uses buttons for adjustment of a transition, both on the interface and on your keyboard. These buttons, shown in Figure 5.9, are mapped to the interface under the Source monitor. They are also mapped on the default Xpress Pro keyboard.

Trim Backward 10 Frames

Trim Forward 1 Frame

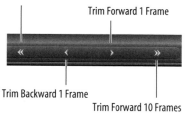

Figure 5.9 The Trim buttons

Trim Backward 1 Frame

Trim Forward 10 Frames

Button trimming is normally used as a nudging device, where each frame advance or reverse can be monitored and played back immediately. Some editors use the 10 frame buttons as a means to move forward in larger increments.

It might seem more intuitive to use the standard keyboard's arrow keys for trimming. Although they can be used for nudging effects, using them in Trim mode will knock you back into Source/Record mode.

Note: The Trim buttons look an awful lot like Play buttons. Try to remember that they can be used only while in Trim mode.

Trimming by Numerical Entry

As you continue to learn and grow as an editor, there will be many times when you will immediately know the solution to common problems associated with trimming. Some editors can determine, based on their experience, the approximate number of frames needed to be trimmed in a transition. There is a certain amount of pride that editors can take in their ability to predict the number of frames by which a transition is "off," or incorrect. For these editors, Free DV and Xpress Pro have the numerical entry option.

If you prefer to directly enter a number of frames to be trimmed, enter Trim mode, select the A side, B side, or both sides of the transition and type the number of frames to be trimmed with a plus (+) or minus sign (−), as shown in Figure 5.10. The transition adjusts appropriately.

Figure 5.10 Trimming numerically

One thing to note about numerical entry: After you enter a number higher than 99, the system assumes that you are referring to seconds and frames; therefore, an entry of 106 would result in a trim of 36 frames, or 1 second and 6 frames (1:06). If you want to enter higher numbers in frames, enter the number and follow it with a lowercase "f" (it absolutely must be lowercase, or else the system will not understand the command) before pressing Enter. This lets the system know that you intend for this entry to be expressed in frames, not in seconds and frames.

Trimming on the Fly

Trimming on the fly is a simple yet elegant way to adjust a transition based on timing with real-time playback. It is based solely on your ability to react as the sequence is played back. When you trim on the fly, the transition loop plays, and you "tell" the transition where to move by pressing a Mark In or Mark Out button on the keyboard (see Figure 5.11). It doesn't matter which Mark In or Mark Out button that you use, as long as it is located on the keyboard. The keyboard equivalents on a standard Xpress Pro and Free DV system are the E, R, I, and O keys.

Figure 5.11 Mark In and Mark Out buttons

To trim on the fly, enter Trim mode and select the transition side(s) and tracks to be trimmed. Play back the trim loop. Before attempting to trim on the fly, you might want to let the loop play back a couple of times so that you can get a feel for the timing of the transition. Otherwise, you could trim incorrectly and have to undo everything. As the loop plays continuously, select the point where you want the transition to move by pressing the E, R, I, or O key. The transition point moves accordingly. If you did not select the appropriate point, let the loop continue to play back and reselect, or press Ctrl-Z/⌘-Z to undo and then continue playback.

If you need to trim past the loop, change your trim settings to reflect a longer preroll or postroll for the trim loop. By doing this, you will give yourself more space in which to make the trim. It also gives you more a bit more "breathing space" while you're attempting to find the correct point for the transition.

Trimming on the fly is normally used for trimming to a precise moment in music or in action. Although it could be said that there are more precise methods, many editors pride themselves on their sense of timing, just as they do in knowing frame counts. Trimming on the fly is a great exercise in creative freedom, and when an editor has good reaction time, it produces great results.

Trimming on the fly takes a little practice before you get used to it. A common mistake when trimming on the fly is to trim too far, obliterating almost all of either the A-side or B-side clip. Sometimes undoing the trim is better than spending time trying to resurrect the partially missing clips. Don't waste time! Undo the trim and try trimming it again.

J-K-L Trim (Xpress Pro Only)

J-K-L trimming is one of Xpress Pro's best features and is, in my opinion, the best reason to upgrade from Free DV to Xpress Pro. (Note to Avid: Mail the check. Repeat: Mail the check.) Actually, it really is an excellent method, and no, Avid didn't pay me to tell you this. The ability to dynamically trim media and view it as the trimming takes place makes trimming simple and precise. Using this method, you can trim and maintain continuity all at the same time, adjust your trimming to maintain continuing action between cuts, establish a proper eyeline between characters, adjust for camera movement, establish audio cues, and so on.

The best thing about trimming on the fly is that both screens (A side and B side) update as you roll through. So if you are trying to line up an event, an eyeline, or anything that gives continuity to the scene, you can roll through with J-K and K-L combinations and watch both monitors to find that specific point where everything lines up perfectly (hopefully so, at least.)

On Xpress Pro, J-K-L trimming is an option. To activate it, select the Settings Tab in the Project window. Double-click the Trim settings. The Trim Settings window appears. Click the Features tab (see Figure 5.12) and select J-K-L Trim.

Figure 5.12 J-K-L Trim option
in Trim Settings

To J-K-L trim, enter Trim mode and press the J, K, or L key to move the transition point.

Remember, as you use the J, K, and L keys, the transition point moves with you. J-K-L trimming, like trimming on the fly, is very powerful. It takes a bit of getting used to, but it can produce rapid and precise results. The keys work the same as they would during Source/Record navigation, save for the fact that they are actually trimming the A and B sides of a transition as the media move.

Note: Keep in mind that the designers of the system recognized some of the pitfalls of using this method. As a result, you can never completely get rid of an entire segment through J-K-L trimming. This is too bad, in my opinion, because I think they are protecting me too much. If I "overrun" a segment through J-K-L trimming, I can always undo it. And it would be great to use it as a tool for getting rid of unwanted segments. Anyway, if you want to delete an entire segment, use Segment mode editing. If you find yourself confused by the amount of trimming you've done during a J-K-L trim, undo.

When there is a need to trim, I almost always find myself using J-K-L trimming because it can be used for small and large trims. For example, if you are extending the tail of the video on shot A to cover some of the dialogue on shot B, you can click the L key, play it in real time to the point where the shot is to be extended, and then press the spacebar to stop trimming. The trim is made instantly. For more close-up and shorter trims, you can use the K and L keys to roll forward and the J and K keys to roll backward. If you place your middle finger on the K key and then alternate the motion using the J and L keys, you can "rock and roll" through the media until you find the point where the trim looks best. As the J, K, and L keys are used, the A and B side monitors show you the last and first frames of the transition.

When you use the J, K, and L keys, start slowly. There is no reason to press the L key and do a trim at full speed. Use the K and L keys first, and move slowly forward. Then stop and take a look at what you've done. If it's a mess, you can always undo it, so there's no reason to be frightened.

Slipping and Sliding (Xpress Pro Only)

Two methods frequently used by film editors are known as *slipping* and *sliding*. If you've done only video work, they may be new to you. Slipping and sliding allow you to trim shots in ways that previously took much more time. In both cases, they are methods of trimming on linear systems that would normally take two or more steps. Although they still can be done using conventional trimming methods, the ease in which they can work makes it more desirable to use these methods.

Slipping

Slipping can be defined as the process of adding and subtracting frames proportionately to a chosen shot. Let's use an example of an event that occurs. We cut to a shot of an explosion. The director likes the duration of the cut but is not satisfied with what occurs when you cut it in. The director wants to see more at the beginning of the cut (so the audience can establish the scene before the bomb explodes) and wants to see less at the end of the shot after the bomb explodes.

In this example, you would ordinarily trim backward on the A side of the transition so that the scene can register, and then go to the end of the cut and take away frames so that the scene doesn't go stale. An easier way to do this is to use slipping.

To enter Slip mode, lasso from right to left covering the entire segment to be slipped (see Figure 5.13). If you want to slip a series of shots, such as in a montage, drag the lasso around the end of the last segment to be slipped and continue until it is around the beginning of the first segment to be slipped. You can control slipping using all the trim methods described previously, including J-K-L trimming.

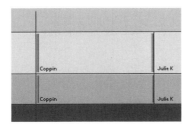

Figure 5.13 Slipping

An alternate way to enter Slip is through the Timeline menus. While in Trim mode, place your cursor over the segment that you want to slip and either right-click (Windows) or Shift-Ctrl-click (Macintosh) to reveal the Timeline menu (see Figure 5.14). You can choose Select Slip Trim or Select Slide Trim using the menu.

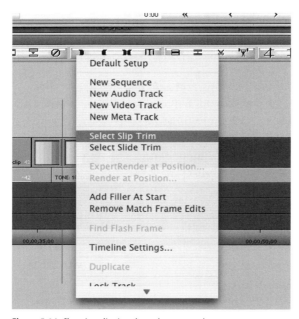

Figure 5.14 Choosing slipping through contextual menus

 Note: You can switch from slipping to sliding by holding Alt/Option and double-clicking the segment.

You may have noticed that, upon entering Slip mode, the interface uses four screens instead of the usual two (see Figure 5.15) because two separate transition points are being affected when you slip. Thus, the first monitor contains the last frame of visual before the slipped shot, the second monitor contains the first frame of slipped shot, the third monitor contains the last frame of slipped shot, and the fourth monitor contains the first frame of the next shot following the slipped shot. As you slip the shot forward or backward, only frames 2 and 3 will update because frame 1 and frame 4 are not changed through slipping.

Figure 5.15 Monitor display during slip

Sliding

Sliding does just the opposite of slipping, affecting adjacent scenes. Here's an example of sliding: We're editing a program in which we have a studio discussion, which leads to a previously edited "roll-in" tape. As we're editing our production, the director becomes aware that we have left the studio a little too abruptly and have returned to the studio too early, with a little bit of "egg on the face" of our studio panel before they begin to speak.

In this scenario, we would normally extend the studio shot a few frames before putting in the edited piece. Then we would go to the tail transition, in which the edited piece goes back to the studio and trims forward some of the B side of the transition so the action from the tape to the studio is continuous.

A faster way is to use the Slide function (see Figure 5.16).

Figure 5.16 Sliding

To enter Slide mode, Shift+Alt/Option-drag to lasso from right to left covering the entire segment to be slid. If you want to slide over a series of shots, drag the lasso around the end of the last segment to be slid and continue until it is around the beginning of the first segment to be slid. Like Slip mode, you can control sliding using all the trim methods described previously, including J-K-L.

An alternate way to enter slide is through the Timeline contextual menu. While in Trim mode, place your cursor over the segment you want to slip and either right-click (Windows) or Shift-Ctrl-click (Macintosh) to reveal the Timeline menu. You can choose Select Slip Trim or Select Slide Trim on the menu.

Like slipping, slide trimming displays four monitors. The first is the tail of the outgoing scene, which is adjusted in Slide mode. The second monitor is the first frame of the scene being slid. The third monitor is the last frame of the slid scene, and the fourth monitor contains the first frame of the next incoming scene. When you slide, the first and fourth monitors are affected. The second and third monitors, which contain the clip that is sliding in the Timeline, do not change.

Here's another example of where sliding can be used: Let's say we put together a program in which there is a fast-cut montage in the middle. Somewhere along the line, the montage went out of sync so that the music was about three frames behind the picture. This has happened to me on occasion. Rather than try to reconstruct the sequence, we can enter Slide mode and slide the visual of the entire montage forward three frames. The correction can be made in about half a minute, and everything will look great again.

There are other reasons for sliding, including moving visuals to match narration or music, adjusting a shot for continuity, and so on. As you gain experience using the slide form of trimming, you'll find more reasons to use it.

If you performed a trim and later realize that you need to go back to Trim mode on that same transition, pressing Alt/Option as you choose Trim mode will bring you back to your last trimmed transition.

More Trimming Considerations

After you master the basic trimming methods, you need to be able to deal with unusual situations.

Analyzing the Transition Using Play Loop

You will often find yourself in situations in which some anomalous audio or video enters the frame and it appears to be right in the middle of your transition. There might be a flash frame of other unnecessary media, or a "blip" sound where dialogue, music, or narration was cut off. This sort of thing is normal and is to be expected when doing nonlinear editing. Again, you are sculpting out a sequence, so a lot of odd things can happen during the process.

In cases such as these, it's really hard to determine where the problem exists because it is so close to your transition. On both Xpress Pro and Free DV, there is a way to more closely analyze the transition to determine whether it came from the outgoing A side or the incoming B side.

You can jockey through the transition using the regular Source/Record navigational tools, but you might still find it difficult to determine which side (A or B) of the transition that the sound occurs. To remedy this situation, the system allows you to play the trim loop, looping only on one side (either A or B, but not both) to determine where the stray audio or video frame is located.

To isolate the trim sides during trim loop, play back the trim loop as you normally would; then select the Q button to loop the A side of the transition only. Only the A side of the transition will play, and you will be able to detect whether or not it has the stray frame. Select the W button to loop the B side of the transition only. By isolating the sides of the transition, you should be able to find the bad frame.

For Xpress Pro users, this process will work only if you have retained the default keyboard mapping of the Go To In and Go To Out buttons. If you have not, instead of using the Q button on your keyboard, press the key that you have assigned for Go To In. Instead of the W button, press the key that you have assigned for Go To Out.

Adding Filler While Trimming

In some cases, you might want to trim on one side of a single track and keep everything in sync (see Figure 5.17). The best way to do it is to add filler while trimming. To add filler while trimming, go into Trim mode and select one side (A or B) of a transition. While clicking and holding on the pink rollers, hold down the Alt key (Windows) or Ctrl key (Mac). This adds or subtracts filler on the unselected tracks so that sync is maintained. Make sure that you have sync locks turned off during this operation.

Figure 5.17 Trimming to add filler

Another way to maintain sync while adding filler is to turn the sync locks on. Whenever you trim a single side and add frames, it adds filler on the tracks to maintain sync. If you try to reduce frames from a single track, it will refuse the edit.

Extend Function

In some cases, you might want to extend a single or multiple tracks forward or backward to a specified point without entering the Trim mode. For example, if cutting a news story, you may add an on-camera sound bite, which in turn can have video extended backward to *backtime* the viewers to the sound. This sort of introduction of a newsperson is fairly common. It is easier to select the video track on the incoming shot and extend it backward to a cue point than to enter Trim mode.

Note: Over the years, a lot of my students have tried in vain to use the Extend mode for trimming. This is like the pie without the à la mode, the pizza crust without the toppings, the … well, you get the idea. Please, for the benefit of your own education and your survival out there in the editing world, do not use Extend mode for such purpose. It takes much more time to do an extend than a trim, and you would be avoiding one of the best features of Free DV and Xpress Pro.

To extend, select the track(s) you want to extend. Find the point in the sequence to where you want to extend the clip. If this point is before the edit, mark an in point (see Figure 5.18). If it is after the edit, mark an out point. Click the Extend button, which is mapped to the P button on your keyboard. The edit is extended in the Timeline.

Figure 5.18 (left) Extending a transition forward; (right) extending a transition backward

Extend edit is an excellent way to perform split edits of L cuts (also known as split edits). After an audio-plus-video edit is made, select the track you want to trim, mark your point, and hit the Extend button on your keyboard. This process is very fast and intuitive.

Extend can be a little hazardous to use because if you have both an in point and an out point marked, Avid uses the in point as the higher priority. Why is this dangerous? If you mark an out point near the transition that you intend to extend, and you have an in point marked at some far-flung location on your sequence, pressing Extend will not do what you intended. Instead, some transition that you aren't even paying attention to will become extended by accident. To prevent this, you can always press the Clear Marks button before marking an edit for an Extend.

The method that I use to quickly determine the direction of the extension is to remember that the rounded part of the Mark In or Mark Out button must be facing the transition in the Timeline.

Maintaining Sync

It seems that whenever a new tool is introduced that can do powerful things, there is an issue of the dangers associated with it. In the case of trimming, constant attention must be paid to avoid breaking sync.

Avid has developed a tool to help: Sync Breaks. Whenever a clip with audio and video is adjusted so the tracks become out of sync, the number of frames out of sync appears on the Timeline (see Figure 5.19).

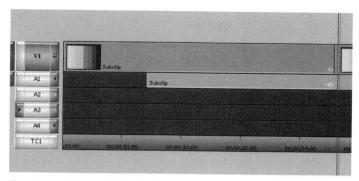

Figure 5.19 Sync breaks displayed on the Timeline

There are two simple rules that I use to avoid breaking sync:

- When trimming on a single track (audio or video) always select Center Trim.
- When trimming an A side or B side, always select All Tracks.

If you have a sequence with multiple video and audio layers, you have to be careful when trimming. Even if you follow the basic rules of maintaining sync, added titles, sound effects, and visual effects can be accidentally slipped out of sync with the rest of your elements. Although this is technically not a sync issue, the elements will not occur where you originally intended them to be. This can be especially treacherous with multiple-layer effects that have been rendered. One bad trim can cause the entire effect to slip out of sync, which requires you to reposition layers and render your results again. However, if you undo or reposition the layers at their original point, you will not have to redo the effects.

The easiest method to prevent slipping out of sync is to add an edit on every video and audio track at the trim point when trimming the video. In other words, if you need to add frames on V1, be sure to add just as many frames on each additional video and audio track. Not doing so will make the other tracks shorter, and the effects or wild sound on those tracks that occur after your V1 trim will appear sooner than originally intended.

To prevent breaking sync, select all your video tracks before entering Trim mode and add an edit. When trimming, make sure that all active tracks are selected. Then, trimming those Add Edit points will add filler on the blank tracks to match the length of the trim that was done on V1, preventing you from losing sync (see Figure 5.20).

Figure 5.20 Trimming on multiple tracks keeps the title on track 2 in sync.

Usually adding the edits would mean cueing up to the transition point, selecting all the video and audio tracks with no media on them, and adding an edit to them by pressing the H button (Add Edit) on your keyboard.

Tutorial: Trimming Sequences

Now that you understand what trimming can do, you can try out your newly acquired skills. In this tutorial, you'll analyze trim sides, use different trimming methods to see how they work, and get comfortable with the Trim tool.

Analyzing Trim Sides

Your first mission is to clean up the blip sequence. First, open up the bin entitled Trim and find your sequences inside. Double-click the blip sequence to load it. Go ahead and play it back—I'll wait.

At every transition point, some anomalous and annoying sound occurs. These sounds are very close to the edit point and need to be analyzed further. First, park your blue cursor on the Timeline near the first edit.

Now you'll enter Trim mode. Here's how you'll do it:

1. Take a deep breath.

2. Click the Trim button located underneath the record side monitor (Figure 5.21). It looks like a little 35mm roll of film.

Figure 5.21 Selecting Trim mode

Viola! You're in Trim mode and located on the first edit.

Play back the transition using the Play Transition Loop button (it's the button located below and center of the B-side monitor). It looks a lot like the Play button, but it has a little slash running through the middle of it.

Your transition will play continuously until you press the Play Transition Loop button again or press the Stop button on your keyboard. Could you tell which side of the transition has the blip noise? I couldn't. Let's analyze the transition by playing back the A and B sides. If you've stopped the Play Transition Loop button, start it up again.

As the transition loop plays back, press the Q button on the keyboard, which changes the Play Transition Loop so that it plays only the A side of the transition. After it plays the A side, it stops and plays it again continuously. Did you hear the bad audio by playing the A side?

Then do the exact same thing over again. Press the Play Transition Loop button again and press the W button. The B side of the transition plays.

Now you know how to analyze both the A and B sides of the transition for better accuracy.

Sync Breaks

In this first transition, you need to trim the B side. Let's try trimming using numerical entry. Because the troublesome frames are on the B side, select the right monitor by clicking it. (Note that the pink rollers in the Timeline are on the B side only.) When clicking the monitors, be careful not to click too close to the middle. If you do, the system will trim on both sides.

Now look at the track selector. You need to trim on all tracks so the audio and video will remain in sync. But before you do, select Video Only so that you can see the sync breaks.

Click the B monitor and enter +3.

Note that the sync breaks appear on the Timeline, indicating that by trimming a single track on a single side of the transition, we have thrown everything out of sync.

Cool, huh?

Let's go ahead and fix our "mistake." Enter –3, and the sequence will remain in its original state.

Trimming Using Numerical Entry

Now we'll do it the right way. Select all the tracks in the Timeline. Just how many bad frames do we have? My guess is three. Enter +3 so that the B side moves forward, erasing the bad frames from the sequence. Now press the Play Trim Loop button again. How does it sound now?

Trimming Using Rollers

Move on to the next transition by clicking on it in the Timeline with the Trim mode on. Notice that the pink rollers all move to that next transition. Be sure that all tracks are selected again. Go ahead and press the Play Transition Loop button.

Using your editorial skills, determine which side of the transition needs to be cleaned up (the side with the bad audio). This time, we'll adjust the edit by pulling on the pink rollers.

You'll need to select the side to be trimmed by clicking on either the A-side or B-side monitor. Using your mouse, click on the pink rollers, moving them forward or backward over the transition point. Note that as you move the rollers, the numbers underneath one of the monitors change from zero to the number of frames you are trimming, along with a + or – sign.

Now release the mouse when you think you've gotten rid of the bad frames. The trim has been made.

Trimming Using Digital Scrub

Move forward to the next transition. Again, using the skills you've learned so far, find the transition side that contains the bad frames. Be sure to select all the tracks.

Now you'll use roller trimming again. But in this case, go ahead and use digital scrub as well. Turn on digital scrub by pressing the Caps Lock key on your keyboard.

Click one of the trim rollers and move it backward and forward. Notice that you can tell when the bad audio plays back. Adjust the trim appropriately and move to the next transition of the blip sequence.

Using the Trim Buttons

In this next transition, you'll use the Trim buttons, which are on your keyboard on the bottom right and on the trim interface underneath the A-side monitor in Trim mode.

Once again, use your skills to determine the side to be trimmed—select all tracks on the track panel selector to stay in sync.

Here is how the buttons work: Each one points in a direction, either backward or forward. Each button with only one direction indicator trims one frame. The buttons with two direction indicators trim two frames. Go ahead and trim using these buttons.

Trimming on the Fly

Here is where it really gets fun. Go to the next transition. Find the side to be trimmed and then select it. Be sure to select all tracks.

In this case, you'll trim on the fly and find out how good your reactions are! Play back the trim loop and place your finger over the E, I, O, or R key on the keyboard. Let the transition play a few times to anticipate where you need to trim. Take your time; you're in no hurry here.

When you think you've found the correct point to update the trim, press the button (I refer to this as "pulling the trigger"). Note that the play transition loop continues to play back. If you messed up the first time, go ahead and let it play and pull the trigger again. Each time you press the key, the transition point updates. It takes a little getting used to this method, but the uses for it are endless.

Now continue to use your skills and finish the entire blip sequence. Be sure to use a variety of trim methods. For Xpress Pro users, the last two transitions can be slipped and slid. You can also try out the J-K-L method of trimming.

Importing, Exporting, and Digital Cut

6

When compared to other applications, Avid Free DV and Xpress Pro's import interface makes the process of importing graphics, both still and motion, relatively very easy. The only true "deal breaker" associated with importing graphic files is the format of the files themselves.

Chapter Contents

Still Graphics
Importing Other Types of Files
Exporting
Digital Cut
Tutorial: Import and Export

Still Graphics

Still graphics are a big part of any production. Examples can include show credits, charts, pictures, logos, and more. Avid has expanded from the original "PICT only" days to offer a very pleasing variety of graphic file formats in Xpress Pro. Supported formats on Xpress Pro include the following:

Alias (.als)	OMFI (.omf)	PNG (.png)	Targa (.tga)
Bitmap (.bmp)	JPEG (.jpg)	QRT (.dbw)	TIFF (.tif)
Chyron (.chr)	Photoshop (.psd)	Rendition (.6m)	Wavefront (.rla)
Cineon (.cin)	PICT (.pic, .pict, .pct)	SGI (.rgb)	X-Windows (.xwd)
Framestore (.fs)	PCX (.pcx)	Softimage (.pic)	Abekas YUV (.yuv)
IFF (.iff)	Pixar (.pxr)	Sunraster (.sun)	Photo CD (Mac only)

Of these still graphic file formats, Free DV can import PICT (.pic, .pict, .pct) and JPEG (.jpg). But never fear—there's a way to convert other formats.

As you can see, there are some formats that might not be on the list. For these formats, you can download a graphic converter application from the Internet. Some graphic converters that offer a stunning array of file format conversions are shareware; others offer a trial use of their application.

Note: Perhaps the most commonly used converter for Macintosh is called Graphic Converter—a unique name, eh? But it handles many different formats and does the job for relatively little expense, around $30 (USD). Graphic Converter from Lemke Software can be found at http://www.lemkesoft.de/en/index.htm. It's a direct download, and like all shareware, you can try and then buy.

Preparing Graphic Files

After you've converted your files into a format that is supported on Free DV or Xpress Pro, you'll need to prepare them so that they fit into the frame properly. A little prep work goes a long way when it comes to still graphics.

When you prep a file, there are certain criteria that need to be understood, including:

- Frame size
- Pixel aspect
- Color levels and color space
- Field ordering (for motion graphics)
- Field dominance (for motion graphics)
- Alpha channel
- Format (already covered)

Let's take a look at some image import settings. If you want to follow along with your Xpress Pro or Free DV, click inside a bin and select File > Import. When the selection menu appears, make sure you select Graphic or Graphic Documents (depending on whether you're using Windows or Mac), and then click the Options button. What follows is a discussion of each of these options.

Frame Size

Frame size is a fascinating thing, especially in light of the newer high-definition television (HDTV) formats (see Figure 6.1). For purposes of standard-definition television (SDTV), you need to know the proper size that Free DV and Xpress Pro accept. The dimensions of the SDTV frame size can be expressed in pixels. Here is where we bridge the gap from the computer world to the television world, from liquid crystal display (LCD) light to an electron beam attacking a phosphorous screen … I could go on, but probably shouldn't.

Figure 6.1 1080 HDTV signal

When importing from still graphics, the important thing is to avoid picture distortion during the conversion. As I indicated, the form of measurement is pixels. The pixels are expressed in width and height. A normal television picture is 720×486; that is, 720 pixels wide and 486 pixels high (see Figure 6.2).

For European and other countries, the correct pixel dimensions are 720×576. The European standard is actually far better than our own, although HD is pretty much the same quality anywhere.

Figure 6.2 (top) NTSC SDTV signal; (bottom) PAL SDTV signal

An important thing to note is that NTSC DV is 720×480. Digital video (DV) has six lines less than the normal picture signal. As a result, you might see some black bars when DV is broadcast at the top or bottom of the screen. You can fix the problem by "blowing up" the picture in an image processor that will fill the screen. In the case of Xpress Pro and Free DV, you can remedy it by using an effect to expand the picture size.

Pixel Aspect

Television signals have long had accepted standards. The idea of standards when creating media is that the picture can have consistent quality no matter where it is produced or who produces it. The current standard used for SDTV is called ITU-601. This standard determines the dimension and pixel sizes of both PAL and NTSC SDTV images. It also dictates other specifications. For example, the 601 standard determines the size and shape of the pixels used in broadcast images.

Surprisingly enough, the pixel defined by the ITU-601 standard is not a square pixel. If you think of an electron gun moving at a constant speed across a phosphorous surface, you see it would be difficult to maintain a square shape. In fact, the shape of the pixel is a little rectangular. This situation makes file imports a little more challenging because almost all computer graphic applications contain square pixels, although many adapt for NTSC and PAL signals.

You can now understand the challenge: If you mapped a square-pixeled image into a rectangular-pixeled image, it would appear to be horizontally stretched-out. To solve the problem, we need to squeeze horizontal pixels in computer graphic applications, so that when the image is mapped to Xpress Pro and Free DV, the resulting image isn't horizontally stretched-out. Adobe's Photoshop CS application has the capability to create and view files for this problem by previewing the corrected pixel aspect. Other applications do this as well.

When you import graphics into Free DV or Xpress Pro, you're given four options for correction of pixel aspect ratios. Avid assumes nothing about what preparation has been done prior to import, so you can choose between these options (see Figure 6.3):

- 601, Non-Square
- Maintain, Non-square
- Maintain, Square
- Maintain and Resize, Square

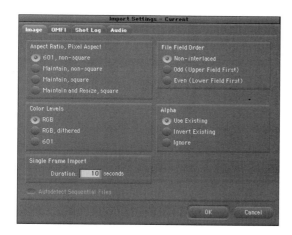

Figure 6.3 Import options

Let's take a look at each of these options as they appear in the import options in your software.

601, Non-Square This option is chosen for graphics that have already been fully prepped for import to Free DV and Xpress Pro. These images use *non-square* (the proper nomenclature for the pixel shape) pixels and the correct size. You can use this option when importing any image with non-square pixels that maintains a 4:3 aspect ratio. If images are not big enough to fill the frame (smaller than 720×486), they will have a black border around them.

Maintain, Non-Square An image that is imported using this option has the correct aspect ratio. It prevents a graphic from being squished or distorted when imported. It is used when the image contains the correct non-square pixels, but might be larger or smaller in dimension. If the image is too big (beyond the 720×480 norm for NTSC DV or the 720×586 norm for PAL DV) the image will be mapped into the shape. If the image is too small (as shown in Figure 6.4), black borders will be inserted.

Figure 6.4 Small image mapped within aspect ratio

Using this option does not resize the image; it is primarily used for importing standard NTSC images, in which the dimensions are 720×486. Using this option will crop six of the horizontal lines, bringing the image down to the DV standard of 720×480. If the image is too large, only the middle of the image will be imported, cropping off any portion of the image larger than the standard import size.

Maintain, Square You can use this import option if you want to maintain the original image size. This option is used primarily for importing logos, icons, and other items that do not necessarily have to fill the screen. With this option, Free DV and Xpress Pro recognize that the original contains square pixels and will adjust to fit the proper aspect, but it will not resize the image to attempt to fill the screen (see Figure 6.5). You can also use this option for normal full-sized files at 720×540.

Maintain and Resize, Square Free DV and Xpress Pro use this option to take an image that was created with square pixels and fill it to the largest dimension possible, adding black borders on the other dimension to maintain the correct aspect ratio. Tall skinny pictures will import so that they fill the screen from top to bottom and have black bars on either side. Wide, horizontal, or "landscape" pictures fill the screen from side to side with a letterbox look at top and bottom.

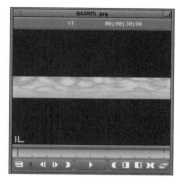

Figure 6.5 A horizontal image with maintained aspect ratio

Color Levels and Color Space

When an image that we view is created, there are certain boundaries for the colors created within them. You may have noticed, for example, that viewing a movie in a theater is not the same as seeing the DVD at home. Aside from cheaper popcorn and Dots, the image of a DVD on even the very best DVD projector or monitor doesn't compare with the vivid color that you see in the theater.

Why is this so? Because the theater uses film.

Every medium has limitations. When a DVD image is displayed, it displays an ITU-601 image, which has approximately 2.35 million different colors. You may have heard other numbers, but after consulting with two of the key color scientists of our time, it turns out that the 32 million colors of RGB, when placed into an NTSC color space, boil down to about 2.35 million colors. And although those are a lot of colors and shades of color, they do not compare with the projection of motion picture film.

Film has around 800 million colors.

So why don't we all put theater projectors in our homes? Well, for one thing, we would need to rent the film from the studio, which is very costly. Most theaters make nothing from ticket sales. The only money made these days is from concessions. The next time you go to the theater, try to help them out by buying something at the concession stand.

With applications such as Adobe Photoshop, the color standard is RGB. RGB color has around 32 million colors, so it's not quite as good as the film variety, but much better than ITU-601.

At this point, your head is probably spinning and you need some aspirin. Go ahead, I'll wait.

When you convert from Adobe Photoshop to Free DV or Xpress Pro, levels have to be monitored and remapped from RGB color to ITU-601. All the math of remapping the color gamut, image brightness and darkness, and so on is extraordinary. Fortunately, we won't be doing any hands-on gamut mapping—the system does it for you, but you need to understand what is happening and why it affects you.

Here's a neat little experiment. Try creating an image in Photoshop using a vivid yellow or Kelly green. Next, try to output the same color to an NTSC monitor. The Kelly green turns into a less saturated green, and the vivid yellow turns more into a mellow tone. Why? Because NTSC doesn't quite have an accurate Kelly green or vivid yellow in its color gamut.

That's a lot of information, but you need to know that what you see in your monitors on the computer can vary when it is sent to an NTSC video signal.

Field Ordering

The NTSC and PAL video frame is composed of two fields, and each field scans every other line in the picture. These two fields "interlace" with each other. For example, if we number each line of video, one field displays the odd-numbered lines: line, 1, line 3, line 5, etc. The other field scans the even-numbered lines: line 2, line 4, line 6, etc. When the two fields are combined or interlaced, they create what we perceive to be a full-resolution frame. Because of a human trait known as "persistence of vision," we think that we see a full frame, even though the image is displayed on a television one dot at a time. If you've ever shot a picture of a television display at high shutter speed, you'll only see a small dot as the image.

But I'm getting ahead of myself here. The question here is this: When a source is recording to videotape or to a file, do the even-numbered lines of the video frame play back first, or do the odd-numbered lines? The order of fields is determined by the playback of the source, which is important because these fields are recorded so that they are "temporally displaced" from each other. In other words, the second field that is recorded, whether it is odd or even, happens later in time than the first field, so if you switch the order, the resulting images can look like a horror show (see Figure 6.6).

Figure 6.6 Poor field ordering. Note the positions of the hockey players in each of the fields.

Allow me to elucidate by example. We shoot a video of Drew Bledsoe throwing a football. As each field is recorded, Mr. Bledsoe's arm moves forward. We record this video with the upper field first. If we were to specify the field ordering as lower field first, Mr. Bledsoe's arm would begin forward, jerk back, jump forward, jump slightly back, and then do the same thing over and over. In other words, the image would jitter backward a lot, but ultimately it would make progress.

A video image that is 24p or 25p has been created so that both fields are combined in a progressive frame. When you import these video files, there is no field ordering.

Images that are created in Photoshop and other still graphic applications will not have field order, so any of these files should also be imported as noninterlaced.

> **Note:** Which brings me to a question: If progressive frames are so great, why is it that each interlaced field offers motion updated 60 times per second instead of 30 as in progressive frames? Wouldn't that be better motion? The answer is yes and no. Yes, an interlaced frame "spreads out" the motion during a given period of a second while the progressive frame contains it in 30 full frames. That is, unless you play it more slowly, in which case you'll also detect the lack of resolution of single fields.

Now that we've learned field ordering, how do we detect whether a video file is upper or lower field first? The easiest way is to talk to the person who originally created the file. If the file was created but the creator doesn't know about field ordering, you can learn which order is the default order used by whatever application it was created in. When in doubt, read the manual!

If there's no manual around or if the creator of the video is clueless, go ahead and try one of the field orders or, if it's a long piece, use just a sample, and study the result. If the image seems to jitter as it progresses, go back and import it the other way and observe. One of them is going to look much better, assuming that there is some kind of motion in the frame.

Field Order versus Field Dominance

Field ordering is commonly confused with field dominance. Although the two terms sound similar, they are very different.

Field dominance is the determination of a cutting point. When we record video, synchronize it, and add timecode with the picture, it takes on certain characteristics, including two fields for each frame. The two fields, when combined, make up a single frame of video and one frame of assigned timecode. Therefore the first field of video that is recorded for a specific timecode is field 1, the second recorded field is field 2, and then the timecode number advances. Field dominance is the determination of which field is first temporally in the edit frame and where each cut will occur. Avid systems always cut before the first field. Therefore it is field-1 dominant. If it were cut on the second field, it would be field-2 dominant.

Field dominance doesn't play a big role in your determinations, unless your source material has cuts within it, of course. For example, if we were to use a line cut (*line cut* is a fancy term for a videotape that has been switched or mixed in a control room) as our source, we would possibly encounter some field dominance issues. If the switch from camera to camera occurred on field 2 instead of field 1, we would need to delete an extra field.

Alpha Channel

When we work with images, the alpha channel determines which parts of the image are seen and which are not. Alpha channels are used when we want to key an image over another, or over a colored background.

For example, if we were to create a logo over a black background and wanted to just show the logo, we would need to create an alpha channel that defined the black background as transparent and the logo as opaque. Both Xpress Pro and Free DV support alpha channels in most file formats.

Note: *Alpha channels* have been called a lot of other names—mattes, holdouts, cookie cutters, and hi-cons—but they are all the same and they all do the same thing: determine transparency.

If you were to look at an alpha channel, you would see a grayscale image. Normally, the white pixels represent areas of the image that will be seen. Black pixels represent areas that will be masked or matted out. Gray pixels represent varied levels of transparency of the image, with lighter pixels less transparent than darker pixels. Alpha channels are represented in this manner for just about every graphic application that has been created.

However, when evaluating alpha channels (such as the one shown in Figure 6.7), Avid systems read them backward, with black pixels representing opacity and white pixels being transparent. Apparently, this variation goes back to film mattes and how they were originally created. Avid chose to go with the film industry standard. Keep in mind that in the early days of nonlinear, the personal computer was relatively new. Not all editors were computer operators, and not all editors used Photoshop.

Advantages of an Inverted Alpha

Although some find Avid's inverted alpha to be a burr in their saddles, there is one distinct advantage to this method. When the alpha channel is inverted, JPEG artifacts along the edge of the matte fall outside of the keyed graphic, guaranteeing a clean matte, even at lower resolutions! So there is a distinct advantage to preparing the matte in this way.

Figure 6.7 Alpha channel
prepped for Avid import

So if you are using graphic files created with a graphics application, there is an invert alpha option.

Importing Graphic Files

Avid Free DV and Xpress Pro's advanced feature set make it easy to import files:

1. First, create a bin in which the imported files will be stored.

2. Select File > Import. The Import dialog box appears (see Figure 6.8). At the top of the screen, you see Enable; choose Graphic Files (Windows) or Graphic Documents (Mac). Now you can navigate to find those files on your system. To import multiple files, Shift-click each additional file (Mac) or Ctrl-click additional files (Windows).

3. After you select the files, choose the media drive in which you want the imported items to be stored. Xpress Pro will take each file and convert it into media that the system can easily read.

Mixing Resolutions (Xpress Pro)

When importing graphics, you need to determine the resolution of the graphic as it is imported. To do this, go to the Media Creation settings and select the Import tab. There you will see the resolution options used when creating import media. You can mix different resolutions in Xpress Pro, but not frame rates (for example, putting a PAL video in NTSC).

Let's say, for example, that you have a Mojo and want to import your graphics at 1:1 uncompressed. The graphic, when keyed over a DV-25 background, will be much more readable because it is 1:1 uncompressed. This is especially nice when doing titles in the Title tool (which we will discuss in Chapter 7). But the artifacts associated with a compressed image (as in DV-25) will not be present in the title, so you could potentially use thin, serif-type fonts. Your only limitation is the resolution of the output itself, which might have some issues with thin fonts or lines.

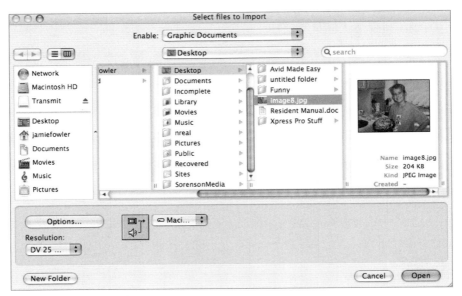

Figure 6.8 The Import dialog box

Single Frame Import Duration

For each graphic import, you can choose how many frames need to be created. For example, if you want to display a still image for 60 seconds, you should type **60** in this option box.

Autodetect Sequential Files (Xpress Pro Only)

Enabling this option (see Figure 6.9) allows Xpress Pro to look for a numbered pattern in the filenames within a folder. This is the method used to import animated sequences. Xpress Pro can import all the files from one of these sequences at once and create a single clip, eliminating the need to string them back together frame by frame in Source/Record mode. To import animated numbered graphic files, you have to select only the first image of the file sequence. You can also import partial sequences by selecting a file from further into the sequence. For example, you could import PICT.030, and that would start the import one second into the image sequence and then proceed to PICT.031, PICT.032, and so on.

Be careful when importing single files. If the Autodetect Sequential Files is turned on, and you have single images numbered in sequence, it will import those graphics as a single frame inside of a sequenced clip, thus making it more difficult for you to find your imported files. This has happened to me many times, so beware!

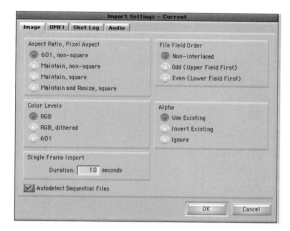

Figure 6.9 Import Settings window with Autodetect Sequential Files selected

Note: The Autodetect Sequential Files option can be a little tricky. If you have two graphics that appear to have a numbered cadence in your graphics folder, Xpress Pro will create them as an animated sequence.

Saving Import Settings (Xpress Pro)

Now that you've established your import settings, save them on your system. If you work with a graphic artist or animation house on a regular basis, it might be a good idea to name the settings after that person or place. Here's how to do it:

1. Go to the Project Window.

2. Select Import Settings.

3. Duplicate the import settings by clicking Ctrl+D/⌘+D.

4. Using the Duplicated Settings file, click to the right of the word Import. A cursor will appear.

5. Enter the name of the setting.

From now on, you can use this setting if you use any files that are similar in nature.

Drag and Drop Importing

After the settings are established, you can do some drag-and-drop importing from your desktop. Using this method assumes a few things:

- Your graphic files have been prepped and ready for import.
- The right import settings have been selected.
- You must drag the graphic to an open bin.

When you drag the image into an open bin (not the Project window), it will import automatically.

Importing Photoshop Graphics (Xpress Pro)

Xpress Pro can work with the layer's capabilities that are normally used with Adobe Photoshop version 6 and above. When importing a Photoshop graphic (.psd file), Xpress Pro will ask whether you want to import it as one flattened layer, a sequence of layers, or a sequence of chosen layers. This third option allows you to ignore layers that you will not use. When you import the file as a sequence of layers, it will produce a matte key clip for each layer and a regular clip for the background.

Xpress Pro also creates a sequence with all the layers in order, just as they were in the original Photoshop file. You can animate each layer (as shown in Figure 6.10) or use the layers with their alpha files over a different background.

Figure 6.10 Photoshop image imported in Xpress Pro. (Note that layers can be animated.)

This new capability has been something that I personally wanted for a long time. Previously, to do something like this was time-consuming and fairly difficult. For example, if I had a Photoshop file with 15 layers and a background, I would normally have to convert each of the layers into separate files and then import them. But with this advanced capability, it takes only a single import to do all the work.

Note: When importing Photoshop files, make sure they are 8-bit files, not 16-bit files. You can check this in Photoshop by opening the file and selecting Image > Mode. If the file is 16-bit, change it to 8-bit and save it before importing. Otherwise, you will get an error screen and no layers when importing.

After the layers are all imported, you can build a sequence for animation or add effects to individual layers. The layers can be used as matte keys over other backgrounds as well.

Note: One thing that is not supported is the blending mode in Photoshop. All layers will be imported with normal blending mode, so if you are trying to create a special effect using a blending mode, try re-creating it using the Effect palette in Xpress Pro.

Batch Reimporting Graphics (Xpress Pro)

When you import graphic files, it is a good idea to store them in a place on your system hard drive so that you can access them again, especially in the event of media erasure. Should you inadvertently lose the media from your imports, Xpress Pro will remember where the import came from. If it came from your hard drive, Xpress Pro can reimport the graphics more easily than if you imported it from a CD or network location that you would have to find again.

Xpress Pro can also be used when editing an offline version of a program in which you want to batch digitize all the clips and graphics in a higher resolution. To batch import your graphics, first select the sequence that contains the graphics to be imported. Then select Bin > Batch Import. The Batch Import dialog box appears (see Figure 6.11).

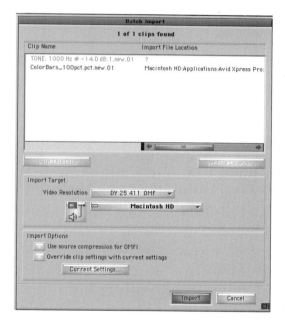

Figure 6.11 Batch Import window

At the top of the Batch Import menu is a list of graphic files that were imported for the sequence that you selected. You can select or deselect each individual file. Next, choose your resolution and clips to be imported. You'll also need to choose a drive for the import. At the bottom of the menu are two key options. The Use Source Compression For OMFI option uses the same compression applied on an original OMFI file when importing OMF files. This allows you to import at a native resolution and do the import more quickly than normal. For graphic files, leave this deselected. The second option, Override Clip Settings With Current Settings, allows you to import files and change their settings to the current settings that you have selected. For example, if your graphics were previously imported at 15:1s and you have changed the import setting to DV25 411, it will import at the DV-25 resolution.

After you've made your settings, batch import the files. They will have their original names, but will be created at the new resolution that you have chosen. You can double-check this by changing your bin to Text view and looking at the resolution of the clips.

Importing Other Types of Files

There are a good many different types of files that your Xpress Pro or FreeDV can import. Now that most commercially available music is on CD, your system is able to import it directly and digitally with no loss of clarity. You can also import QuickTime files. In the past, QuickTimes were considered inferior for their small size. But these days, you can import high-resolution files from QuickTimes.

Importing Audio from a CD

When using audio CDs it is very beneficial to copy the tracks to a project file, just as you did when importing graphics. By using this method, you have the ability to use the audio without having to track down your CD again.

 Note: While we're on this subject, let me remind you that using any CD music for public display is not a good idea. (My attorney just heaved a sigh of relief.)

Importing audio from an audio CD works much like importing graphics, except there are fewer options. To import an audio CD track, select the target bin and then choose File > Import. When the import browser comes up, select Files of Type > Audio (Windows) or Enable > Audio Documents (Mac). Navigate your way to the audio CD (see Figure 6.12) and select the track.

Figure 6.12 Importing from an audio CD

Music CDs use a sampling rate of 44.1 kHz. If you want the sample rate to match that of your project, choose Settings > Import Settings and select the first check box (see Figure 6.13) to convert the source sample rate to the project sample rate on import.

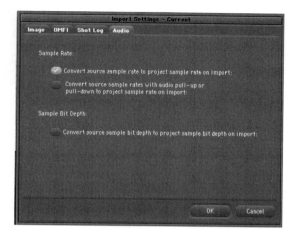

Figure 6.13 Setting the import sample rate to match the project sample rate

Importing QuickTime Files

Importing QuickTime files in Xpress Pro and Free DV is a very simple procedure. Before you import, make sure to set your Media Creation tool so that it will import files at the resolution that you are using for the rest of your sequence.

To import a QuickTime movie in the proper way, you'll need to have the same codec on your system that was used when exporting the file originally. Codecs are compressor-decompressors, and there are a lot of compression schemes out there. Examples of codecs are Sorenson, Sorenson Pro, Animation, Component, and so on. (We will discuss these in more detail later in this chapter.) The export of files is the driving force when discussing codecs.

To import a QuickTime file, select a target bin in your project and choose File > Import. The Import screen appears. Select Graphic Files and then navigate to the QuickTime file to be imported. Select the file and press Open. The file will import. Many of the same rules about field order, color space, aspect, and alpha channels from the Still Graphics Import section of this chapter apply to QuickTime files.

There are two types of QuickTime files: dependent and nondependent. If you try to import a file that is dependent, it doesn't work. Dependent files use another larger file and work much like aliases work on your desktop.

Importing OMF and AAF Intermediary Files

You can import Open Media Framework (OMF) and Advanced Authoring Format (AAF) intermediary media into your bins just as easily as a QuickTime or graphic file.

Be sure to select the format of the file on the Import menu, or else it won't show in your file browser.

The concept behind intermediary files is simple: take an OMF or AAF file and use it in After Effects, Discreet Smoke, or Premiere—any application using media files. The problem is that not all applications comply with the use of the file type. Some prefer their own formats. Intermediary files usually consist of two types of file. The first is a composition, which contains all the information about the file. You can compare it to a sequence that contains information about your media, how it will play back, timecode numbers and clip information, and so on. The second part is the media itself.

- OMF stands for Open Media Framework. These files were the first to be developed by Avid. They are used by Avid, Digidesign, Adobe, and other software vendors.

- AAF stands for Advanced Authoring Format. Xpress Pro is now compatible with AAF files as well as OMF files. But OMF is the native format of both Free DV and Xpress Pro.

To import the OMF or AAF intermediary files, Select File > Import. When the Import menu appears, select the file format (either OMFI or AAF, depending on the format you want to import). Navigate to the file and select it. Free DV and Xpress Pro will import both metadata (information about the media, such as timecode) and the media itself.

Exporting

With Free DV and Xpress Pro, you can export media, data, and information about your sequences, projects, still graphics, QuickTime files, and more. When you add more video and audio codecs and digital media applications to your system, the export options seem limitless.

Free DV diverges quite a bit when it comes to exports versus Xpress Pro. Still graphic exports are limited to JPEG only, whereas Xpress Pro can export in all the formats that it uses to import.

Graphic options allow you to choose between Windows-based graphics (bitmaps) or Mac-based graphics on both applications. There are some limitations. For example, certain PICT files made on a Macintosh cannot be imported into Windows-based applications such as Photoshop.

Still, there are a lot of things that you can do with the exporting abilities of both. You can export the following:

- Individual frames from clips and sequences

- AVI, QuickTime, DV Streams, or Windows Media

- Audio files for mixing on a digital audio workstation (DAW)

With Xpress Pro, you can also export the following:

- Sequences for use on other systems

- MPEG streams for use with DVD authoring

- Export files for a transfer between Avid systems

- Sequences to other applications for use

Save files to Avid Links, such as Audiovision, D\S Compositions, or Pro Tools formats.

Export Settings Templates

With Xpress Pro and Free DV, you have three export templates that were created for you. To look at these, click the hamburger (Fast menu) in your Project window in the settings area and select All Settings. These templates are as follows:

- Fast Export as QuickTime Movie

- Macintosh Image

- Windows Image

Let's go over each of these preset options and discuss.

Fast Export as QuickTime Movie

Using this setting creates a fast export of a QuickTime movie using the Avid DV codec. It creates a movie that is Same As Source, meaning that the exported QuickTime will be the same size as the captured source footage when you are using the Avid DV codec. If you have the optional Mojo, you can export an uncompressed sequence to Quick-Time as well.

A lot of old-timers like me once thought that QuickTime was a dubious sort of file format. These days, it is not only essential to use QuickTime, it is quite a lifesaver. QuickTime formats are used for everything, all the way to film size (4K) files.

Macintosh Image

When you use this setting, it exports a single PICT file that is determined by your marked in point in the sequence. Photoshop for Windows reads rasterized PICT files only. However, some other Windows applications can open it.

Windows Image

This setting exports a single BMP file. Like its Macintosh counterpart, a marked in point determines which single frame is exported. To simplify my own personal settings, I changed the Windows Image Export Setting to BMP and the Macintosh Image Export to PS MAC.

Creating Your Own Settings

You can create new export settings as well as use the ones described here. Duplicate your PS Mac settings (Ctrl+D/⌘+D) and open them up by double-clicking them. Select JPEG as the file type and make sure that Sequential Files is deselected. Use Marks should be selected. After you set it up, rename the setting to JPEG. Now you have a few export options in your arsenal, both standard and custom (see Figure 6.14). These settings can be imported with your other settings and used for easy drag-and-drop exporting without even having to create new templates!

Figure 6.14 User-created export settings

Of course, this isn't so exciting for Free DV users, because the number of export formats is limited. If you do a lot of exporting, it might be time to start saving your pennies so that you can get Xpress Pro.

Graphic Exports

Avid Free DV and Xpress Pro have the capability to output single frames and multiple frames in sequence. These frames can be used for a wide variety of reasons.

Keep in mind that the image quality of single-frame exports is severely handicapped by the resolution of NTSC and PAL. If you've never worked with print before, here's a brief explanation: A standard definition frame export from Xpress Pro is 720 pixels wide and 540 pixels tall. The most basic printed image usually contains a minimum of 300 dots per inch (dpi). Many printers prefer 600 dpi. So if you do the math correctly, your exported image would best be suited for print at a size of anywhere from 1.2 to 2.5 inches wide.

This is based on the presumption that you would even use a video image for print. A more common use for exported graphics is its use in a graphic-editing application. In some cases, you might need to export a sequence of frames for animation, compositing, rotoscoping, or some other dynamic media imaging. Either way, Xpress Pro and Free DV can handle these types of exports with ease.

Single-Frame Graphic Exports

Xpress Pro can export a lot of different file formats. Free DV, on the other hand exports fewer formats. Do you Free DV people feel robbed? You shouldn't, for three very simple reasons:

- *Helloooooo?* It's called *Free* DV for a reason.

- You can download graphic converter applications very easily from the Internet and convert these files to just about anything.

- If you *really* want to get crazy with graphics, there are some inexpensive graphic converter applications that will convert to every file format known to man- and womankind.

The first order of business is to determine which format you'll need to export. To see the variety of options, find the frame where you want to export. It can be from a clip, subclip, sequence, or effect. You can export from either the Source or Record monitors. When your Avid system exports a graphic, it chooses whichever monitor is selected, so be sure to enable the correct one. Any frame works. After you find the frame, place a mark in on it. The mark lets Free DV/Xpress Pro know which frame is to be exported. From there, select File > Export. If you have other things to do before exporting, be sure to click on the frame before accessing this menu because the Export menu is conditional. In other words, if you were to click on a bin, the system would assume that you were trying to export a bin or perhaps a sequence (depending on exactly what was clicked in the bin), but it wouldn't know that you are trying to export a frame.

When the Export menu comes up, select the Options pull-down menu. From here, select Graphic, and the Graphic Export menu appears. To the right of the menu are the Use Enabled Tracks and Use Marks selectors.

Multiple-Frame Graphics Exports

Exporting a multiple-frame graphic sequence works much like exporting a single graphic with one exception: You can create multiple individual files, one for each frame. If you work with animators or do much *rotoscoping* (that is, painting frame by frame) this is probably of common use for you. Individual frame exports can, for some applications, be easier to work with than a QuickTime movie or other streaming media. The frames need to be contiguous in the sequence to be exported in this automated fashion. If they are not contiguous, you can edit a new sequence together and make them that way.

To export multiple frames in a sequence, choose Sequential Files on your Export Graphic Options menu.

If you are only exporting a portion of your sequence or a clip, be sure to make a mark in and out at the intended start and finish and then check the Use Marks box in the export settings; otherwise, the entire piece will export. When you save a sequence of files, put them in a separate folder. Otherwise, they could dump all over your desktop. And a messy desktop makes for sloppy work. Maybe it's the military kid in me, but I find this method extremely inefficient.

Exporting files over a network directly to a server or directly to a CD-ROM or other removable storage medium is not necessarily the best solution if the write speed to that storage medium or server can't keep up with how fast Xpress Pro can export. Instead, export to the fastest drive you can send to. After the export is completed, you can then transfer the saved files to the removable medium or server.

As you export sequential frames, Xpress Pro will take whatever name you assigned in the Save dialog box and add a number, beginning at 001. So, for example, if you export sequential files with the name Untitled Sequence, Xpress Pro will name the first exported file Untitled Sequence 001, then Untitled Sequence 002, and so on until it finishes unloading each single frame in the marked sequence. From there, they can be moved for whatever purpose you intend.

It's good to remember that some file formats produce larger files than others, so make sure that you have plenty of drive space for the export. Unlike QuickTime and streaming media formats, in the event of a power outage, whatever individual files were exported will be usable. Continue the export with a new mark from wherever you left off. Or better yet, purchase an uninterruptible power supply. In the long run, you'll be thankful, anyway.

Exporting Audio Files

Now we will discuss the options when exporting single clips or sections of audio without the complexities of needing to define your sequence, individual audio edits, and transitions. You can create single audio files with Free DV and Xpress Pro that can be used with a variety of applications, from the high-end audio workstations to a simple audio application.

Xpress Pro also has the ability to export individual or entire sequences of audio files. Select the sequence or the clip of the audio that you want to export. You'll want to make marks and enable tracks according to your needs.

You can select a clip, sequence, subclip, or any other form of audio media. You can also select the audio by selecting it directly from a bin, but be mindful of the no-brainers: If you select Use Marks in your Export dialog box, and the clip in the bin has no marks, there will be no audio exported.

There are two choices of audio format when exporting: WAV files and AIFF-C files. WAV files originated with Windows PCs and now are compatible with Quick-Time. Thus they can also be used with Macs. The other format, AIFF-C, is pretty much the professional audio industry standard. Almost all audio workstations and applications that use audio will accept an AIFF-C format.

You also have a sampling choice (see Figure 6.15). If you intend to create a file for an audio CD, you'll need to use 44.1 kHz sampling. If you're doing an export of DV material not intended for audio CD using four channels of sound, 32 kHz is the normal sampling rate. And if you have audio sources sampled at the higher (and thus superior) rate of 48 kHz, you can use them for the file. Again, the end purpose will normally define which setting to choose. You can also default to the sample chosen for your project.

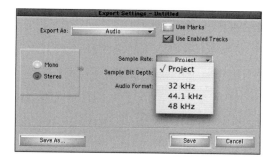

Figure 6.15 Audio sampling rate selection dialog box

Audio files can be exported as either mono or stereo. Any stereo exports will include panning that was set in your edited sequence or source clip. Be careful not to inadvertently cause volume to double by panning one track center and the other to one side. When using stereo, it's WYHIWYG (what you hear is what you get). Fortunately, most audio exports go fairly quickly. So if you mess it up, you can go back and re-export the file.

Finally, you must select a sampling size. Audio editing has developed to the point where sampling size is incredibly accurate. As a result, the old industry standard of 16-bit audio has been superseded by 24-bit audio, which is superior (but not that detectable to most non-audiophiles).

You can choose the larger sampling, but before you do, make sure that wherever the file goes, the equipment can support it. Some audio facilities still use 16-bit audio and have no intention of changing that standard anytime soon. Better to contact the audio facility than to export the wrong sampling size. Audio post facilities also frequently have the capability to downsample. For most consumer audio uses and programs, you are probably safest at 16-bit audio.

Exporting QuickTime

Before we discuss exporting frames and audio files, let's get right to the most elaborate kind of export: your sequence. Although exporting single frames is a relatively easy process, exporting a sequence can be a bit more tasking. There are many formats and options. Let's start by taking a look at QuickTime, which you should have already installed on your system.

QuickTime is a media playback system developed by Apple Computer. The QuickTime Player has become quite a versatile tool for digital artists. If you haven't used it yet, you might be surprised at how much it can do. QuickTime Pro offers a lot of other options that you wouldn't normally have: more codecs, exporting capabilities, and more (see Figure 6.16). And the best thing about QuickTime Pro is that it is relatively inexpensive.

Figure 6.16 Choosing the QuickTime movie type

Note: For more information about QuickTime Pro, go to Apple's website, www.apple.com.

Two Types of QuickTime Movies

There are two different types of QuickTime files: QuickTime reference movie and QuickTime movie.

QuickTime Reference Movie Exporting sequences as a QuickTime reference movie creates an alias file that references the media already on your system. The OMF files that Xpress Pro uses are played back within a QuickTime wrapper, making the reference file very small. This type of export takes little time because the media has already been compressed and is easily accessed. The instruction set used in this file is so small that there is very little concern for drive space. However, it is absolutely dependent on the media that you already have on your system. If you move it to another computer without the media, the reference file is worthless, bupkis, nil, naught, nothing.

The most common reasons for using QuickTime reference movies are speed and file efficiency. If you need to export a reference file to be imported into Adobe After Effects or Apple Shake for compositing, you can easily do this with QuickTime reference format. The media is already on your system, and there are no compatibility issues. It saves time for the export and drive space for media, and you can go right to the next application. This is also an excellent option for files that you intend to compress or reformat further using a program such as ProEncode or Cleaner.

Note: My own personal preferences divert here. For whatever reasons (age, fear of computers, and so on), I prefer to use the second type of QuickTime file.

QuickTime Movie The second method of QuickTime export is as an independent QuickTime movie with media created by a codec. Creating this type of file depends on the codec and settings that you choose. It is much larger than the reference file, but it is also a freestanding file, meaning that you can copy it to another system and it will play back fine without concern over a reference file and the dependent media.

Codecs

When I first learned the basics of Adobe's Photoshop application, I was told that the key to manipulating single images was through plug-ins. The more plug-ins you had, the more things you could do. As a result, I probably have purchased at one time or another just about every commercially available plug-in for Photoshop. Plug-ins do a lot for photo manipulation.

Codecs, for lack of a better analogy, work as the plug-in when it comes to QuickTime files. There are dozens, maybe even hundreds of QuickTime codecs that are out there. Even more are being developed as we speak (or read). Think of a computer geek with a QuickTime development kit, creating a new codec. I guess for programmers the creation of new codecs is necessary, because I am frequently introduced to them.

For QuickTime, the codec is king. The more codecs you have, the more versatile QuickTime becomes. Those who die with the most codecs win. Have you ever downloaded a video and wondered how on earth they made such a beautiful picture on such a small file? It is almost always because of the compression-decompression scheme. Codecs make the difference between a very good QuickTime file and a very bad one.

There are some codecs that come with QuickTime when you install it (see Figure 6.17). Other codecs can be added as you need them. These third-party codecs, including Avid codecs, allow you to create media in different styles as needed.

Name	Date Modified	Size	Kind
AvidAV1xCodec.component	Oct 11, 2004, 2:24 PM	44 KB	Component
AvidAVDJCodec.component	Mar 17, 2005, 11:44 AM	264 KB	Component
AvidAVdvCodec.component	Mar 17, 2005, 11:44 AM	348 KB	Component
AvidAVUICodec.component	Mar 17, 2005, 11:44 AM	104 KB	Component
AvidDVCodec.component	Oct 11, 2002, 9:33 PM	200 KB	Component
DesktopVideoOut.component	Apr 22, 2004, 2:55 PM	--	Component
DivX™ Video 5.component	Aug 24, 2002, 11:02 AM	432 KB	Component
DVCPROHDCodec.component	Apr 9, 2004, 9:18 PM	--	Component
DVCPROHDMuxer.component	Apr 22, 2004, 2:55 PM	--	Component
DVCPROHDVideoDigitizer.component	Apr 22, 2004, 2:55 PM	--	Component
DVCPROHDVideoOutput.component	Apr 22, 2004, 2:55 PM	--	Component
DVCPROHDVideoOutputClock.component	Apr 22, 2004, 2:55 PM	--	Component
DVCPROHDVideoOutputCodec.component	Apr 22, 2004, 2:55 PM	--	Component
FCP Uncompressed 422.component	Apr 7, 2004, 6:00 AM	--	Component
LiveType.component	Apr 9, 2004, 2:16 PM	--	Component
Sorenson Video Pro OSX.qtx	May 12, 2004, 5:17 AM	472 KB	Locati...odule
ToastVideoCDSupport.component	Feb 4, 2002, 7:28 PM	1.5 MB	Component

Figure 6.17 Codecs in my QuickTime library

Which codec is best? It usually depends on how you'll use the file. There are codecs that work on older and slower computers, codecs that demand high-performance new computers, and so on. If you use a high-performance codec and play back the movie on an old system, the results can be catastrophic.

When you select a codec for export, you're given several options on how the codec will write the file, including the quality level that you want the file to be. The best idea when using codecs is to test them on the same type of computer that they are targeted for.

Using and Copying Codecs

The most common QuickTime Export error is the lack of similar codecs on the target computer. Both the export and target computer need the same codec to work properly.

If you're running Xpress Pro on Windows XP, your codecs are located in the folder [drive name]:Windows/System32/. Normally, these files are hidden in the folder, but you can get Windows XP to reveal them. If you're running Xpress Pro on Macintosh (OS X), the codecs are located in the folder Macintosh HD/Library/QuickTime. The Avid QuickTime Codecs are for Meridien Uncompressed, Meridien Compressed, the Avid DV Codec and another QT codec for ABVB and Nuvista Avid media. All these codecs cover the gamut for exporting to every Avid system ever made.

The type of codecs available for your computer will vary, depending on whether you're running a PC or Mac. In other words, some codecs are created exclusively for only one platform. That's rare these days, but there are still issues with some codec files.

Exporting Sequences

Let's start by exporting a sequence. From here, we'll go through all the options and dialog boxes. At first, this may seem a bit cumbersome—there are a lot of questions that the system needs to have answered before exporting—but after you create settings and are satisfied with the results, exporting sequences can be a drag-and-drop operation.

Here is a checklist to use as we export a sequence:

All Media Online Make sure that all your media is online. A quick way to check for this on your sequence is to load it into the Record monitor, click on the Timeline hamburger (Fast menu), and select Clip Color > Offline. Any offline clips will show in the Timeline. You'll need to find them and import, capture, or relink them before exporting the sequence.

Audio Sample Rate If any clips contain sampling rates different from the one you chose as the default rate for your sequence, you need to convert them before exporting. You can view the sample rates of each clip in your bin and then select Bin > Change Sample Rate to convert any mismatches.

Audio and Video Levels. What you see is what you get (WYSIWYG). All audio levels, pans, video levels, effects, and anything else you did to the sequence will be exported. Make sure that these levels are all to your satisfaction. Despite any false hopes you might have, exporting will not improve your work.

Render Everything If you render it now, it won't have to be rendered during export. If you don't, you could be in for a long export. Bottom line is that although Free DV and Xpress Pro can play back in real time, there is no real-time support for other file formats. As a result, the system will have to "think" through every unrendered effect during export and render it.

Drive Space A partial QuickTime file is not a QuickTime file. It is worthless, void, zilch, nada, naught. For a QuickTime file to work, it has to be completely exported. You'll want plenty of drive space to make sure that the export comes all the way through. If the system runs out of space, it'll tell you. If your sequence is very long, you might consider breaking it up into segments before exporting.

Exporting a QuickTime Reference Movie (Xpress Pro)

Now that we've completed our checklist, let's export a QuickTime reference movie. Exporting a QuickTime reference movie is done with a few easy steps.

First, select all the tracks in the Timeline track selector panel that you want to export. If you want to export the entire sequence, clear all the in and out marks. If you're exporting only a portion of the sequence, determine the exported section using a Mark In and a Mark Out.

Now, select File > Export. A box with Export As appears. Click the Options button. The Export Settings window appears. Here you will find the extensive array of settings. At the top, there is also an Export As setting. Click on it to reveal all the different file types available. Choose QuickTime Reference. Once chosen, you're given some new options below. For now, let's select everything, with the exception of Network Referencing. Be sure to select Use Enabled Tracks so the right media references will export. You'll flatten the video tracks; insert black in the blank spaces; render all effects; and go with your project settings for audio sampling, file format, and sample size. You'll also use the Avid codec.

You may have also noticed that there is a setting entitled Digital Mastering (Xpress Pro only). The options in this pull-down menu are shortcuts to choosing the export options already in the menu. There are two choices with this menu: Digital Mastering and Fast Draft.

Digital Mastering flattens the video tracks, fills blank spaces in the sequence with black, mixes down the audio tracks, and renders all effects. The other option is Fast Draft, which gets the sequence out more quickly. It fills blank spaces with black and flattens the video tracks. The only problem with Fast Draft is that if the effects are not rendered, they will not show up in the resulting QuickTime.

When creating a QuickTime reference, one of these selections—Fill Spaces with Black—is very important. If this isn't done, the resulting reference file might have difficulty playing back any blank spaces in your sequence. Always select this option.

Saving the Export Settings

Notice the Save As button at the bottom left of the Export Settings options (see Figure 6.18). This button is not for saving the export, but rather a method to save your export settings. Go ahead and click it to save these settings. You'll notice that this is now in your settings menu as one of your export options.

Figure 6.18 Setting saving in the Export menu

Drag-and-Drop Exporting

You can export using drag and drop much as you did with your importing previously. First, activate the export settings that were created in the Settings tab of your Project window. There should be a check mark next to those settings. Now, select the sequence in its bin and drag it off to the desktop.

Another Way of Exporting: Send To (Xpress Pro)

With Xpress Pro, you can export a QuickTime reference (or for that matter, any type of export) and then send it to another digital application as long as it is on the same machine. This method of export goes directly from the Xpress Pro bin to the target application. The function is called Send To. Here's how you do it.

First, make sure that your export settings are correct. You want to export as a QuickTime reference file, flatten tracks, and fill spaces with black. After you create the setting, make it active, select your sequence in its bin, and then select File > Send To.

The Send To menu appears (see Figure 6.19). You have to show Xpress Pro where the other application exists. Choose Make New and find the application that you want to use. You'll probably want to enable the tracks on the Timeline and make marks before you do this. After you find the application, Xpress Pro will export it to wherever you choose.

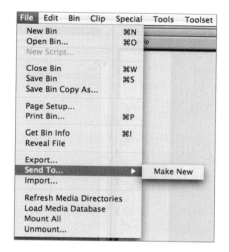

Figure 6.19 Choosing Send To

The only real advantage of using Send To is that you can launch the next application automatically from Xpress Pro. In some cases, the application will automatically load the sent export file as well.

Exporting QuickTime Movies

Now that you know how to make reference files, it's time to do a QuickTime movie export. Let's move media! (That's a phrase that is used at Avid. I'm, umm, still waiting on that check, guys …) A QuickTime movie export puts a QuickTime wrapper on media files created with your codecs. Here, the number of options available is abundant.

To start, prepare your sequence, as mentioned previously. Now take a look at the sequence in your Timeline. If you want to export only a portion of the sequence, be sure to mark an in point and an out point. You'll select the Use Marks option in the Export options. If you want to export specific tracks from the sequence, make only those tracks active. You'll want to choose the Use Enabled Tracks option in the Export options.

With the sequence selected (either by clicking on the Timeline or the Record monitor) select File > Export. You can name the soon-to-be-exported QuickTime here and then click on the Options button.

> **Note:** Choose before you export. If you forget to select the Record monitor or Timeline, whatever was last selected on the interface will be exported. The Export menu is conditional, depending on whether a bin, sequence, clip, or other media is selected. Whenever you're unsure, it's easier to just stop the export, click on the proper item, and begin exporting again.

The Export Options button leads to a variety of different formats, which in turn leads to even more specific formats. First, click the Export As pull-down menu. There is a list of different types of media exports available on your system, everything from OMF and AAF to the QuickTime formats. Are there any tilde keys in front of the formats in your menu? The tilde (~) indicates that this export option has not been qualified with Xpress Pro and is not supported by Avid. Nonetheless, the option exists, and you can try it out as an export if you wish.

Select QuickTime Movie and take a look at more options. While you're near the Export As menu, be sure to select the Use Marks and/or Use Enabled Tracks options if needed. Just below is the Save As Source option. When you save the QuickTime movie the same as its source, you're putting a QuickTime wrapper on Avid media. There are two options here: to save it as source or to customize the QuickTime. If you customize it, the Use Avid Codec button deflates, and you're given yet another options button: Format Options.

Format Options

When you customize your QuickTime export, you have a myriad of options, which primarily are concerned with which QuickTime codecs will be used. There are both audio and video codecs. Click on the Format Options button, and you will see another window, in which the current options are displayed. Here the audio and video are separated, and there are settings that can be made. Keep in mind that this myriad o' options depends upon the number of codecs that your system has and is capable of using. You also have a filter and size option for video and some streaming options if you intend to use your QuickTime on the Internet. The streaming options can be deselected if Internet use is not intended.

Video Settings

When you click the Video Settings button, a Compression Settings pull-down menu appears, in which you can choose the QuickTime codec that best suits your needs. The number of settings available depends upon the type of computer, the enabled media capabilities, and the amount of software that you own. My system is lacking in this department, yet I have a choice of 27 different codecs. After your codec is selected, you can select a quality setting below the pull-down menu.

With some codecs, you have even more options! Are you counting how deep the option menus go? So far, we're up to number four. Try this: Select the Avid Meridien Compressed codec and then click yet another options button below the quality adjustment. Now you have a choice of even more ways to compress the media (see Figure 6.20). There are so many codecs on the market that it would be impossible to discuss the details of each one here.

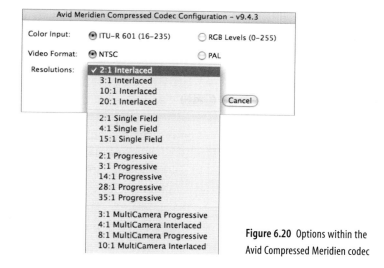

Figure 6.20 Options within the Avid Compressed Meridien codec

Audio Codecs

You can choose from a variety of audio codecs. Uncompressed is usually the way to go, unless you have a need to compress the audio in a different format for a special purpose. Be sure that the sampling rate and sample size are the same as your audio project sample to avoid downsampling issues. Audio files do not take up a lot of space, so you can be bold here.

Prepare for Internet Streaming

The last item on the list of Format Options are the choices that can be made when creating a QuickTime for video streaming (see Figure 6.21). There are three:

- Fast Start
- Fast Start–Compressed Header
- Hinted Streaming

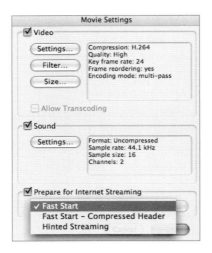

Figure 6.21 Format options

Finish that sandwich and we'll go over each option.

Fast Start Fast start allows your QuickTime to begin streaming on the Internet before it is completely downloaded.

Fast Start–Compressed Header This method of preparation is actually a bit better for Internet streaming. It works exactly the same as Fast Start, but with one major advantage. The header portion of the QuickTime is compressed so that it can be read more quickly by the Internet client. The QuickTime will not stream until the header is completely read. A smaller header allows for a faster start on the stream.

Hinted Streaming This type of preparation is for use on video servers. The file does not begin streaming until it receives a hint track for each track of video and audio. The hint track allows the server to divide the file into packets for more efficient Internet delivery. When selecting this option, you either need to know how your video server works or contact someone who does. The encoding, packet size, and method of delivery will need to be chosen in later option menus.

After you select the audio and video codecs, filters, frame sizes, and Internet options, save the QuickTime movie. It might take a while to export, depending on the codec and the length of your sequence.

Other Movie Exports

You can also export your movie in other formats, such as DV Stream or MPEG formats, when available. These formats are readable on a QuickTime Player, but are not specifically created for QuickTime.

DV Streams come in two flavors: standard DV-25 (NTSC or PAL) and DVC Pro (also in NTSC and PAL). When you choose to export to DVC Pro, the audio automatically locks to 48 kHz, the DVC Pro standard.

Exporting OMFI Files

Open Media Framework Interchange (OMFI) is a file format that can be transferred to other platforms and other applications. It was developed primarily by Avid and is supported by a group of OMFI partners, developers, and software companies that cooperate with the standard to allow import and export of files and information using OMF formats.

As stated in the Import section, the intention is to allow one digital media application to allow the import and export of files and compositions to another. By allowing the applications to "speak" to one another through importing and exporting, we, the users, don't have to deal with extreme measures, third-party software, and any "undocumented solutions" to move media from, say, an editing application to an animation application.

Acceptance in the marketplace of OMF has been mixed, but one area that immediately embraced OMF was audio. Almost every audio workstation made has some form of OMF capability. As a result, exporting audio files and compositions through OMF is quite common.

OMF comes in two flavors: Version 1.0 is supported by older audio workstations and works quite well in most situations; version 2.0 was developed a little later and incorporated some changes. The result is that more applications can use OMFI. Once again, before deciding on whether to use 1.0 or 2.0, the best bet is to call the facility that will be using the file and talk directly with the engineer who will be using the files. Once you've created a successful test, name the Export Setting for the name of the facility it's going to.

Exporting AAF Files

Another form of export is Advanced Authoring Format (AAF), which is very similar in concept to OMFI and it essentially does the same thing that OMFI does. Using AAF, you can export sequence information (compositions) compositions with embedded audio and video media.

The two different standards are based upon the fact that software developers, like any other committee of persons, cannot agree on everything. Whenever you get commercial software developers to allow some form of access to proprietary compression and functionality, it gets a little slippery. Some applications are OMF-compliant; others are AAF-compliant. Your Free DV and Xpress Pro have both. As long as there is some method of moving media from one application to another, it's good, right?

Whether your target application is OMF- or AAF-compliant, the methods of export are exactly the same.

Exporting OMFI and AAF Compositions and Media

Let's see how you can export AAF and OMFI files

First, click the Options button, and the Export Options window appears. Select your format in the Save As pull-down menu (see Figure 6.22). You can choose between OMFI 1.0, OMFI 2.0, and AAF. The types of options for each format are exactly the same, so you're just determining which type of interchange file will be created.

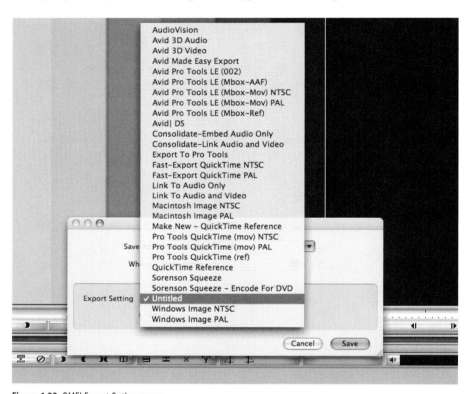

Figure 6.22 OMFI Export Option menu

The next tasks are to select what you want to export to the interchange format and to determine how it will be exported.

Export an OMFI or AAF File with Links to the Current Media Choosing this method creates a composition file that has links to the media that is already on your system. If you choose this method and send this file to another system, the application that uses it has to be able to recapture the media to bring it online. Compositions are very small files, so this method is great for sending through Ethernet or small media drives.

Copy Media and Link to Copied Media This method allows you to make copies of the media on another drive and create a composition with links to that media in its new location.

Consolidate Media and Link to Consolidated Media When you have a sequence that is long, you can consolidate it so that it doesn't have huge amounts of media files from the original clips. Doing this makes the resulting media files fewer and smaller. This option, like the Copy Media option, creates links between the composition and the resulting media files. Normally, it is used for moving media onto a separate drive when the project needs to go to another system.

Embed Media This function creates one single file with both the composition and the media files. As long as you have a drive big enough to support it, embedding is a good way to keep track of your media. Make sure that the target application can support it. This makes a nice clean package to deliver, but it definitely "puts all your eggs in one basket." It's a big file that will take a while to create. If that single file becomes corrupt, the whole thing is useless.

Consolidate and Embed Media This last export option will consolidate the media first, so that you do not have a lot of extra media embedded in the file; it will then embed it into a single file.

After you choose a method of export for audio and video files, save and export.

Digital Cut

A digital cut is a method of export in which the system feeds video and audio to a recording deck. This deck could be everything from a professional DigiBeta deck to an inexpensive DV cam. Any type of equipment that can record real-time playback would be used for the digital cut. I mention this because there are so many new ways to record video, including DVD recorders and mini-DVD recorders. Some refer to digital cut as a "print to tape." Either way, they are the same thing.

Preparing for a Digital Cut

When you perform a digital cut, there is a bit of setting up to do. Here is a handy checklist to get you started:

- Edit bars and tone before the sequence begins.
- Edit a slate to identify your material.
- Render effects.
- Convert audio sample rates.
- Calibrate the signals going from Free DV/Xpress Pro to the record deck.
- Configure your input deck in the deck configurations setting.
- Output using the Digital Cut tool.

Editing Bars and Tone

A lot of people skip this task, but I highly encourage putting bars and tone before your edited work. SMPTE bars work like the ISO rating on a roll of film. Using bars, you tell the recipient of your work how to adjust the brightness, contrast, hue, and saturation of the picture for optimal viewing. When we add tone to the sequence, we are giving the recipient of this digital cut a level to use when setting up the audio for playback.

Of course, there are some situations in which you wouldn't add bars and tone—when a client receives a "viewing copy." I've never been a fan of the viewing copy, because it usually ends up creating situations in which the client comes back to the editing suite, only to discover that the finished piece looks good, but his or her television needs to be calibrated.

Case in point: A client came back to me, complaining that the images were too green. After we played back the same tape on a calibrated monitor, the client realized that his television hue had been tweaked by his four-year-old son, who apparently was trying to make the Teletubbies change colors. But whether we like it or not, the client is always the boss, so things like this can happen.

Some production companies have standard formats for their bars and tone. These choices depend on who you work for and the type of finished work produced. For example, the quiz show *Jeopardy* records bars and tone at timecode 58:30:00 for one full minute, cuts to black for 10 seconds, displays the slate with announce for 10 seconds, and then cuts to black for another 10 seconds. So its setup looks like Table 6.1.

▶ **Table 6.1** Bars and Tone Formatted for Television

Source	TC In	TC Out	Duration
Bars and Tone	00:58:30:00	00:59:30:00	00:01:00:00
Black	00:59:30:00	00:59:40:00	00:00:10:00
Slate	00:59:40:00	00:59:50:00	00:00:10:00
Black	00:59:50:00	01:00:00:00	00:00:10:00
Program	1:00:00:00		

If you do the math, you will note that the show begins at 1:00:00:00. There's a very good reason for this: When editing the show, timing has to be precise. When the show begins at 1:00:00:00 and you edited 20 minutes of material, the timecode will read 1:20:00:00.

When editing commercials, the format changes. First, we edit commercials in non–drop frame timecode because most commercials run 30 seconds, so there's no need to use drop frame to stay in time. Commercials (see Table 6.2) usually have a minute of bars, an eight-second countdown slate, and two seconds of black, followed by the commercial.

Source	TC In	TC Out	Duration
Bars and Tone	00:58:50:00	00:59:50:00	00:01:00:00
Slate/Countdown	00:59:50:00	00:59:58:00	00:00:10:00
Black	00:59:58:00	01:00:00:00	00:00:10:00
Commercial	1:00:00:00		

There is no true standard for applying bars and tone, but these are the most common. Motion pictures use an SMPTE leader when counting down. No doubt you have seen this many times. For some films that are transferred to video, this leader is still used. There is a QuickTime of the SMPTE leader for you in this chapter's folder on the *Avid Made Easy* companion DVD.

When adding bars and tone, you might have to change your starting timecode in the sequence to make sure that the program starts at the hour. This is a simple procedure:

1. Click the monitor that has your sequence.

2. Press Ctrl+I/⌘+I on the keyboard. Information about the sequence appears, including your start timecode.

3. Type in your new starting timecode and close the window.

Creating a new start timecode does not move anything in the sequence; it just changes the start number. So you'll have to move everything down when you put in the bars and tone. Don't forget to edit on all tracks, or else your higher channels of video (video track 2 on Free DV and video tracks 2–24 on Xpress Pro) will shift out of sync with your other program material.

Adding the Slate

The slate is a means of identifying a sequence in its current state (that is, it needs to have a unique identifier to serve its purpose). You might edit 15 different versions of a commercial spot. What makes this one unique? Usually you can tell by identifying it on your slate.

For example, suppose that you edit a commercial for a big soft drink company. The director has worked with you on this spot and has 15 different versions of it. The director is not sure which one will run, so you are asked to do a digital cut of all the different versions.

Usually, a spot has some form of identification—a number to differentiate it from other spots. The soft drink spot has the identifier 118-05-CCN. So you could name them 118-05-CCN-A, 118-05-CCN-B, and so on. Without the slate, it could be difficult to note the subtle variations between each version.

Some people like to get fancy with their slates. I personally prefer a simple black background with white sans serif fonts, which is readable and easy to identify. I find it funny that some people like to advertise with their slates. Usually the only person who sees the slate is the person creating duplicates of it at the dub house. Everyone else tends to fast-forward through the slate to view the program.

Rendering Effects

After you complete bars, tone, and slate, you need to render all the effects in your sequence. Mark an in point at the beginning of your sequence and an out point at the end. Select all your tracks. Click the Digital Video toggle above the Timeline so that it is blue. From there, select Clip > Render In to Out. This will render all your effects.

One of the keys to shortening your render times is to render the top track only. If any effects exist underneath the top track of effects, they will be rendered, too.

If the client is in the room when you have to render, this is a good time to catch up on the latest office gossip. The best editors keep track of what interests their clients. If your sequence is long and effects-laden, you're going to have to do some serious talking.

While rendering, you might notice that the system updates you on the percentage of effects rendered. Press T on your keyboard, and the information will shift to show you the estimated time left before the render is complete. This number can change drastically, especially if you are rendering a really big sequence of effects with multiple tracks.

Convert Audio Sample Rates

The fourth and final step in digital cut preparation is to convert audio sample rates to the project sample rate that are established in your audio settings.

Normally with a DV project, the sampling rate is set to 48 kHz, but if you added any CD audio (44.1 kHz) or audio from other sources, you have to convert the sample rate.

To do this, select Bin > Change Sample rate. A menu will appear with a pull-down button that allows you to choose the sample rate, the quality of audio, and the target drive in which the media is to be stored.

Three Methods of Digital Cut

Now that we've covered how to set up for a digital cut, let's go through the procedure. First, you need to determine which kind of digital cut to do. There are three different ways to perform a digital cut:

- Insert edit
- Assemble edit
- Crash record

Let's take a look at each one and determine how and why they are used.

Look Busy!

If the sequence is really long and it takes more time than you anticipated, here are some additional stratagems for keeping the client distracted:

- Ask the client about the next project.
- Go over the editing timesheet and verify the times logged.
- Make more coffee.
- Run to the restroom.
- Tell a joke or perform a magic trick.
- Ask the client to show you a picture of their kids or grandkids.
- Query the client on their favorite hobby or subject.
- Dust the monitors.

I'm sure that some of these things may sound ridiculous (especially if you've never edited with the client present), but they work. In one instance, I was editing with a client who had tried another editor at the same facility. I tend to rake my fingers across the keyboard from time to time. This makes a busy little clacking noise. The client told my supervisor that I was really much faster than the other editor. Yet, on the timesheet, I took just as much time to do the same things.

My point here is that looking busy can make the client more comfortable. If you just sit at the machine and watch the render, the client perceives you as being slow and unproductive. Above all, when rendering, at least *look* busy.

Insert Edit

To do an insert edit digital cut, you need a tape that is timecoded and blacked. This method is dependent on the deck that you use. Most decks cannot perform insert edits. So if you're dumping your sequence back to a deck, you cannot use insert mode. Almost every FireWire-controlled deck cannot do an insert edit. Keep this in mind.

There are some hitches when performing an insert digital cut. The most important is that the tape that you record to must have a continuous stream of black and timecode. The timecode does not have to match the timecode of your sequence, but it is a pretty good idea to do this, anyway.

Note: So how do you record a continuous stream of black video and timecode? The easiest way is to purchase a black burst generator. These can cost anywhere from $100 to $300 (USD). Connect the output of the black-burst generator to the video input of your machine and record. Some people think that recording black from your Avid is just as good as getting a BBGen. Not true! The highest-quality pictures are made from a source with real black, as opposed to a black still frame from your system.

For example, if you start bars at 00:58:30:00, you could start the timecode on your tape to 00:58:20:00 to allow the tape to preroll before the edit point. That way, you could find elements more easily if there are any changes to be made to the show. This brings me to another advantage of the insert method. If you decide to change a single shot after recording your digital cut, you can do another insert digital cut of the changed shot in the sequence. This method avoids having to perform a digital cut of the entire piece all over again.

Assemble Edit

In an assemble edit, the deck goes into a recording mode and adds new signal and time-code as it goes. The assemble edit is "invisible," just like it is in insert edit mode, but the deck again has to be able to do an assemble edit. The difference between assemble and insert edit is that with assemble editing, the tape needs to be blacked and coded only up to the starting timecode. From the point of the digital cut, assemble editing creates new timecode, video, and control track. In the case of assemble editing, the control track continues recording where it left off previously. As a result, an assemble edit looks smooth, but actually contains a new sync recording.

To determine whether your deck supports this mode, go to the deck configuration settings and look at the description of your deck. In the deck settings window, there is a space for notes. Usually, Avid will describe compatibility with assemble editing, time-code accuracy, and other issues that affect both input and output from your deck.

To use assemble editing, it must be enabled in your deck preferences first. When you open your deck preferences (from the settings tab in your Project window), select Allow Assemble Edit for Digital Cut.

So, which decks and cameras support these two modes? The best way to find out is to look at the Avid website, www.avid.com. There are so many decks and cameras out on the market that it would be impossible to list all of the supported decks in this book. Some decks are partially supported—that is, they may be able to do insert edits but not assemble edits—and others are fully supported.

FireWire (IEEE 1394) protocol is not always frame-accurate. There is a lot of dependency on the deck, the transcoder (if necessary), the FireWire card, and the software. As a result, if you are controlling your deck by FireWire, assemble and (sometimes) insert digital cuts are not supported, because to make frame-accurate edits, Free DV/Xpress Pro needs a recorder that can make frame-accurate edits! If you use RS-422 control of your deck, you may have frame-accurate remote control of your deck, but again, the deck must be able to make insert or assemble edits.

Crash Recording

Many decks are configured only for hard or "crash" recording, which is the third method of making a digital cut. Crash recording is simple: Hit the record button on your deck and play back the digital cut. In almost every case when you are using a camera as your record deck, you use this method of recording. If you choose this method—by far the easiest of the three—you will want plenty of black at the head and tail of your sequence. Otherwise, the untidy crash record will be seen, which is never good at presentations. In the case of crash recording, you can set your deck to Local control on the Digital Cut tool and start recording as you press the Play button for the digital cut.

Crash recording is a way to do a digital cut to a deck that is not controlled by Xpress Pro. There can be many reasons for doing a digital cut with this method. The most common is that not all decks are controllable by Xpress Pro. For example, VHS decks normally have neither FireWire nor RS-422 serial controls.

Configure the Record Deck

Before performing a digital cut, make sure that your deck is connected and properly configured.

There are two different control interfaces that can be used in deck configurations which were discussed earlier, RS-422 (also referred to as Direct) and OHCI (IEEE 1394, or FireWire) With either of these protocols (see Figure 6.23), the communication is two-way, and your Xpress Pro can poll the deck or camera to determine its model and make.

Figure 6.23 Selecting the proper channel for communication with your deck

After you add a channel, you can select a deck. When adding a channel, the system asks if you want to autoconfigure the deck (see Figure 6.24), which allows the system to determine which type of deck (name and model) that you are using. The deck templates for an Avid system are numerous. When it finds the deck (by polling it and determining the make and model), it loads the correct template. There are times, however, when Xpress Pro does not properly identify the deck or camera, particularly when using OHCI. Keep in mind that there are now many decks and cameras on the market, and although the protocols are common, the methods of implementation are not. So the best thing to do is to go to your deck configuration settings and do it yourself.

Figure 6.24 Autoconfiguring your deck—it doesn't always work with FireWire configurations.

First, go to the Project window and click the Settings tab. Locate the Deck Configuration settings and double-click.

It may take a moment or two for the deck templates to load. The deck templates contain information about how to control the most commonly used decks. If your deck is not among the templates, you can still use a generic template and configure it for your deck.

If this is your first time using Deck Configuration, you need to click the Add Channel button. The Channel Options appear. You can choose between Direct (RS-422) and OHCI (IEEE 1394, or FireWire).

On Windows machines, usually an RS-422 to RS-232C adapter, such as Addenda's Rosetta Stone, is used for controlling the deck. The deck is therefore connected to one of the two RS-232C serial ports built into your system. On Windows systems, you must choose between the Com 1 and Com 2 RS-232C ports.

On Mac Systems, RS-422 control can also be established. It requires either a serial-to-USB adapter such those made by Keyspan or a third-party card, such as Gee Three's Stealth card. The Keyspan adapter and the Stealth card (and many others like them) allow direct connection between the RS-422 connector on the deck and the card on your Mac. In Deck Configuration, this is shown as the Direct choice.

If you are using a hardware codec or a Mojo and want RS-422 control, you should choose either the Com 1/Com 2 selection (Windows) or the Direct selection (Mac).

After you add your channel, it's time to add a deck. Click the Add Deck button, and the Deck Selection window appears. In order to properly select a deck, you must choose the manufacturer first. For example, if your deck is a Sony DSR-11 (see Figure 6.25), choose Sony. The list of Sony configured decks appear. Scroll down the list and select DSR-11.

Figure 6.25 Selecting a deck

If your deck is not listed under the manufacturer's name, you might be able to find the template on Avid's website. Avid frequently adds or creates new templates because new decks and cameras come out frequently.

Another option is to select a Generic deck, which follows standard protocols for controls of OHCI and RS-422 controllers. It is not particularly sensitive to the full capabilities of a specific deck, but it can fulfill the needs of just about any deck.

If your deck has neither RS-422 nor OHCI capability, you need to control the deck manually. In cases such as these, there is no need to configure a deck because the deck cannot be controlled by Xpress Pro. When you access the Digital Cut tool, select Local for deck control. In the Deck Control section, you'll notice that No Deck appears where timecode would normally be.

Deleting Deck Configurations

If you need to delete a previous deck configuration, do the following:

1. Go to the Project window and click the Settings tab.
2. Select Deck Configurations.
3. Click the deck and Shift-click the channel. Or you can lasso them both in the Deck Configuration tool.
4. Press Delete. The deck configuration disappears.

Okay, so we have finally gone over the options and are ready to actually take a look at the Digital Cut tool.

Digital Cut Tool

The Digital Cut tool will look different, depending on whether you have a software-only system or a system with the optional Mojo. To open it, choose Clip > Digital Cut (see Figure 6.26).

Figure 6.26 Selecting Digital Cut

Software Only (without the Optional Mojo Interface)

Let's take a quick tour of the Digital Cut tool (see Figure 6.27) and spend some time on the key elements.

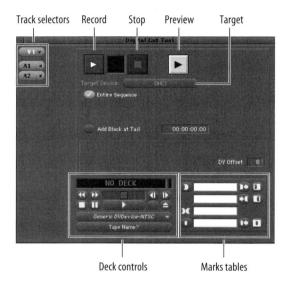

Figure 6.27 The Digital Cut tool

Notice a track selector at the top left that is much like the one on your Timeline (see Figure 6.28). If your deck is configured to a FireWire device, there is a single column, representing the enabled tracks in your sequence. You'll also see a single column if you are using a locally controlled deck. If your deck is a non-FireWire device with RS-422 control, there is a second column of tracks in which you can select the channels that will be recorded on the deck.

Figure 6.28 Selecting tracks for digital cut

The big buttons to the right of the track panels control the digital cut (see Figure 6.29) When you click the red button, the digital cut will begin. Much like the Capture tool, you'll get a blinking light (to the right of this button) when the digital cut is in progress.

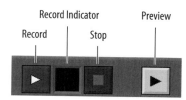

Record Indicator Preview

Record Stop

Figure 6.29 Digital Cut control buttons

To the right of the blinking light is a blue Stop button. When recording or previewing a digital cut, you can click this button to stop the process (you can also press the Escape key on your keyboard).

The yellow button is used to preview your digital cut. If you are inserting the sequence onto a tape that already has materials on it, it is highly recommended that you preview the digital cut. It is better, in fact, if you try the digital cut on a blank tape first. There is nothing like that all-is-lost post-apocalyptic feeling that you get when you've ruined a master tape. If it has never happened to you before, trust us, it's not pretty. When you do this preview, you want to monitor the output of the deck, not the output of the Avid. Monitoring the deck will show you what the preroll and postroll will look like. And take one more moment to make sure you are not assemble editing.

Below the buttons is a Target Device pull-down menu. If you are using a remote-controlled deck with FireWire, this would normally be OHCI. This menu lists all the target device types that are currently connected. If it is grayed-out, Xpress Pro doesn't see your deck. If you're doing a crash edit in Local mode, it normally would be grayed-out.

Below that are two check boxes. Select the top one if you are indeed outputting your entire sequence. If not, leave it deselected and be sure to mark your in and out marks on the sequence. The second check box is for adding black at the tail of your digital cut. If you're doing an assemble edit or controlling the deck locally, this is especially important. An assemble edit ends by stopping the deck in a crash record mode, so you'll want to add plenty of black at the tail to keep the sequence looking smooth for a while after the sequence has played. Usually 30 seconds is good. Some tape duplication facilities require two minutes of black after program end. Look at it this way: If your sequence will be played back in a conference room, and some manager type is doing a presentation around it, there very well could be a minute or more before the manager stops the tape.

You might also consider adding some black at the tail if you are doing an insert edit. Even if the tape already has black on it, often the level of black doesn't match the output of your Xpress Pro. As a result, the end of the sequence, which normally fades to black, could look like a glitch where Xpress Pro stops recording and the black from the tape continues playing. Mismatched levels are common in broadcasting, and they don't look particularly good. However, if you are inserting footage into the *middle* of a sequence, make sure you do *not* have Add Black at Tail selected.

If you chose an insert or assemble edit, Xpress Pro has a pull-down menu that determines where the digital cut will take place. The menu gives you three options: Sequence Time, where the tape timecode matches the sequence timecode exactly; Record Deck time, where the digital cut will begin at the exact timecode where the deck is parked before you begin the digital cut; and Mark In time, which can be determined by marking an in point using the timecode registers near the bottom of the Digital Cut tool.

 Note: If you are doing NTSC video, be sure that the tape timecode and your sequence timecode use the same frame code mode—that is, they both need to be either drop frame or non–drop frame timecode.

Again, if you are remotely controlling the deck, there should be a menu next to the right of the previous menu, which selects whether you are insert or assemble editing. If there is no menu here, you have selected Local mode. If the menu does not have the Assemble option in it, you need to adjust your deck preferences accordingly to enable it.

Below the pull-down menu is the custom preroll time (see Figure 6.30), which might need to be adjusted to properly make an edit on your deck (again, only if remote-controlled) and a DV Offset. The DV Offset is used when doing a digital cut using FireWire. Sometimes, when doing a digital cut to DV-25, the audio and video do not arrive at the same time. Adjusting the DV Offset will fix this problem. For your deck, there is a predetermined offset built into the template. If you use a transcoder, the chances of a delay are even greater. Many of the more common transcoder templates are listed in the deck configuration menus. When one is chosen, the default offset is automatically selected.

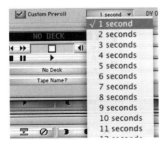

Figure 6.30 Selecting a custom preroll time

Although it looks like a direct entry box, the DV Offset is controlled through your deck preference settings. If you do a digital cut, but the audio and video don't seem to be in sync, you'll need to open your deck preferences and override the recommended DV offset with a number of your choosing. The bad news about overriding the recommended offset is that you have to determine the correct number of frames through trial-and-error. The good news is that it should remain consistent, as long as you use the exact same equipment. So after the settings are made, save them. An easy way to determine the offset is to lay a sequence off to tape that consists of a few seconds of filler, followed by a beep synchronized to a single frame of white or bars or video, followed by more filler.

Note: If you receive the error "No coincidence point found" it probably means that your deck, your tape, or both are "write protected" or "record inhibited." Pop or slide the record inhibit button on the tape or flip the record inhibit switch on the deck and try again.

The rest of the Digital Cut tool should be familiar to you (we covered it in Chapter 2). Be sure that the right deck and tape name are selected. If you are controlling the digital cut locally and doing a crash record, none of this is necessary. No marks need to be in the marks register unless you are recording your digital cut at a specific Mark In timecode. One slight difference is that there is no Mark Out button, because the length of your sequence or marks on the sequence determines the outpoint, plus any black filler you've added.

Digital Cut with Mojo

The Mojo accelerator allows a few more options when you create a digital cut. It can work as a transcoder to Composite, Component, or S-Video analog decks. It can output real-time effects. It can output uncompressed video.

The greatest advantage of a Mojo is the lack of rendering required when completing a digital cut. Although all the preparations should be completed as with a digital cut without a Mojo, you do have the capability of playing back uncompressed video and some real-time effects.

Once connected to your deck via FireWire from the Mojo, Xpress Pro can control the deck. The only significant difference that you will see on the Digital Cut tool when used with Mojo is that you can enable Effects Safe mode. Effects Safe mode will determine which effects need to be rendered before performing a digital cut. Enabling Effects Safe mode will prevent video underruns or other playback issues. With Effects Safe mode selected, click the Record button for the digital cut to begin. After rendering, the system will perform the digital cut.

Tutorial: Import and Export

There are several graphic files and QuickTime movies on the accompanying DVD. Try to import each one of them and then export them using the options described in this chapter. After you finish, we'll move on to digital cut and video output.

Still Graphics

There are several still graphics in the Import folder of your DVD. Take a look at each one and determine which of the import options will be needed when you import into Free DV/Xpress Pro.

As you import, you can see how the Avid handles material. Be sure to watch out for stretched graphics. In some cases, the file is oriented horizontally and vertically out of the pixel aspect ratio. You will have to determine which option to choose.

Note that one set of graphics is sequential. How do we import a sequential set of graphics? If you forgot, go back to the Import menu and take a look in the bottom left.

If you can't successfully import these graphics, try reading the Import section over again, particularly the Options section.

QuickTime Movies

Try importing and exporting the QuickTime movies in the Import menu. After you finish, try exporting a QuickTime reference movie. Take the exported reference file and using Get Info (Mac) or Properties (Windows), note the small file size. The original is much larger, isn't it?

Adding Tone

To add tone:

1. Select your audio tool (Ctrl+1/⌘+1).

2. Click the Peak Hold (PH) button.

3. Select Create Tone Media.

   The Tone Media menu appears (see Figure 6.31).

Tone Media Level in dB The tone media levels are preset at -14dB (see Figure 6.32). This is an incorrect rate for digital audio standard levels. Some digital systems are set for -20dB. On most systems, -20dB digital equals 0 VU analog.

Figure 6.31 Tone Media information menu

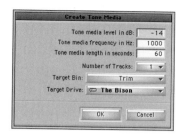

Figure 6.32 The Default tone level is −14. (Change it to −20.)

Tone Media Frequency The tone media frequency is preset at 1000 Hz, which is the standard for most recorded video media. However, some audio post houses prefer using a variety of tones at different frequencies. If your digital cut is going to an audio house for sweetening or for mixing, it's a good idea to check with them first before adding tone to your digital cut. You can also add a series of tones to properly identify individual audio tracks.

Tone Media Length in Seconds This setting controls the amount of tone media created. Sixty seconds is the default and the standard.

Number of Tracks The number of tone tracks to create should be determined. If the output uses discrete tracks going to separate channels, tone media should be created for each track, including stereo pairs.

If the output uses a mono output, tone should be put on only one channel. This is done to avoid adding volume to the tone. Two tone tracks mixed together would be additive, creating a louder tone signal than desired. If the tone is placed on a single channel only, it will be mixed into a mono signal that registers correctly on the audio input of the record machine.

After these items are selected in the Create Tone Media menu, you will need to select a bin for the tone clip and a drive where the tone will be rendered.

Adding Bars

SMPTE bars, the most commonly used test pattern, is imported to Xpress Pro as a PICT file. You can find the SMPTE bars in the Avid\Avid Xpress Pro\Supporting Files\Test Patterns folder. There are several other test patterns available in this folder.

Before importing the bars, you should change your import settings so that the right amount of media will be imported. To do this, follow these steps:

1. Go to the Project window and select the Settings tab.

2. Select Import Settings.

3. Under the Single Frame Import heading, change the number of seconds to 60. This will add 60 seconds of bars media when the SMPTE bars are imported.

   To import SMPTE bars, do the following:

1. Select a target bin for your bars clip.

2. Go to the File menu and choose Import.

3. Make sure the options are set as follows:

Option	Value
File Type	Graphic
Aspect Ratio	601 non square
Color Levels	601
Field Order	Non-interlaced
Alpha	ignore

4. Navigate to the Test Patterns folder and select SMPTE Bars.

5. Import this file. The new bars clip is added to the bin.

Now you can edit your bars and tone into your sequence. Be sure to select All Tracks and Splice.

Adding a Slate

Adding a slate will help you identify the sequence, creation date, total running time, and other information. The slate (see Figure 6.33), which can be created in the Title tool, doesn't have to be too fancy. In fact, some of the most incredible commercials and video trailers for motion pictures use plain old black background slates with white Helvetica type. But you can decide for yourself. Be sure to allow 10 seconds of black after the slate.

Figure 6.33 A typical slate

In some cases, you might want to add a countdown from 10 seconds to 2 seconds before the program begins. This is usually done for broadcast only. Again, you or your producer can decide what is adequate. A countdown can be generated using the Title tool. Some effects footage libraries have fancy countdowns. Of course, no one will see this except the client, yourself, and whoever uses the tape.

Render Effects

Xpress Pro's Expert Render can determine exactly how many of your effects need to be rendered in your sequence before you do your digital cut. Expert Render tends to work on the safe side, so your sequence should play back without failure. If you really want to play it safe, and you have the time, you can render everything.

Rendering with Software Only (Xpress Pro)

If you're using the software only, choose Special > Enable Digital Video Out (see Figure 6.34).

Figure 6.34 Enabling
Digital Video Out

You'll notice that your Digital Video Toggle may have switched colors. The reason is that for output, you have to turn off real-time effects. What does this mean? Well, you're going to be rendering all the effects in your Timeline. This might take a while. We highly recommend a thorough study of the Appendix and Glossary of this book while rendering. Who knows? You might learn something new.

Before you go any further with your digital cut procedure, let's talk about offline resolution. If you used 15:1s, you will not easily be able to get a digital cut out of Xpress Pro. When you select Special > Enable Digital Video Out, Xpress Pro beeps at you and informs you that only DV-25 sequences can be used when non-real-time mode is selected. What does this mean? Basically, Xpress Pro does not want to output single-field, poor-resolution video.

There's a workaround for this, but it will take a little time. And keep in mind that your sequence will still look like 15:1s video. It's the same thing you heard about any computer process: garbage in, garbage out.

You can transcode your sequence from low resolution to DV-25. To do this, you could select the 15:1s sequence in your bin and then select Bin > Consolidate/Transcode (see Figure 6.35). When the Consolidate/Transcode menu appears, select Transcode and make sure that DV-25 is selected (see Figure 6.36). You'll also need to select a target drive. In this case, you'll be creating a new sequence. Transcode the sequence. A new sequence with the suffix ".transcode" will appear in your bin, along with all of the clips.

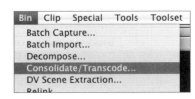

Figure 6.35 Selecting the
Consolidate Transcode window

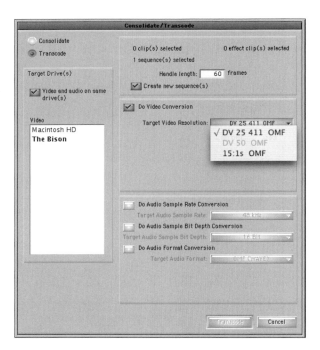

Figure 6.36 The Consolidate/Transcode window with DV-25 selected

After the transcoded sequence is made, load it into the Source monitor and again select Special > Enable Digital Video Out. This time, the toggle button should turn blue without any errors.

Mark an in point at the beginning and an out point at the end of your sequence. Select Clip > Render In/Out. You could also select Clip > Expert Render In/Out, but let's face it, you'll render all the effects with software only. Fortunately, you're using a very fast computer so this won't take much time at all … ight?

Please note: You can also use this procedure with 28:1 if you are working with 24p or 25p projects.

Rendering with Mojo

If you're using the optional Mojo, you can rely on Expert Render to let the system determine which effects need to be rendered in order to play back your sequence. Here's how to set it up: Mark an in point at the beginning of the sequence and an out point at the end; then highlight all your tracks, both video and audio. Select Clip > Expert Render. The Expert Render menu appears. Select the Prepare Effects For Digital Cut option at the bottom of the menu and click OK. The system will render the necessary effects, and you're ready to proceed.

Caution! When working with 1:1 media, the Mojo will play only a single stream of video in real time instead of multiple streams as is available with DV-25 media. Transitions such as a dissolve require two streams of video. The Expert Render setting Prepare For Digital Cut incorrectly misses the rendering of transitions. You must either render all or render the transitions manually. Effects Safe Mode in the Digital Cut tool will also not detect transitions that must be rendered for a 1:1 sequence to play back correctly to tape.

Converting Audio Sample Rates

Before performing a digital cut, you have to convert all audio sample rates to the same spec. To do this, follow these steps:

1. Select your sequence in its bin.

2. Select Bin > Change Sample Rate (see Figure 6.37). You could optionally right-click/Ctrl-click the sequence and choose Change Sample Rate.

Figure 6.37 Changing the sample rate

3. Choose the correct sample rate and the quality of audio that you want to create. (For a final layoff, this should always be High.)

   You can also choose to delete the original audio. If you do not choose this, duplicate clips will be generated with the new sample rate.

   Xpress Pro creates new media for clips in the sequence that do not have the correct sample rate. Your conversion is complete.

Calibrating for Output

Before outputting, you'll want to measure the output of the audio tone using the Audio tool against input meters on your record deck. If the deck has adjustable levels for record input, optimize your levels appropriately. Usually this means simply zeroing the level of tone, but you should also test the levels going to the deck using the loudest portion of your sequence to make sure no clipping occurs and to ensure that the tone is truly representative of your program levels.

Effects and Transitions

You might think it pointless for me to write a whole chapter about effects. When I taught classes for Avid, I found that many editors bypassed the Effect classes, assuming that they were simple instructional procedures on how to drag and drop. And yet when my phone rings, it is common for an editor to be whining about a special effect that he or she thinks goes beyond the Avid array. The answer is always the same: The effects palette is a lot more powerful than originally perceived.

Chapter Contents

Motion Effects
Titles
Palette Effects
Effect Editor
Editing with Keyframes
Building Vertical Effects
Real-Time Playback
Nested Effects and Collapsing (Xpress Pro)
3D Warp (Xpress Pro)

Motion Effects

A motion effect is an effect that changes the speed at which a clip would normally play. Xpress Pro can create three distinct flavors of motion effects, described in the following sections.

Timewarp Effects (Xpress Pro) Timewarp effects are applied to segments in the Timeline directly from the Effect palette (see Figure 7.1). The rate of motion is determined by the effect. In other words, a timewarp effect is an effect that has specific motion speed in specific parts of a chosen clip. It's an effect with variable motion, but the determination of when the motion changes pace is dictated by the effect itself.

Figure 7.1 Timewarp effects in the Effect palette

Freeze Frames Freeze frames are applied to clips in the Source monitor and create a new clip that must then be edited into the sequence.

Standard Motion Effects Motion effects are applied to clips in the Source monitor. Each motion effect plays at a consistent speed that is determined by the user or is fitted to fill a required space. Like freeze frames, after the motion effect has been applied to the source clip, a new clip is generated and must then be edited into the sequence.

Note: If you're using Free DV, there aren't a lot of effects available; then again, the software is free. On the other hand, Xpress Pro has an awesome 100+ in its palette. There is also a whole separate category of very powerful effects created by third-party companies called AVX effects. These effects can almost bring your humble Xpress Pro up to the power of a Symphony. Sadly, AVX effects are not available on Free DV, so you'll have to upgrade to gain that capability.

Motion Effects Interpolation

Each motion effect can be interpolated in different ways. Interpolation determines how frames and fields will be blended, combined, or displayed in the motion effect. Interpolation can determine how good a motion effect will look when played back. In the past, you might have noticed slow motion replays on television that look poorly constructed. In the old days, we used fields when playing back slow motion. As a result, single fields looked pretty awful when played back slowly. Currently, the entire frame is used if modern equipment is utilized. For example, most major league sports use slow-motion relays in full-field mode.

There are four different modes of interpolating motion effects (see Figure 7.2). Some, as indicated, are not available for every type of effect. They are:

Figure 7.2 Selecting an interpolation mode

Duplicated Field A Duplicated Field interpolation method consists of taking one field of a frame and duplicating it, which halves the resolution of the image. This method is not recommended for broadcast, but works fine for single-field projects that are intended for the Web, or in some cases, CD-ROMs.

Both Fields Selecting Both Fields uses both fields of the video frame. In some cases, this method will work fine, but not for fast-moving action. Often there are artifacts that develop from interfield motion. As a result, this type of interpolation could appear jittery.

Interpolated Field Interpolated Field uses both fields and blends them. To be more precise, it uses field one for the first field of video and then blends field one with field two for the second field of video. Rendering an Interpolated Field motion effect is more time-consuming, but it works better for shots with interfield motion. However, when used with freeze frames, Interpolated Field might result in a softer image.

VTR-Style VTR-Style interpolation is used only on timewarp and motion effects and is not available on freeze frames for reasons that will be obvious. A VTR-Style method of interpolation emulates slow-motion playback on VTRs by shifting field information by a scan line so that the fields are aligned. This results in a smoother motion without detail reduction, which would be noticeable in a Duplicated Field mode. VTR-Style interpolation renders slightly faster than Interpolated Field interpolation, but in some cases can create some noticeable jitter at slower speeds because of the line shifting.

Freeze Frames

Freeze frames in Free DV/Xpress Pro are clips that contain a single frame of video that can be displayed for a set duration that you choose.

To create a freeze frame:

1. Load the master clip or subclip containing the image that you want to freeze into the Source monitor.

2. Find the frame that is to be frozen in the Source monitor.

3. Choose Clip > Freeze Frame (see Figure 7.3). A menu of preset durations will appear. Choose a duration or select Other to set a customized time for the freeze frame.

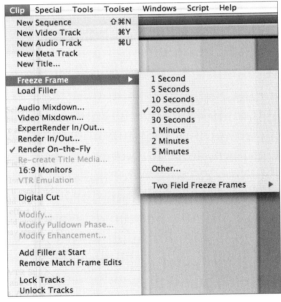

Figure 7.3 Creating a freeze frame

4. Choose a method of interpolating the freeze frame from the drop-down menu that appears

After making your selections, the system will ask where you want to store the media for the new clip. Select a volume (a drive) and click OK. Next, the system will ask which bin the freeze frame clip is to be stored in. Choose the bin or create a new bin, then select OK. The freeze frame appears in the bin and is also automatically loaded into the Source monitor for editing into your sequence.

Standard Motion Effects

Motion effects play back clips at a nonstandard, nonvariable rate. They can also utilize a strobing effect, in which a frame is frozen and held for a predetermined amount of time.

To create a motion effect:

1. Load the master clip or subclip with the media you want to manipulate into the Source monitor.

2. Mark an in and out point for the media that will be used to create the motion effect.

3. Choose the Motion Effect button under the Source monitor or, if you're using Xpress Pro, from your Command palette (Ctrl+3/⌘+3). Or map it to your keyboard or the user interface. The Motion Effect dialog box appears (see Figure 7.4).

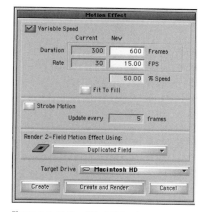

Figure 7.4 Motion Effect dialog box

4. Under the Variable Speed heading, select the duration or the speed (rate) of the motion effect.

5. If you want to strobe the motion, select the Strobe Motion option and select the number of frames between strobes.

6. Select an interpolation method for the effect.

7. Choose Create. The Bin Selection dialog box appears. Select a bin and click OK. The motion effect is created and stored in the bin.

Titles

Avid's Title tool is the same in both Free DV and Xpress Pro. If you've worked with any kind of text editing or desktop publishing applications, you'll find the Title tool to be a very simple but handy tool.

To access the Title tool, choose Clip > New Title (see Figure 7.5). Xpress Pro users can map the Title tool to their keyboard, but unless you create lots of titles, this might not be useful.

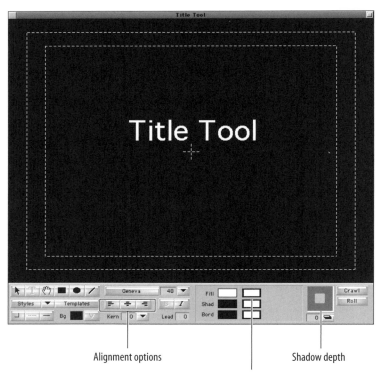

Alignment options

Shadow depth

Fill, shadow, and border transparency

Figure 7.5 Title tool

Object and Alignment Menus

When the Title tool appears on your desktop, note that two additional menus appear above. These two menus, Object and Alignment, allow you to manipulate objects in the tool and align them. They might be familiar to you from other applications that you use.

The Object menu allows you to take individual objects that you create in the tool and prioritize them so that one object is on top of another. The Object Menu also allows you to group together and ungroup individual objects (or, if you prefer, elements) that you create in the tool.

The Alignment menu allows you to align objects relative to the Title tool space as well as within the object's given space.

Title Tool GUI

When teaching the Title tool to others, I usually start on the first button and pretty much describe them all. So let's get started.

- The arrow tool ▚ is pretty self-explanatory. It allows you to grab and move objects in your title.

- The T button 𝐓 is your text tool. When selected, you can enter text right onto the interface.

> **Note:** When creating text, it's a pain to move the mouse to the bottom of the title interface and switch from the text button to the arrow button. A faster way to do this is to press the Alt or Option key on the keyboard and click. The text cursor turns to an arrow cursor so that you can instantly move the text rather than mousing around the Title tool interface.

- The hand tool 🖐 is a holdover from the days when you could not place the entire video screen in the interface. It's not really useful today, unless you have to make your Title tool smaller to fit it on your screen. It was created in the days when monitors were of extremely low resolution. If you have one of those monitors, do yourself a favor and donate it to a school or a museum.

- The three geometric buttons ▫ ● ╱ allow you to place squares, circles (as well as ovals), lines, and arrows on your title. They don't look like much, but you can come up with some fairly creative titles using them. These objects can be drawn on-screen and saved as templates, which we'll discuss later. To create a perfect square or circle, hold down the Shift key before drawing. If you've already drawn a square or circle, you can click it with the arrow key and, while holding the Shift key, maintain its aspect ratio while making the circle or square larger or smaller.

- The styles button ▭Styles ▼ allows you to save and store fonts, shadows, fill colors, and borders. You save styles by clicking the down arrow button. You can also click the styles button and tear off the menu (Figure 7.6), expanding it to reveal each saved style. When you click the downward pointing arrow, a menu appears asking which aspects of the style that you wish to save. You can select one or all of these options.

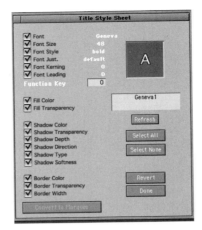

Figure 7.6 Title styles tear-off menu and style sheet

The idea of the style menu is that you can create a look (or style) for your titles and store it. But if you want to save all objects (including the aforementioned geometrics) and placements of objects, you should use the Templates button.

- The Templates button Templates allows you to save, edit, or include templates that you produced previously. The template is saved as a .pct file and can be recalled or included for use on another system. Essentially, the system is using these files as a base plate for your work. Any time you need a particular template that has been saved, you can edit it, reuse it, and save it again.

- The three bottom row keys assign attributes to boxes and lines. When you click the corner tool ⌐ , you can select a corner radius or customize one yourself (see Figure 7.7). If you select the dotted line at the bottom, it allows you to enter a custom number of lines in the radius.

Figure 7.7 Customizing a box corner

- The same can be said for the middle button, which is the line size tool ⋯ . Select a preset line size or customize the thickness of lines using this tool.

- The arrowhead tool ▬ is like the two others, with custom size at the bottom and preset sizes for arrowheads. If you want a line to include arrowheads, you can use this tool.

- Next to the arrowhead tool is the background swatch Bg ▪ . You can click this to determine a color for the background, assuming that you do not want to put video underneath your title. It uses a fairly common method of color picking, but if you like the more traditional circular color wheel, you can select it by clicking the circle button in the tool. You can also tear off this color palette (see Figure 7.8) and use it while you work.

Figure 7.8 Color picker tear-off menu

- There is also an eyedropper tool. If you want your background to match an object on the screen, click the eyedropper and click it again when you move it over the desired color.
- The last button in this group is the V button , which determines whether you want the Title tool background or a video background underneath your title. When you want video, the V on this button should light up with green. When deselected, the V is white.

Now we'll move on to another group of objects that define fonts, alignment, kerning, and leading.

When clicked, the font key will show you all the available fonts for your tool. Before we continue, let's talk about fonts a little. Fonts come in two varieties: screen fonts and printer fonts. Printer fonts are used for printing; screen fonts for displaying. Simple, right? So, for example, if your client brings you a font to produce titles, he or she must give you the screen font (and the printer font, if you're going to do some desktop publishing or anything like that). So if a font looks jaggy to you with ragged edges that were not intended (see Figure 7.9), it's probably because your system couldn't find a screen font.

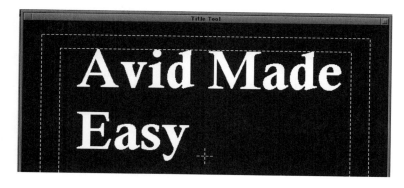

Figure 7.9 Jaggy fonts on-screen indicate that a printer font was used.

Next to the font key is a size register ![48]. You can enter a custom size or click the arrow to use a preset size for your font.

The alignment keys (![alignment keys]: left alignment, center alignment, and right alignment) are object-oriented keys that align your text relative to the object that you created. In other words, these keys do not align your text relative to the screen (see Figure 7.10) but instead to the text object that you created when typing them.

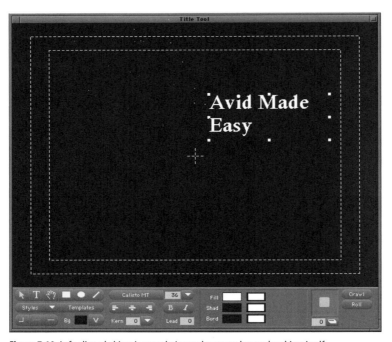

Figure 7.10 Left-aligned object is not relative to the screen but to the object itself.

The next key is the kerning key ![Kern 0]. Kerning is the adjustment of horizontal space between letters. When using the Text cursor and selecting letters, you can move them closer or farther apart. Some fonts have situations in which kerning is needed between certain characters. You can also use kerning to achieve a look or style with the font by expanding it or contracting it. You can either use the kerning presets (normal, loose, or tight) or type a number in the register. Negative numbers produce tight kerning (see Figure 7.11), positive numbers create loose kerning, and 0 denotes no kerning.

To the right of the kerning register is the leading key ![Lead 0]. Leading (pronounced as led-ding, or if you're an old hippie like me, Led as in Led Zeppelin) is the space between lines of text. You can create each line of text and move it closer or farther away from the others (see Figure 7.12) or you can use this key.

Just like kerning, negative leading numbers create tight spaces and positive leading numbers loosen the space between lines.

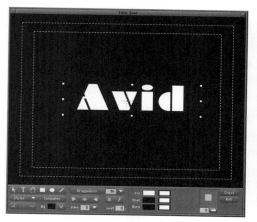 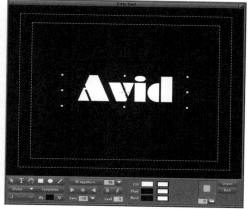

Figure 7.11 (left) Font with normal kerning; (right) font with tight kerning

Figure 7.12 (left) Font with normal leading; (right) font with tight leading

The next two columns determine the fill color and opacity, shadow color and opacity, and border color and opacity of a selected object. This object can be text or any of the geometrics mentioned previously (boxes, circles, and lines).

The color swatches are to the left, and the opacity swatches are in the right column. If you click the color swatch, a color picker will appear, just as it was when we looked at the background color. When you click the right column, the opacity of an object's fill, shadow, or border can be adjusted. In addition to these, you can create a wash between transparencies for a more stylized approach by using the two small swatches to the right.

Palette Effects

Every effect can be placed into one of two categories: transition effects and segment effects. Transition effects are effects that are used or applied at the transition point between two separate clips. Examples of transition effects can be wipes, fades, and dissolves. Segment effects are specific effects that are applied to the segments of your sequence. Examples of segment effects are masks, pictures in pictures, and resizes. Some effects can be in both categories. For example, you can use a circle wipe as a tool to vignette, but it can also be a transition.

Using the Effect Palette

All the effects available in Free DV and Xpress Pro can be accessed through the Effect palette (see Figure 7.13), which can be accessed by selecting the Project window and clicking the Effect tab, or you can choose Tools > Effect Palette (Ctrl+8/⌘+8).

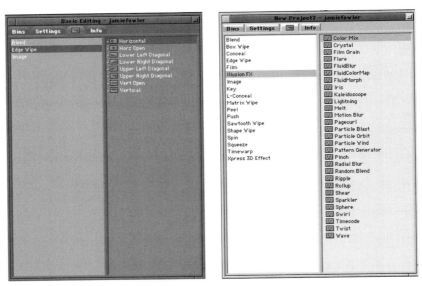

Figure 7.13 The Effect palette in (left) Free DV and (right) Xpress Pro

The Effect palette has two columns. The left column contains a list of categories. As each category is chosen, the list on the right changes. The list on the right is a list of effects within the chosen category on the left.

For example, if you were interested in looking at Blend effects, you would first click the Blend category in the left column. The right column would display the different types of blends available on your system: Dip To Color, Dissolve, Fade From Color, and so on.

Applying Effects

Applying effects to your sequence is a simple drag-and-drop operation, just as I described previously. To apply an effect:

1. Open the Effect palette and choose an effect category from the left column.

2. Choose a specific effect from your category in the right column.

3. Click the effect and drag it into the Timeline to its desired location. The effect is applied.

When an effect is applied through drag and drop, certain defaults will take place:

- If the effect is a transition effect, its duration is one second long (30 frames NTSC or 25 frames PAL).

- The effect is centered so that its midpoint occurs at the original cut point. The effect would occur 15 frames before the transition in its default state and would overlap 15 frames into the cut point.

Removing Effects

To remove an effect:

1. Place the blue position indicator on the effect in the Timeline. Make sure that the track where the effect is located is selected.

2. Click the Remove Effect button under the Record monitor. The effect disappears.

You can also remove a segment effect by using the Timeline Segment editing modes. To do this:

1. Select either Extract/Splice or Lift/Overwrite (the yellow or red buttons at the bottom of the Timeline).

2. Click the effect—or even Shift-click multiple effects—that you want to delete.

3. Click the Delete button. The effect or effects are deleted.

Real-Time Playback of Effects

Real-time playback can be achieved on some effects because of the fact that CPUs are getting faster. Almost all the Avid effects in your Free DV/Xpress Pro system can be played back in real time, right after you apply them. However, third-party AVX plug-ins (available on Xpress Pro only) must be rendered to enable playback of the effect. Both Free DV and Xpress Pro have the capability of playing back up to five real-time effects simultaneously.

Note: There are more details on real-time effect playback later in this chapter.

Your system will vary depending on its configuration. Although it might seem pointless to have the ability to enable or disable real-time effects, there are some trade-offs to be considered. When you enable real-time effects

- You cannot output an NTSC/PAL video signal
- Your external NTSC/PAL monitor (if you have one connected) will be blacked out

Real-time effects are great for editing situations in which either you or a client needs to judge the results of applied effects. After that is done, and the effects are all approved, you still eventually have to render them before outputting a digital cut to video.

To enable or disable real-time effects, click the Toggle Digital Video Out button on the Timeline. When the button is green, real-time effects are enabled. When it is blue, they are not enabled.

 Note: If you are using Xpress Pro with the optional Mojo, the Toggle Digital Video Out button is not on the interface because real-time effects are always enabled, and digital video out is also available.

Transition Effects

A transition type effect creates an effect between two clips in the Timeline. This can be one of many different effects, including dissolves, wipes, and pushes. The effects are all different, but they have many common characteristics, including the duration of the transition and the position of the transition relative to the two adjoining clips.

When referring to a transition, the outgoing clip is commonly referred to as the A side of the transition, and the incoming clip is referred to as the B side. When working with transitions, you have four choices for the positioning of the effect:

Starting At Cut When Starting At Cut is chosen, your transition effect will begin at the cut point between the A and B side. Thus, a 30-frame transition would start at the cut point and end 30 frames into the B side. If you've worked with linear video editing systems, Beginning At Transition is probably what you're used to.

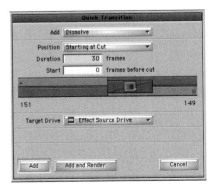

Ending At Cut Ending At Cut allows the effect to begin before the cut point. The number of frames in the transition is the determining factor as to when the effect will occur. For example, a 30-frame transition will occur 30 frames before the original cut point and end at the cut point.

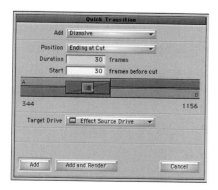

Centered On Cut When an effect is Centered On Cut, it utilizes equal sides of both A and B and is centered at the cut point. For example, a 30-frame transition effect will overlap 15 frames on the A side and 15 frames on the B side. The actual center point is located at the original cut point. Traditionally, film editors have used centered transitions.

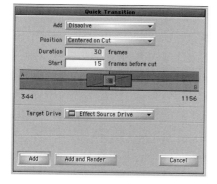

Custom A Custom transition effect is neither centered on nor begins at or ends at the cut point. Custom transitions use an unequal number of frames from A and B sides to complete the transition. There are a number of reasons for creating custom transitions:

- Insufficient source media on either the A or B side of the transition
- Undesired frames adjacent to the transition on the A or B side

Segment Effects

Segment effects are different from transition effects in that they are applied to entire clips in a sequence. Segment effects affect the picture for the entire duration in the Timeline.

To apply a Segment Effect, open the Effect palette and drag the Segment Effect to the clip in your Timeline.

Whew! That was hard. Give me a minute to catch my breath. I'm really out of shape with this effect thing.

Notice that as you drag the effect, the entire clip becomes highlighted. After the effect is added, an effect icon appears in that clip in the Timeline.

The Effect Editor

Each effect in the Effect palette has parameters—characteristics that are particular to the effect that can be adjusted and customized. Those parameters are controlled by the Effect Editor (see Figure 7.14). To open the Effect Editor, click the Effect Mode button.

Figure 7.14 Effect Editor

For ease of use, another way to do this is to change your toolset. Remember the toolsets? Changing to Effects Editing does not automatically switch to Effects mode unless your blue indicator is parked on an effect in the Timeline. But you can enter Effects mode by selecting the Effect Mode icon. To switch to the Effects Editing toolset, select Toolset > Effects Editing. Although the contents of the Effect Editor differ for each effect, the editor layout is always the same. The Avid Title tool and some third-party

AVX effects such as Boris FX and SpiceMASTER have extended editing interfaces of their own. To open this interface, click the small rectangular icon that appears with these effects in the upper-left corner of the Avid Effect Editor.

Adjusting Parameters

The Effect Editor lists different groups of adjustable effect parameters in collapsible twirl-down menus. A twirl-down menu is indicated by a triangle icon pointing at each specific parameter. When clicked, the triangle twirls down, pointing downward to reveal specific parameter sliders of each parameter group. If you click the triangle again, it twirls back to its original pointing position at the parameter group, and the individual parameters disappear.

Each adjustment of a parameter is controlled by a slider. You can control the adjustment of each parameter using three different methods:

- Click the slider and move it to the right or left.
- Click the slider, type in a numeric value for the adjustment, and press Enter.
- Click the slider and adjust it in increments by using the left and right arrow keys on your keyboard.

Note: When adjusting parameters, you can move 10 increments by holding down the Shift key when pressing the left or right arrow button. You can also move from slider to slider by using the tab key. Tab moves to the next parameter; Shift-tab moves to the previous parameter.

The result of changing a parameter is WYSIWYG (what you see is what you get). The Record monitor should update to the resulting image.

Each individual effect has adjustable parameters. The number and type of parameters will vary greatly, from the simplest wipe (which might contain only a few parameters) to the most intensive AVX plug-in effect (which can contain dozens).

Although it would be impossible to cover all of the effects that are available for Free DV and Xpress Pro, many of the parameters work and operate the same way. What follows is a review of some of those parameters.

Border

Many effects—such as wipe, conceal, squeeze, shape and 3D effects—contain a border parameter. The Border parameter allows you to adjust the color, blend color, softness, and width of the border of an effect.

BORDER COLOR

The Border Color and Blend Color parameters let you set the color for the border. Adding a blended color allows you to create a gradient border. There are three values that create the border colors: They are:

Value	Explanation
Hue	The shade of color as defined in value ranges between 0 and 255.
Sat	Saturation: the intensity of color. The value range is again 0 to 255, where 0 represents no saturation (color) and 255 is fully saturated color.
Lum	Luminance: the brightness of the border. Values are 0 to 255, where 0 represents black and 255 represents white.

There are three ways to adjust Border Colors:

Parameter sliders By clicking and moving individual sliders, the parameters will change. Adjust the hue, saturation, and luminance to the desired color. You can preview the color of the border either by looking at the color preview box to the right of the parameters or by previewing the effect.

Eyedropper This is a great way to sample a color from existing images in your effect. To use the eyedropper, click and hold the mouse over the color preview box. Slide the mouse over to your image in the Effect Preview monitor and release the mouse on the color you wish to select. The color register box changes to the sampled color.

Color Selection tool This allows you to pick colors using color selection. To access the color selector, click the icon next to the color preview box. When you find the color you like, press OK.

BORDER BLEND COLOR

You can add and adjust the border blend color in the same way as the border color, using the sliders, eyedropper, and Color Selection tool. Keep in mind as you select your border colors that the gradient will contain colors in between the primary border and border blend colors.

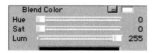

When using the eyedropper tool on your border color, both the border and blend colors change to the selected color. To prevent this and allow the system to keep the existing blend color, hold down the Alt/Option key while selecting the border color with the eyedropper. The system does not change border color when the eyedropper is used to select a blend color.

Acceleration

Acceleration determines the type of motion and fluidity between keyframes of an effect. Linear acceleration moves at a constant speed and motion and is indicated in the Acceleration parameter as 0 Acceleration.

The opposite of linear acceleration is smooth acceleration, which eases in and out of motion between keyframes. This is indicated in the Acceleration parameter as any number between 1 and 100. Thus a smooth acceleration starts at the keyframe and gradually accelerates, then slows as it arrives at the next keyframe. A linear acceleration does not change speed as it leaves one keyframe or arrives at the next. Smooth acceleration is much more natural, and linear is much more mechanical.

There are times to use each of them. An example of linear use is when you have images in boxes moving across the screen at once. If smooth acceleration is used, their speed and proximity to each other vary, and the result is something akin to a massive freeway collision. Using linear acceleration allows you to keep the images uniform in motion, provided that proper keyframing is used.

Smooth acceleration can be used when zooming in a picture to cover another. The acceleration increases as the image comes closer, then slows down to rest at its full screen position.

Although Acceleration can change the motion of the effect overall, you cannot vary the Acceleration parameter between keyframes. Acceleration is intended to be used over the entire effect.

Background

The Background parameter is used to determine background colors when used with Resize, Mask, Picture-in-Picture (PIP), and other similar effects in which the image is scaled, and a background source is needed to fill the screen. The Background parameter can also be used with transitional effects such as Dip To Color, in which a color is needed to be defined as a source.

Much like the Border parameter, Background utilizes Hue, Saturation, and Luminance parameters. It also uses a Color Selector icon and an Eyedropper.

Scaling

When the Scaling parameter group is present, the foreground image can be adjusted in size using the X and Y axes. The X axis (Width) controls the horizontal size of the image; the Y axis (Height) controls the vertical size of the image. The image scale can be adjusted between values of 0 and 400, where 0 is no invisible and 100 is 100% of normal image size.

Keep in mind when scaling images that you are working with video, so any enlargement of the image causes serious degradation of the overall picture.

Below the X and Y axis adjustments is a Fixed Aspect button. When selected, the Fixed Access button maintains the aspect ratio between horizontal and vertical axes so that the image maintains its original shape and is simply scaled down or up in size. Thus, when the horizontal (X) axis is adjusted, the vertical (Y) axis follows when this feature is selected.

Note: Although both Scaling and Position parameters use different terminology, it is a good idea to get used to the concept of X, Y, and Z axes when discussing effects. Those terms are used here, despite the names used on the effect, to clarify for those users who are more "effects savvy."

Position

The Position group of parameters allows you to position the image from top to bottom and left and right in the screen. The parameter values vary from -999 to 999, where a 0 value is center screen. The horizontal position (X axis) is called H Pos. The vertical position (Y axis) is called V Pos. For horizontal positioning, negative values of H Pos move the image to the left of center. Positive values of H Pos move the image to the right of center. For vertical positioning, negative values of V Pos move the image up from center screen. Positive values of V Pos move the image down from center screen.

Crop

The Crop parameter is useful for removing unwanted elements from a picture such as a boom microphone or other nuisances. The Crop parameter can be of great assistance when substandard images are used. For example, when VHS or U-Matic tapes are captured, there sometimes are muddled elements in the bottom of the picture (some people refer to this as flagging, but it is actually the point in the picture where head switching occurs between the two video heads that scan the tape). In some cases, the vertical blanking might show at the top of an image when it is scaled down for an effect. In cases like these, the Crop parameter is a necessity.

Crop values range from 0 to 999, where 0 is no cropping, and 999 crops the entire image. The Crop parameters are T, B, L, and R.

T   Top of the image
B   Bottom of the image
L   Left side of the image
R   Right side of the image

Cropping can be an exacting task, and the parameter sliders aren't always as precise as you might want them to be. To move the sliders in smaller increments, use Shift-Ctrl/Shift-⌘ when clicking and moving the sliders.

Saving Effect Templates

Every good editor has an arsenal of effects that they have saved and can drop into their sequence. After you create an effect with elaborate keyframes and parameters, you can save the effect as a template to be applied to other segments and Timelines. To save an effect template, do the following:

1. Create a new bin for the template. This is optional, of course, but is a good idea from an organizational standpoint.

2. In the Effect Editor, drag the Effect icon from the top-right corner of the window into the bin. This saves the effect.

After you save all your keyframes and effect parameters and dragged the effect template into the bin, you should name it. By default, the template is given the name of the type of effect; for example, Picture In Picture or Dip To Black. Give it a descriptive name.

In addition to the listing of templates in your bin, the name of any bin that contains effect templates is listed at the bottom of the Effect palette, giving you direct access to your custom effects from within the Effects palette.

Applying Effect Templates from a Bin

To maintain effects continuity, you can apply an effect template directly from a bin to your Timeline. You can also apply a template directly from the Effect palette, much as you would any other standard effect in Xpress Pro.

To apply an effect template from a bin, follow these steps:

1. Drag the effect template from the bin to the segment or transition in the Timeline where it is to be applied.

2. As you drag the template into the Timeline, note that each segment and transition that it passes over is highlighted.

3. When you find the correct location in the Timeline, release the mouse. The effect is applied.

Keep in mind that with segment effects, the effect will vary based on the duration of the effect, so it might move faster or slower than it did when previously applied. You can go into Effects mode and adjust the keyframes to make the effect more to your liking. Adjusting the effect in the Timeline in no way affects the template.

Applying Single Parameters from an Effect Template

In some cases, specific parameters of an effect might be needed. In cases such as these, you can apply just a single parameter from an effect template. When you apply a single parameter, Free DV and Xpress Pro use only the first keyframe in the template as a guide. The target effect, which should already be in the Timeline, is affected only on selected keyframes. To apply a single effect parameter:

1. Select the effect in the Timeline and go into Effects mode. The Effect Editor appears.

2. Twirl down the parameter menu for the desired effect parameter to be replaced.

3. Select the keyframes that you want to change. If you click in the Effect Timeline, you can use Ctrl+A/⌘+A to select all the keyframes.

4. Select the effect template in the bin and drag it to the parameter pane of the parameter that you wish to change.

5. The effect is applied to only that parameter on all selected keyframes when you release the mouse.

Saving an Effect with the Source

In addition to saving just the template, you can save the effect template with the source material included. To do this, Alt-click/Option-click the Effect Template icon and drag it to a bin. When the template is saved with the source, it will indicate it in the template name; that is, Resize with Src.

Some effects actually work in exactly the opposite way; for example, matte keys and Title effects. To save these effects without the source, you drag them to a bin.

Timecode Navigation

In Effects mode, the Timecode display window above the record window changes (see Figure 7.15). Two new elements are added: Effect Duration and Current Position.

The position number is particularly of interest because it not only refers to frames but it also refers to fields. Thus, 12.2 would be the 12th frame, second field. You can navigate by typing frame numbers in Effect mode much as you would navigate by timecode in Source/Record mode. Type a plus (+) or minus (-) followed by any two-digit number, and the frame will move forward or backward by the number of frames that you indicate.

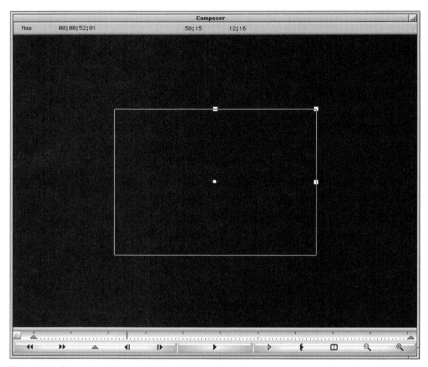

Figure 7.15 Timecode window with effect times

Editing with Keyframes

Keyframes are the backbone of any effect. In scientific terms, the keyframes define the principle of moments in any effect. Normally, a simple effect such as a wipe would have only two keyframes: one at the beginning and one at the end. With Free DV and Xpress Pro, all effects have a beginning and an ending keyframe—they cannot be deleted, but they can be adjusted. You can also manually define other keyframes.

Each keyframe allows you to adjust or change effect parameters. Wherever you feel the parameters need change, you can add a keyframe. The system determines what needs to be done between keyframes to make the effect flow properly. The process of in-betweening from keyframe to keyframe is called interpolation. At first, adding keyframes might seem a bit challenging, and you might not get exactly what was intended. Over time, as parameters are learned, your ability to use keyframes will improve.

Keyframe indicators are shown in the Effect Timeline underneath the Record monitor (see Figure 7.16). The indicators are small triangles ⟨⟩. The Active keyframe—the keyframe that is being currently adjusted in the Effect Editor—is indicated by a bright pink color. Inactive keyframes are grayed-out.

Figure 7.16 Keyframes below Record monitor

When adjusting a keyframe in Effect mode, it is important to notice which keyframe(s) is active. Often the blue position indicator under the Record monitor is placed close to a keyframe, but that keyframe is not selected. If this is the case, you could be adjusting another keyframe blindly by moving the parameter sliders but seeing little or no result. Always be sure to check for the active keyframe before adjusting parameters.

Adding a Keyframe

When you add keyframes, the effect does not change. The effect is altered only when that keyframe is selected and parameters are changed. You can select a keyframe in the Timeline by clicking it. To add a keyframe:

1. Move in the Timeline to the position where you want to add the keyframe.

2. Click the Add Keyframe button below the Record monitor or press the N key on your keyboard.

Selecting Multiple Keyframes

To select more than one keyframe:

1. Click the first keyframe that you want to select in the Timeline underneath the Record monitor.

2. Ctrl-click (Windows) or Shift-click (Macintosh) any additional keyframes. Multiple keyframes are selected.

You can also use Ctrl+A/⌘+A to select all the keyframes in an effect. You cannot deselect all the keyframes of an effect. The closest thing to do is to click a single keyframe to select that keyframe and deselect all others.

Deleting a Keyframe

To delete keyframes, click the keyframe to be deleted in the Timeline underneath the Record monitor. The keyframe becomes highlighted. You can also Shift-select or Ctrl/⌘-select multiple keyframes for deletion. Then press Delete on the keyboard. The keyframe is deleted.

Moving Keyframes

In some cases, you may need to move the position of a keyframe in the Timeline. To do this, first select the keyframe to be moved in the Effect Timeline. Then Alt/Option-drag the keyframe to its new position. The keyframe is moved. On some slower systems, you'll want to make sure that the keyframe has updated to the correct position before you release; otherwise, you will have moved your keyframe only part of the way to your desired location.

Copying and Pasting Keyframe Parameters

After you've defined your keyframes, you might want to copy and paste the same parameters from one keyframe to another. To do this:

1. Select the source keyframe on the Effect Timeline by clicking it.

2. Copy it (press Ctrl+C/⌘+C).

3. Select the target keyframe on the Effect Timeline by clicking it.

4. Paste it (press Ctrl+V/⌘+V). The keyframe parameters from the source keyframe are pasted.

Advanced Keyframing (Xpress Pro)

One of the disadvantages of the keyframing tool in Effects mode is the inability to control keyframe parameters independently of each other. For example, when flying a Picture In Picture effect across the screen, it might be advantageous to add more scaling parameter keyframes while not affecting positioning keyframes.

Enter advanced keyframing (see Figure 7.17), a new capability on Xpress Pro and other Avid systems. Advanced keyframing allows additional keyframes to be set on single parameters; thus, many keyframes can be added to the Scaling parameter without affecting the motion path or any other parameters.

Most effects have no need for advanced keyframing. It is available on Picture In Picture, 3D, and Resize effects. To enter Advanced Keyframing mode, click the Advanced Keyframe button on the bottom right of the Effect Editor in a Picture In Picture, Resize, or 3D effect. The Advanced Keyframe icon is symbolized by a vertical double pink Timeline.

The Effect Editor expands to display several parameter rows with individual Timelines and keyframes. You can use the twirl-down menus for each parameter to show the sliders. As you work your way down the menus, you will notice that for each parameter slider there is a minitimeline to the right. To select a parameter, click the slider or the minitimeline for that parameter. At the bottom of the Effect Editor is an Add Keyframe button ![icon]. With a parameter selected and the blue indicator in the middle, try clicking that button. You'll notice that the keyframe is added to only that parameter.

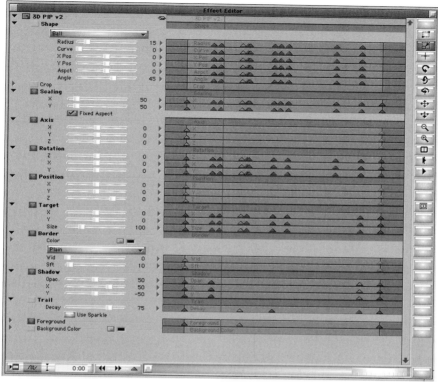

Figure 7.17 Advanced keyframing with PIP effect

Over time, you will find many situations in which advanced keyframing is beneficial. The control over individual parameters can make for more exacting effects quality.

> **Note:** The newest addition to the Avid line, Xpress Pro HD, has even more advanced keyframable effects than before. See the Appendix to get the lowdown.

Dual Split Button (Xpress Pro)

Selecting the Dual Split button displays a "before" and "after" image of your effect in the Record monitor. The "before" image is indicated by white corner brackets. To remove the Dual Split display, press the button again. The white corner brackets can each be dragged to a new location if it is more important to see the split horizontally instead of vertically.

While building your effects, you might find it useful to zoom in and out of the effect monitor for a more through examination of your effect. To zoom in, Ctrl/⌘-click in the monitor. To zoom out, Shift-Ctrl/⌘-click in the monitor. You can also map the Reduce and Enlarge buttons onto your interface. You'll especially find the zoom tools helpful if you use the Outline Path button. For effects that move on a path across the screen, the Outline Path selection will allow you to see the movement of the effect from keyframe to keyframe. Each gray dot in the path represents a keyframe.

In some cases, you might find it difficult to navigate your way from keyframe to keyframe through complex effects using the small Timeline underneath the Effect Preview monitor. Just to the left of the monitor is a very handy keyframe scale bar. By adjusting this slider, you can zoom in on the effect Timeline and see all the keyframes. In the regular configuration, keyframes can easily get lost. Zooming the Effect Preview Timeline allows you to analyze the keyframes more effectively.

Another method is to use the fast-forward and rewind keys. Normally, these keys function so that you can jump forward and backward between each locator on your track. If you hold down the Alt/Option button and use them, they would normally jump from transition to transition in your Timeline. However, when you map them underneath the Effect Preview monitor (and they must be under the monitor, not on the Timeline buttons for this to work), they will jump forward or backward to each keyframe so that you can see and examine the parameters for each one.

Building Vertical Effects

In the "Basic Editing" chapter, we covered how to add video tracks (Ctrl+Y/⌘+Y) and how to monitor video tracks (by clicking the monitor button next to the track name). Building vertical effects such as multiple Picture In Picture tracks, keys, resizes, and titles is fairly simple, at least in theory. The key to building vertical effects is a concept referred to as previsualization.

Prior to creating any type of complex effect, it's a good idea to sketch it out on a piece of paper. Try to determine which effects will be used, how each track will be assigned, what sources will be needed, and what resources will be required. Sketching out an effect can be as simple as drawing on a cocktail napkin or as complex as creating a spreadsheet with a storyboard visual reference. It's up to you, the effect designer, to determine which tools are necessary.

Previsualization is mentioned here only because so many picture editors can become overwhelmed with 24 vertical video tracks. The effect in itself is a fairly simple thing. Manipulating an effect and understanding its interaction with other effects is entirely different. When you previsualize, try to break down your effect design to its most simple elements and draw it on the page. When you attempt the effect in Xpress Pro, you can add each element step by step and then preview it to see whether it works.

When you create effects, you may have to determine whether elements are within the title safe or action safe areas. Using the Grid button will allow you to turn on and off a grid over the monitor so that you can see these areas. Title safe is the inner grid; no titles should extend beyond or over this area. Action safe is the outer grid, which covers most of the video image. In general, no significant action should take place outside of this area because it won't show up on some video monitors and televisions.

Real-Time Effect Playback

The better your understanding of Avid systems, the easier it is to determine how your system will perform using vertical layers of real-time effects. To play back a sequence, Xpress Pro will do three things:

- Build the pipes
- Load the RAM buffer
- Begin playing back

Building the Pipes

When you press the Play button, the system immediately begins a process known as "building the pipes." This is the function of "reading" the sequence and determining what media it will need to play back, what effects will need to be preloaded, and so forth.

In many cases, it will take an insignificant amount of time to build the pipes; the process goes unnoticed in the background. But when a large amount of media is accessed, when there are many cuts, or when the effects are fairly extensive, the time between pushing Play and the media actually playing can be long and frustrating. In cases such as these, the PlayLength toggle button (Xpress Pro only) comes in handy.

The PlayLength toggle switch **PL** allows the system to build the pipes for only one minute. This way, it will take a shorter amount of time to build the pipes and play back the sequence.

Xpress Pro indicates that PlayLength is active by switching your Play button from its normal color to white. When PlayLength is toggled again, the system returns to normal playback mode, and the Play button resumes its usual characteristics.

Loading the RAM Buffer

Although one might assume that Xpress Pro reads media directly from the drives, this isn't the case. The system will normally preload 20 frames into a temporary RAM buffer before beginning playback. This RAM buffer allows your system to catch up with itself by preloading the frames ahead of time. If it has difficulty reading media, as opposed to other systems, it will use the "look-ahead" function of RAM to prevent dropped frames.

In some cases, the RAM buffer gets behind because of a system bottleneck. System bottlenecks can be common with computers based on a variety of factors, including your video card, bus speed, RAM speed, and CPU speed.

If you encounter a situation in which Xpress Pro is having difficulty playing back a stream of real-time effects, you can give the system more time to fill the RAM buffer.

1. Go to the Project Window and select the Settings tab.

2. Double-click the Video Display settings (see Figure 7.18).

3. Under the Pre-Filled Frames selection, enter **10**.
   The system spends an extra 10 seconds prefilling the buffer.

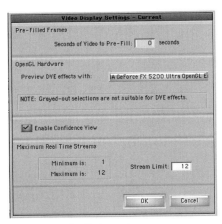

Figure 7.18 Video Display settings

Playback Stress Indicators (Xpress Pro)

When Xpress Pro has difficulty playing back effects sequences, it has the ability to indicate exactly why and how the system is encountering difficulties. These stress indicators are located in the Timecode track of your Timeline, and they will show you what and how to remedy playback problems.

After playing back your sequence, take a look at the Timecode track. You may notice some tiny colored bars just above the timecode numbers. These bars indicate problem areas of the sequence. The color of the bars determines the problem encountered.

Red Bars Red bars indicate a taxed system. In these areas, Xpress Pro dropped frames to play back your sequence. Generally speaking, red bars indicate that your CPU isn't working fast enough to play back the problem-affected area. The only solution is to render this area.

Yellow Bars Yellow bars indicate areas in which the system is stressed to its limit, but did not fail to play back all frames. You should consider making some kind adjustment to alleviate the problem. Pre-filling frames, freeing up extra memory by exiting from other applications, and other CPU-freeing methods can be used. If you're concerned about playback performance, and the edits in this area are pretty well locked in, it might be wise to render.

Blue Bars Blue bars indicate that the drives on your system reached a high stress level, but that everything played back okay. You might consider using a faster drive or reconfiguring the drive in some manner to assure faster access to media.

Using ExpertRender (Xpress Pro)

If you just played back a sequence that dropped frames, you can have ExpertRender fix your problem areas. ExpertRender is Xpress Pro's smart render engine. It knows the rules of rendering and will only select those items which need to be rendered to ensure playback for different situations.

To fix dropped frames, play back your sequence and immediately choose Clip > ExpertRender.

The Laws of Rendering

Let's face it: Rendering is painful. The whole concept of random-access nonlinear computerized editing means that it takes less time to do and is more fun. So here are a few axioms about rendering to consider.

Render as little as possible. You might be surprised by how few actually do this. When you add a non–real-time effect and already know it will work, render it when you're done with the sequence. You can always adjust it later, if necessary. If you have a choice between using a real-time effect or a non–real-time effect (and it doesn't matter which is used), choose the real-time effect. If you're building a multilayered effect that exceeds your maximum streams limit or contains non–real-time effects, don't render until all the layers are added. If you can wait until the sequence is finished before doing a render, wait.

For multilayered effects, rendering the top layer will also render the effects below it. This is much less time-consuming than rendering each individual track. Let Xpress Pro do the work for you. Whenever possible, use Expert Render.

Nested Effects and Collapsing (Xpress Pro)

Effect nesting is a powerful feature of Xpress Pro that utilizes its ability to build an effect within an effect. Before we go too far, let's discuss one of the most common problems associated with vertical effects: transitions.

When we make the shift from linear to nonlinear editing, there are always a few hitches, and the transition from multiple tracks is one of the trade-offs. Allow me to elucidate: You build a show on video track 1. The titles are on track 2. Along the line, your producer decides to dissolve from your video on track 1 to another piece of video on the same track. No problem, right? But it just so happens that you have a title up on the screen on track 2, so you'll need to dissolve that out as well.

This is what separates a good editor from a precise editor. Some editors (and you know who you are) just add a dissolve to track 2 as well as track 1 and allow the fades to vary. That's not precise. And besides, it ain't pretty, either.

The easy way is to use collapse. Collapsing conserves tracks and allows for clean transitions on a single track. Collapse can be used on simple two-track titles with backgrounds or complex 20-track effects that need to transition to a single adjacent clip.

Here's how to collapse tracks:

1. Using either of your Segment mode buttons, select the clip on V1 and the title on V2. (If you're using several tracks, click all to select them.)

2. Click the Collapse button ![collapse button] and voilà: You collapsed all your selected tracks into a single track. Now all you have to do is add the transitions to the clips on either side. No worries about matching the timing and durations between the two tracks, because they're all rolled into one track now. You have achieved precision. Congratulations. Let's move on.

So now you might be wondering—when you collapse tracks, where do they go? When you collapse tracks, they become subnested. That is, both tracks still exist separately, but they are nested underneath a Submaster effect. You can access these tracks by entering the nest, which we'll describe later in this chapter.

Submaster Effect

The Submaster effect ![Submaster icon] is a great tool. You can add a Submaster effect and nest inside of it by using collapse, or you can add it to a higher track to create an effect that can be used over several clips.

For example, let's say you have a piece with a dream sequence that recurs again and again, changing ever so slightly from the dream sequence before it. You want to maintain the same look over each of these sequences. The scene (according to the director, who always has the last say) needs to be tinted blue with a letterbox over it. For the first occurrence, you create tracks with the blue tint on V2 and the letterbox on V3 with your video source on V1. Now you can collapse the V3 and V2 tracks into a Submaster and save the effect as a template. That way, you never have to re-create your effect for each recurrence of the dream, and you collapsed it into one tidy effect that can be placed over the video as many times as you require it.

You can do this same type of effect on higher tracks for simple snappy transitions. For example, you can create a gate flash (that's a fancy term for what happens in telecine when a film is overexposed) effect on filler above your video tracks to transition from one scene to another. Rather than incorporate it on the same tracks as your clips, you can place this filler effect on a higher track and save it in an effect bin that can be used any time.

Now that we've shown how you can collapse tracks and inadvertently build a nest, let's explore how you can build one manually and why you would want to do it.

Step versus Expanded Nesting (Xpress Pro)

There are two different methods of working with nested effects. The first method is called step or simple nesting (see Figure 7.19). Step nesting allows you to focus and isolate a single effect, stepping inside of that effect to its core.

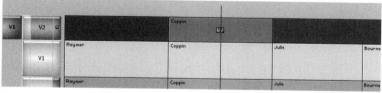

Figure 7.19 (top) The Matte and Fill tracks of a title created with the Title tool; (bottom) How the title effect appears on the Timeline without nesting

The second method, expansion nesting, expands the Timeline to reveal the inside of the nest, as well as the rest of your edited sequence (see Figure 7.20). Although they basically do the same thing, there are advantages for each method.

Step nesting allows you to monitor inside of the effect where you are nesting. So if you are adding something to the inside of a Picture In Picture effect, the monitor shows you the video that is inside of the Picture In Picture, not the result of the effect. This inner view is important for placement and adjustment of parameters of any added effect.

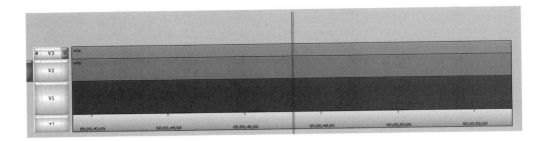

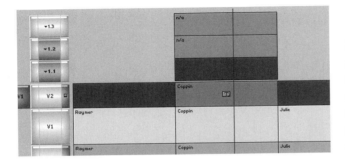

Figure 7.20 (top) A title effect opened using step nesting. Note the lack of adjacent clips and the two tracks—one is the matte and the other is the fill. (bottom) The same title effect opened using expansion nesting. Note the two tracks vertically above the effect.

Expanded nesting shows you the tracks within a nest, but keeps the monitoring the same. With expansion nesting, you still monitor the entire Timeline with effects added, so it isn't particularly good for closeup work within the nest. On the other hand, expansion nesting allows you to monitor audio, patch source tracks to tracks that exist outside of the nest, view all levels of a nest, and see the entire Timeline—not just the element that is being affected in the nest.

These descriptions might sound a bit complicated, so let's take a look at an example of each method and how it can work.

Step Nesting

Here's a simple example of a step nested effect: Suppose that you have a Picture In Picture effect in your sequence. This effect uses two tracks of video: one for the background, a wide shot of a newscaster; the other for a graphic, a map.

In this scenario, there are parts of a map that need to be identified. You decide to add a title on track 3. So you add a track of video and build your title, and everything is going just great. You might even get done early tonight, for a change. You edit the title onto track 3 and start playing back your finished sequence. Just when it looks like a walk in the park, you get a sinking feeling of impending doom as you realize that you created the Picture In Picture effect transition over the shoulder of the newscaster as a zoom from infinity to its normal size.

You enter Effect mode, scale the first keyframe of your title back to infinity, and leave the second one in the final resting position. Another playback, another problem.

When played back, the title doesn't exactly emulate the path of the Picture In Picture effect because it was created originally off-center, resulting in an effect that begins off axis but lands in the right position.

You could continue chasing your tail, creating a new title in the center of the frame and again emulating the motion of the Picture In Picture effect, but life is short. And this is a great opportunity to nest.

If you could place the title inside of the Picture In Picture effect, it would track just fine. Here's how to do it. Build the Picture In Picture as you normally would, but before building the title, select the video track with the Picture In Picture effect. Be sure that your blue position indicator is over the effect.

Now, click the Step In button on the bottom of the Timeline ⬇. The button is a downward-facing arrow, indicating that we are going down into the effect, spelunking our way through it. The Timeline changes to reflect the Picture In Picture clip only. The sequence monitor image will also change to reflect the source of the effect in Full Screen mode.

From here, you can add another video track inside of this nest and create the title, editing it into the nest as you would any normal sequence. When you're inside of a nest, all the normal sequence rules apply. You can build 24 tracks of video in this nest, just as you can with any sequence. In this example, the source clip of the effect is in Full Screen mode while you are in the Step In mode, so you can position the title more correctly when building it. Once you've created the title, step out of the nest by clicking the Step Out icon ⬆. The sequence will reappear and your title will be inside the Picture In Picture. Wherever the Picture In Picture effect goes, your title will follow.

Expansion Nesting

Now we'll take a look at expansion nesting and an example of when you should choose this method over step nesting. Let's start by taking an image that we want to integrate into a documentary. The image is faded, the color has a blue cast to it, and the shot has been transferred with the negative reversed. So we'll need to fix it and we want to pan across the screen, all the while incorporating a letterbox matte. As we build the nested effect, we need to pay attention to an audio cue in the narration track, which tells us when to start the pan of the image from one person across the entire group.

In this scenario, expansion nesting is the best solution. There are two reasons: We need to hear an audio cue, which we would not normally hear by using the step method; and we are adding effects to an entire picture, thus there is no need to focus on any specific image within a group of images.

To begin, I like to add a Submaster effect to the top and then expand the Timeline to reveal the added effects inside. The reason I choose the Submaster effect is simple: The Submaster effect has absolutely no characteristics, but it implies that there is something underneath. In essence, it's just a wrapper for nested effects. Some other NLE products call them "containers."

After you place the Submaster effect on the segment, you can select one of the segment-editing buttons on the bottom of the Timeline. It doesn't matter which one is chosen, because it's only a method of expanding the Timeline to show the nest. With the Segment mode selected, double-click the Submastered clip in the sequence. The Timeline expands vertically, showing a video track V1.1. (You can also do this by going into Effects mode first and then double-clicking without using Segment mode.) We'll drag and drop a mask on top of this segment.

Now double-click track V1.1. It expands to show track V2.1. In this case, instead of counting vertical tracks, Xpress Pro is counting nested tracks, differentiating between V2, and V2.1. Here we'll add the Flop effect, which reverses the picture horizontally.

Now we'll add more to the equation. Double-click track V2.1 and expand to track V3.1 (see Figure 7.21). Here we'll add a color effect. Finally, we'll double-click V3.1 and expand it, revealing V4.1. Here we'll add our pan and zoom, so that the picture will be imported from its original file and panned on the audio cue, as we discussed earlier.

Figure 7.21 Expanded nest on the Timeline

So the processing order goes like this: Pan & Zoom > Color Effect > Flop Effect > Mask > Submaster > V1. And the whole process is in front of you, so you can pick each effect and adjust it with the Effect Editor. The audio will play back normally, and you can still see the entire nest.

Now that you've made the adjustments, how do you get the nest to disappear back inside of V1 on the Timeline? Again, using a segment-editing mode, double-click V1. The nest disappears. In this instance, you have created about five layers of effects on one piece of media. Can your system play it back in real time? Probably. Because you are not dealing with five separate streams of video, it is much easier for Xpress Pro to play back, even with five different effects on the single stream.

Nesting Order and Autonesting

The order in which you build your nests within nests is very important. For example, if you want to add a color effect and a matte to a picture, the color effect would need to go inside of the matte effect. Otherwise, the matte would show evidence of the color effect as well. Your ability to prevent these issues before they happen will increase through experience and previsualization.

Even when a multiple nest effect has been poorly planned, Xpress Pro has a solution to easily fix this. You can change the order of nested effects inside of the Effect Editor. When an effect is nested inside another effect and Advanced Keyframe mode is selected, the Nesting Priority icon appears for each effect nested inside of the original effect.

In order to use this feature, the base effect on the Timeline must have advanced keyframing capability. Without it, you cannot reorder the nest. In the earlier example of expansion nests, we used a Submaster effect, which does not have advanced keyframing. To solve this problem, we'll need to add an effect on top of the Submaster.

Autonesting

You can also place an effect on top of a nest. This is referred to as autonesting. Using Segment mode, click the base track of your nest (V1, for example.) Go into the Effect palette. We're going to use a Resize effect, which has advanced keyframe capabilities. To autonest the Picture In Picture on top of the Submaster effect, press Alt/Opt and double-click the Resize icon in your effect palette. The resize icon should appear on the base track of the Timeline. The reason we chose the Resize effect is because it defaults to 100 percent screen size, so no actual adjustments are necessary.

Effect Priority

Now we'll take a look at the Resize effect in the Effect Editor. At the bottom of the screen is the purple layered icon used to promote the effect to advanced keyframes. Click this icon, and the Effect Editor expands. You should also be able to see all of the nested effects inside. To the right of each effect is blue layering icon. This is the Effect Priority icon, which allows you to determine the nesting order. You can click and drag the effects vertically to change the order in which the effects are processed by Xpress Pro. Try grabbing the color effect and moving it below the Avid Pan and Zoom. If you do this, the color is added before the image is imported for Pan and Zoom. As a result, the color adjustments won't show! The same is true when placing the Flop or Mask effects at the bottom.

3D Warp (Xpress Pro)

Xpress Pro has additional effects that emulate 3D space. Let's go over some basic concepts and then look at each type of effect.

We've already discussed how we can manipulate the horizontal and vertical axes, respectively known as X and Y. Now let's focus on the depth axis, known as Z. To give objects depth on the screen, the Z axis can be adjusted so that what normally is a flat item (such as a video image, which is flat) needs to be manipulated so that pixels emulate the effects of a third axis, showing depth.

We emulate a third axis frequently when using the scale parameter of an effect. For example, if we want an image to fly from infinity to full screen, we can adjust a resize effect so that an image enters at zero size and increases to 100 percent, giving us the impression that it is coming toward us.

But the problem with this type of faux 3D effect is that there is nothing to indicate that there is any true depth of space in the picture. The scaled image is flat, so there is nothing to show that there is a true dimension. As a result, these effects seem rather tired.

To allow us to create that third dimension of depth, 3D on Xpress Pro takes form in three different shapes: page folds, balls, and slats (see Figure 7.22).

Page Fold Page folds have been used in video effects for decades. They give the impression that a page from a book is being turned, complete with the sense of depth in the curled portion of the video. Video editors have commonly used this effect to indicate a change in subject or scenery.

Balls A 3D ball is not just a circular wipe: It can show portions of a picture with a true Z axis, forming what appears to be depth in the picture. The image is distorted in a circular fashion to express depth, and it can be spun, to a degree, to implicate a ball shape. The parameters within the Shape parameter can further affect the 3D look of the 3D ball, changing the amount of distortion that is applied and other parameters.

Slats Without a Z axis, the slat shape would appear to be a horizontal wipe. The difference here is that as the slats come onto the screen, the image is distorted so that there appears to be some depth from the "front" of the slat where the image is closer to us, and the "back" of the slat, where it is farther away.

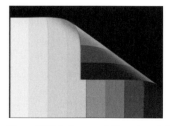 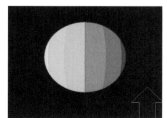 

Figure 7.22 Left, a page fold; center, a ball; right, a slat

Some existing effects can be promoted to 3D type effects. These effects are Titles, Picture In Picture, and imported mattes. To promote them to 3D, click the 3D button in the Effect Editor [⬛]. You now can adjust these effects by choosing one of the 3D shapes. Promoting a title or a Picture In Picture effect is important. On most high-end, video-effect editing systems, the smooth page turn and 3D transitioning is standard operating procedure. Without 3D promotion, Xpress Pro would have little to match these systems.

Experimenting with Effects

Most video editors have their own arsenal of effects. You can store these templates in a bin of favorites, then transfer that bin to a thumb drive, disk, floppy, or Zip drive. Using previously created effects can add a lot of "wow" factor to your sessions and impress clients.

Once you've built up a pretty good effects bin, be sure to copy it and take it with you. Go into the Avid Projects folder, find the project in which you created your effect bin, and copy it to your favorite portable storage format.

It's hard to edit projects that have a lot of information and little eye candy, and effects can't always save the day. But in many cases, a solid effects arsenal can make all the difference between a sleepy presentation and a glittering performance. And for you, the editor, it can be a challenge to keep your material lively and your job interesting.

What's New in Xpress Pro HD

Avid has developed a new Xpress Pro system that is capable of editing and outputting DVC Pro HD video, as well as standard-definition media. This system integrates some of the latest technology and allows the user the freedom to integrate HD into standard-definition projects and vice versa.

Xpress Pro HD is available for both Windows and Mac OS. The latest release, version 5.1, goes far beyond any recent updates in the history of Xpress Pro. If you are still using version 4.6 or other previous versions, here are some features that may entice you toward upgrading.

Appendix Contents

Real-Time DV-25 Bitstream Output

New Resolutions

More Effects Supporting Advanced Keyframing

AVX 2.0 Support

Marquee Titles

Film Enhancements

Real-Time DV-25 Bitstream Output

The newest version of Xpress Pro HD is capable of a DV-25 bitstream output. What is a DV-25 bitstream output? Well, in the case of Xpress Pro, it is a DV-25 decompression and recompression of the video output. Why would you need it? If you have a Mojo, it doesn't really matter if you use real-time bitstream, but it is possible to use. If you have no Mojo, it means real-time effects in your timeline will *not* have to be rendered! (As long as you have a fully qualified Avid system that meets the basic requirements for Xpress Pro.)

With a Mojo

If you have a Mojo and want to use a DV-25 bitstream output, you need a separate FireWire card on a different bus to use Xpress Pro HD with the Mojo. Make sure that your computer has a separate bus before you add the card. If you do not have a separate bus, you'll have to use the Mojo the same as before.

When you use a Mojo with the new DV-25 bitstream, you have to first select the new DNA/1394 Toggle button . (DNA stands for Digital Nonlinear Acceleration, an Avid marketing term.) When the button is in DNA mode (which is the default), a Mojo works normally as before, but all outputs are turned off and you cannot output a DV-25 bitstream. However, you still have monitoring capabilities. But you can configure it for bitstream encoding via FireWire, and the output is turned on.

> **Note:** A Mojo cannot show HD resolutions. You can, however, edit with the Mojo. It does not give you an HD output.

Without a Mojo

If you do not have a Mojo, the DNA/1394 toggle button will be in 1394 mode and cannot be toggled. From there, you have to configure for a bitstream output. Once configured, real-time effects play back without a Mojo.

Configuring the Bitstream

Whether or not you have a Mojo, the configuring for a real-time bitstream output is the same—except in the case of a Mojo, the DNA/1394 Toggle should be set to 1394. Without a Mojo, it automatically is set to 1394, as stated previously.

First, right-click the Video Quality button at the bottom of the Timeline (see Figure A.1); choose Realtime Encoding, right-click again, and choose Format > DV 25 411 (4:1:1 is just the subsampling rate). You also have the option of DV-50 if the source is truly a DV-50 device. Otherwise, it will not work. Currently, only DV-25 real-time bit-stream encoding is supported. You also need to choose Output To DV Device.

Figure A.1 Selecting real-time encoding and choosing a DV format

You have to elect Video Settings in this menu. Because encoding is possible, the video is delayed (see Figure A.2). Generally, you should try setting the Desktop Play Delay to about 15 frames to set the in order of playing it back in sync. Remember that when selecting this option, playback is delayed by whatever duration is set. Take a look at the NTSC monitor to verify that the video is in sync. After the delay is set on your output, you should be able to make a digital cut any time.

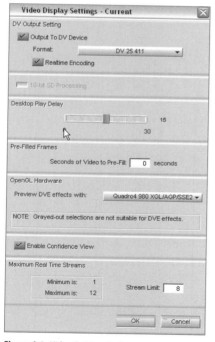

Figure A.2 Video Settings tool

Digital Cut Tool Changes

The Digital Cut tool has also changed somewhat. Note that there is a choice of device: either DNA or IEEE 1394 (see Figure A.3). When you choose DNA, it outputs through the Mojo. When you select IEEE 1394, you output directly through FireWire and have a choice of the outputs listed below.

Figure A.3 Device choices in the Digital Cut tool

In Xpress Pro HD, real-time bitstream encoding of DV-25 media is enabled, allowing you to output without doing any rendering of real-time effects. This feature is dependent on your computer's RAM and CPU speed, but any Avid-recommended system should work.

The caveat here is that there could be issues if your system does not meet Avid standards. In cases such as these, it may not have the power to encode in real time.

When doing a digital cut, you have the choice of four output modes (see Figure A.4).

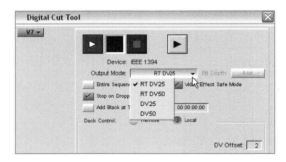

Figure A.4 New modes of output in the Digital Cut tool

DV25	The same as earlier DV-25 output in Xpress Pro
DV50	The same as earlier DV-50 output in Xpress Pro
RT DV25	Real-time bitstream encoding (no rendering of real-time effects is necessary)
RT DV50	Real-time bitstream encoding (no rendering of real-time effects is necessary)

New Resolutions

Xpress Pro HD accepts two new resolution types:

- DVC Pro HD
- DNxHD

DVC Pro HD can be captured directly to Xpress Pro via FireWire. DVC Pro HD is the only HD format that is supported for capture with Xpress Pro HD, although you can use media captured from Adrenaline HD systems, as long as it is 8-bit encoded. Xpress Pro HD does not support 10-bit encoding.

Avid DNxHD resolutions must originate from an Avid Adrenaline system because they are not native to Xpress Pro. However, Avid recommends the use of this resolution whenever possible because these HD resolutions and media were created specifically for Avid systems and work well with Xpress Pro.

The following resolutions and frame rates can be used from this media:

- 1080i/59.94
- 1080i/50
- 1080p/23.976
- 1080p/24
- 1080p/25
- 720p/59.94
- 720p/23.976

All resolutions available on Adrenaline can be played back (but not captured) on Xpress Pro HD, with the exception of 10-bit media.

More Effects Supporting Advanced Keyframing

With previous versions of Xpress Pro, only a few effects supported advanced keyframing. In the new version 5.0, advanced keyframing is supported on many more effects. These effects include the following:

- All blend effects
- Chroma, luma, and matte keys
- 3D titles
- 3D imported matte keys
- All mask effects
- Color effects
- All wipe effects
- All conceal and L-conceal effects
- All peel, push, spin, and squeeze effects
- All film effects
- AVX 2.0 effects

AVX 2.0 Support

Xpress Pro HD supports the new AVX 2.0 category of effects, which consists of third-party effects vendors like Boris FX and others.

Marquee Titles

Xpress Pro HD utilizes the Marquee title system (see Figure A.5). In many cases (especially with HD video), the Marquee titler is more suitable for graphics in Xpress Pro than the Title tool. The interface is more robust, the 3D capabilities work well, and you can even use the new AutoTitler, which takes a text document and treats it much like a database—inserting repetitive titles from text editing in an instant.

Marquee, which was originally a Windows-native application, has now been ported to Macintosh and is available for Xpress Pro HD use on either platform.

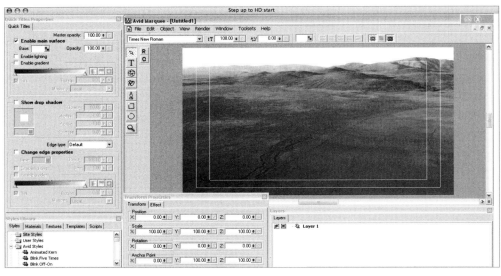

Figure A.5 Marquee title system

Film Enhancements

Xpress Pro HD now supports 3-perf film. Previously, 3-perf was difficult to manage and was not compatible. Now the system not only supports this format but also reflects those changes in FilmScribe.

Another film enhancement that is brand new is that Xpress Pro now allows for mixed film gauges within the same sequence. This is a new function that was added primarily for documentaries and any programs in which mixed gauges of film are used.

Glossary

absorption The retention of light without reflecting or transmitting.

Academy leader A leader placed at head of release film prints, counting from 11 to 3. As opposed to SMPTE (Society of Motion Picture and Television Engineers) leader.

achromatic Having no color; gray, white, or black.

A/D converter Acronym for analog-to-digital converter. A device that transforms an analog signal to digital samples.

adaptation The process of the human visual system's adjustment to light and color conditions in which the eyes are exposed.

add edit A function on the Avid Control palette that, when added between consecutive frames in a sequence segment within the Timeline, can separate segments into subsections for individual manipulation.

additive color A color formed by adding a mixture of primary light sources: red, green, and blue.

ADO Acronym for Ampex Digital Optics. A video digital effects system manufactured and sold by Ampex.

ADR Acronym for automated dialog replacement in film. Also called looping.

AES/EBU Acronym for Audio Engineering Society/European Broadcasting Union.

AIFF-C Acronym for Audio Interchange File Format-Condensed. A sampled-sound file format for audio data.

ALE Acronym for Avid Log Exchange: a format used for converting telecine files. Also an application for converting telecine files created by Avid Technology. ALE is used as a log import format for Avid and other non-linear editors (NLEs).

alpha channel An 8-bit, grayscale representation of an image that determines masked areas for keys. Also referred to as hi-con, holdout, cookie cutter, key channel, and mask.

ambience A production sound used where there is no dialog to establish a setting. More traditionally, ambience refers to outdoor locations, and room tone refers to interiors. Also referred to as room tone or presence.

A-mode A linear method of assembling an edit decision list (EDL). In an A-mode EDL assembly, the editing system performs edits in the order in which they will appear on the master.

analog A continuously variable electrical signal.

analog recording A common form of magnetic recording, in which the recorded waveform signal is transferred electronically via an analog signal to media.

anti-aliasing A computerized process of digitally smoothing the jagged lines around lower-resolution graphic objects or titles. Anti-aliasing is usually achieved by blending pixels.

ASA An exposure index defined by the American National Standards Institution. Originally defined for black-and-white films, it is also used for color films.

aspect ratio The ratio of picture width to picture height. 1.85:1 is the most common film aspect ratio in the United States; 1.66:1 is more common in Europe. Standard-definition television is 4:3. Most high-definition television (HDTV) pictures are 16:9.

assemble list A cut list that includes all the edits in a sequence in the order in which they occur chronologically. Used for conforming negative or work print. Also known as the cut list.

ATM Acronym for Asynchronous Transfer Mode. A network technology based on transferring data in small packets of a fixed size. Used as a means to transmit video, audio, and computer data over a network. Packet delivery ensures that no stream of data will tie up the line.

ATR Acronym for audiotape recorder.

ATSC Acronym for Advanced Television Standards Committee. The group that is developing standards for high-definition and digital television as well as compression schemes for broadcasting them. Currently, there are 18 different types of high-definition television (HDTV).

Attic folder The folder containing backups of bins. Everytime bins are saved by the user or are autosaved by the Avid, copies of the bins are placed in the Attic folder.

audio scrub The process of shuttling through and monitoring segments of audio at various speeds. Originates from earlier analog audio days when audiotape media was "scrubbed" against the play head of an ATR to monitor cue points.

audio sweetening The mixing of sound effects, music, and announcer audio tracks with the audio track of the edited master tape, usually during the mixing stages of a production.

audio timecode Longitudinal timecode (LTC) recorded on track normally used for audio.

AutoSave A feature that saves your work at intervals you specify using your Bin settings. Backups are placed in the Attic folder.

autosync Feature that allows for synching and combining of separate audio and picture clips on an Avid nonlinear editor (NLE).

AUX Auxiliary source. Used normally in linear video systems, AUX refers to an arbitrary external video or audio source.

backtiming A method of calculating the in point by subtracting the duration from a known out point so that, for example, music and video or film will end on the same note.

bandwidth Refers to the upper limit of data that can be transferred within a single channel or medium.

batch capture An automated process in which groups of clips, sequences, or both are recorded digitally from source media.

batch digitize Same as batch capture.

batch list Import log format for Final Cut Pro. A telecine log must be converted into a batch list before it can be digitized into a Final Cut Pro NLE. The equivalent of an ALE file for Avid or Power Log file for Media 100.

Bézier A type of curve that you can use for segments in some types of effects keyframes. A Bézier point on a curve allows you to control the smoothness or sharpness of the motion of the keyframe.

bin A container where film workprint is stored hanging from pins. The editor's completed scenes are normally stored in a separate bin.

A bin normally consists of a series of hooks that overhang into a nonfibrous bag. The clips are attached to cardboard trim tags that visually identify the scene, take, edge numbers, and a short description. The tags and clips are hung on pins and cascade into the bag. nonlinear editors (NLEs) have virtual or electronic bins, where pointers to media files (clips, sequences, and subclips) are located. NLE bins are used in much the same way as film bins, with the added feature of the ability to copy clips into several different type bins.

bit A contraction of a binary digit, normally having a value of 0 or 1. The smallest unit of information that a computer can store.

black and code The process of recording black video, timecode, and control track onto videotape stock. This process is also referred to as striping or blacking.

black burst A black video signal with no other luminance or chrominance. Black burst can be used as a reference signal for synchronizing video and audio components.

black burst generator An electronic device that emits a black burst signal, usually with multiple outputs so that devices can be referenced or synchronized electronically together.

blacked tapes *See* black and code.

blue screen A special effects procedure in which a subject is photographed in front of a uniformly illuminated blue background. A new background image can be substituted for the blue during the shoot or in postproduction. Also referred to as chroma key.

B-mode A method of assembling an edit decision list (EDL). In a B-mode EDL assembly, the editing system performs all the edits from tapes that are currently assigned to the decks

and then finds the next tape sequentially in the list for full assembly of all of its edits in the list, leaving gaps for material to be filled by subsequent tapes. Also referred to as "checkerboard" assembly.

bps Acronym for bits per second.

brightness A visual stimulus that gives the observer a perception of more or less light.

bumping up The transfer of a program recorded on a lower-quality videotape to a higher-quality videotape; for example, a recording from DV to Digital Beta.

burn-in Refers to character-generated numbers superimposed on video and telecine transfers. Typical burn-ins include video timecode, audio timecode, and key numbers.

BVB Acronym for Black-Video-Black. A preview mode in linear editing systems that displays black, newly inserted video, and then black again. Used for checking for flash frames when longitudinal timecode (LTC) is used.

B–Y One of the color difference signals in the component color system of the National Television Standards Committee (NTSC) video standard. The signal formula is:

B–Y = 0.299R (red) – 0.587G (green) + 0.886B (blue)

calibrate To adjust levels or instruments for maximum precision.

calibration The process of correcting any deviation from a standard set of specifications.

camera roll A roll of motion picture film used in production, usually 400 feet or 800 feet in length. Each roll is assigned a unique number for reference. Also called cam roll.

camera report A report issued for each camera roll by the camera department of a motion picture production. Includes scene numbers, takes, circled takes, footage, and other information. A copy of this multicarbon form should be sent to the editorial department.

capture To input video and/or audio into a nonlinear editor (NLE) format. Also known as digitizing or ingesting.

CCD Acronym for charged coupling device. A sensor used in digital video cameras and other photoelectric devices to convert light into electricity.

CCIR Acronym for Consultative Committee for International Radio, an international body that sets television standards. Now referred to as ITU-R.

CCIR 601 A document issued by the CCIR that recommends specifications for digital component video. Now referred to as ITU-R BT.601

CCIR-709 A document issued by the CCIR that recommends specifications for high-definition television signals. Now referred to as ITU-R BT.709.

CES Acronym for color encoding specification.

change list A list of instructions comparing an updated cut of a sequence to its previous version. Simplifies changes for the person conforming by only listing updated revisions and new edits.

changeover The point at which the projectionist switches between reels during display of a motion picture. Changeover cue marks must be made 24 frames before the last frame of action (LFOA).

character generator A device that creates alphanumeric characters that are superimposed on video.

characterization The process of defining color characteristics for a model of input or output device; used with color management modules.

charge-coupled device A sensor used in digital video cameras and other photoelectric devices to convert light into electricity. Also referred to as a CCD.

chroma The color component of a video signal.

chroma curve Graph used in Color Correction mode that adjusts color values.

chromadynamics The human response to color: psychological, physiological, or cultural.

chroma key A special effects procedure in which a subject is photographed in front of a uniformly illuminated blue background. A new background image can be substituted for the blue during the shoot or in postproduction. Also referred to as blue screen.

chroma subsampling A technique for sampling image information, usually for storage on videotape, in which luma is stored at full resolution but chroma components are reduced. Often referred to by ratio, in which 4:2:2 would refer to 4 pixels of full luminance, 2 pixels of horizontal chroma for each channel of chroma information, and 2 pixels of vertical information for each channel of chroma information.

chroma wheel Controls used in Color Correction mode to adjust hue and saturation.

chrominance Refers to the properties of color.

chunking A method of transferring media files to a workgroup in segments so that users can begin using the files without the entire file having been sent.

CIE Acronym for International Commission on Illumination (abbreviated from its French title: Commission Internationale de l'Eclairage); the committee responsible for international recommendations for colorimetry. An organization that defines color spaces; for example, CIE LAB and XYZ tristimulus values.

circled takes Refers to method of circling takes that the director wishes to print during production. Takes are circled on camera and sound reports as well as on facing pages in the script supervisor's notes. When referring to the film, circled takes are also known as A neg. Noncircled takes, not normally telecined, are called B neg. These terms are not to be confused with A roll and A/B roll methods of conforming film.

CIS Acronym for color interchange standard, a method of interchanging color values between color spaces.

clapper The two striped sticks used on a slate that aid in establishing sync on a shot. By clapping the two sticks together, recorded visually on film and aurally on audiotape, visual and aural reference for sync can be established on film.

clip Data that points to segments of source material recorded or digitized into your nonlinear editor (NLE) system.

clip name A name given to a shot used in a nonlinear editor (NLE) to identify it. Clips are usually named after a scene and take number, e.g., "16/1" for scene 16 take 1.

clipping In video, a condition in which the variation of input luminance signals can produce no further variation of an output signal. Usually occurs when brightness is overdriven, causing little or no variation at the highest point of luminance in the signal. In audio, a type of distortion caused by excessive levels, resulting in harsh, loud, and unpleasant sound.

C-mode A linear method of assembling an edit decision list (EDL). In C-mode EDL assembly, the editing system performs edits by source tape number and ascending source

CMX The most common format for edit decision lists (EDLs), CMX was the brand name of one of the first computer-controlled editing machines and a pioneer in nonlinear editing machine development. CMX 3400 EDLs have two audio tracks; CMX 3600 EDLs have four. Originally a co-venture of CBS and Memorex.

CMYK An acronym for cyan, magenta, yellow, and black (K) inks used in the subtractive color process.

codec A compressor/decompressor, based upon a specific compression scheme, such as motion JPEG, MPEG, and so on. Codecs come in both hardware and software form.

colorant A dye, ink, or other agent used to create color to a material.

color balance The adjustment color signals to produce the best quality image.

color bars A standard color test signal that is recorded onto videotape as a reference for video levels in the program content and then adjusted during playback to achieve standardized imaging results.

color correction The process of adjusting film colors using a color correction system. A component of telecine and, more recently, of nonlinear editing systems.

color encoding A numerical specification for color information, usually device-dependent.

color gamut Referring to the full range of colors that can be captured or reproduced by a device, represented by a color space.

colorimeter An instrument that measures color.

colorist A person who adjusts electronic processing equipment in the transfer of motion pictures to video or data in order to manipulate color. In the industry, one who is a color artist and craftsperson with an extensive background in image manipulation with a high degree of understanding of color management.

color management The appropriate use of color hardware and software to control color in an imaging system.

color primaries (additive) Light sources comprised of red, green, and blue that combine to form various colors.

color primaries (subtractive) Colorant sources comprised of cyan, magenta, and yellow that absorb light.

color timing Also called timing or grading. The process of adjusting color balance for each scene from a conformed negative.

color wheel A circular graph, similar to a vectorscope, used in the Color Correction tool as a control for making hue offset and secondary color-correction adjustments.

component video Video signal that separates the various components (that is, chrominance, luminance, or other variables) rather than combining all elements, as in composite video.

composite video A video signal in which chrominance and luminance are combined.

compositing The process of combining two or more images to form a single image.

composition Term used to refer to finished pieces in other applications and with Open Media Framework Interchange (OMFI). In many compositing and effects programs, a "comp" is the equivalent of a sequence.

compression The process of reducing data file sizes for storing images.

cones Photoreceptors in the retina of the eye that receive the information that initiates color perception.

console window The Avid window that displays function, operational, and system information.

consolidate To copy media files or portions of media files. Used for archiving and moving media.

continuity reports A term that refers to notes made by a script supervisor regarding script continuity. Also refers to reel continuity, in which an editor reports durations of reels, last frame of action, and last frame of film.

control point The location on a Bézier curve that controls direction.

control track The portion of a videotape on which synchronous control information is placed. The control track contains a pulse for each video field and is used to synchronize the tape and the video signal.

contrast A degree of dissimilarity of luminance in two or more different areas of an image.

CPU Acronym for central processing unit. The "brains" of a computer that is the center of its functioning ability. Normally confined to a single chip or twin chips.

crash edit An electronically unstable edit, or any edit made in Record mode that creates a new control track on the tape that is not synchronous with the previously laid control track. Also be referred to as crash record (for example, in the Avid Digital Cut tool).

crawl The function of the Title tool that creates text that moves horizontally across the screen versus a vertical title roll.

cropping The redefining of image boundaries. Cropping can be done by removing portions of the image or by masking them.

crossfade An audio transition in which two sources are swapped electronically, one fading out as the other fades in. Also called audio dissolve.

CRT Acronym for cathode ray tube.

cue To advance a videotape to a specific location.

curves graph Used in color correction, a curves graph plots input color values on the horizontal axis and output color values on the vertical axis.

cut An instantaneous transition from one visual source to another.

cut list An edit decision list (EDL) for film. Instead of timecode numbers, edge numbers are used.

cyan A subtractive primary color which absorbs red light and reflects or transmits blue and green light.

DAC Acronym for digital-to-analog converter.

DAE Acronym for Digidesign Audio Engine. Used for audio plug-ins.

dailies The results of a single day of shooting. Usually refers to workprint made from a single day of shooting, but can also refer to a videotape transfer of the footage. Referred to as dailies because of the traditional method

of shooting, developing, and printing overnight. Same as rushes.

DAT Acronym for digital audiotape. Audiotape recording format used by many sound recordists and audio engineers. Society of Motion Picture and Television Engineers (SMPTE) DAT is most commonly used.

datacine A telecine capable of scanning and creating large image files that go beyond the constraints of standard-definition television (SDTV) video. Datacines can be used for storing color-corrected frames of film and the files they create can be scanned back onto film, avoiding the need for traditional color timing.

daylight A combination of skylight and direct sunlight.

daylight illuminant A device that reflects or transmits the same spectral characteristics as daylight.

decibel (dB) A unit of measurement for sound pressure (audio volume) level.

deck controller A tool that allows the user to remotely control a deck using standard functions such as shuttle, play, fast-forward, rewind, stop, and eject.

decompose To create new master clips based on material used in an Avid-edited sequence.

degauss To demagnetize (thus, erase) all recorded material on a magnetic tape. Can also refer to demagnetizing a monitor that might have some outside magnetic interference.

delay edit Linear video editing term for an L-cut or overlap edit.

depth shadow A solid shadow that extends from the edges of a title or shape to make it appear to be three-dimensional.

diffuse Referring to scattered light.

digital A signal that contains information in a binary form. Digital signals are often perceived incorrectly as being lossless. However, some are compressed, others are not.

digital cut An output to videotape of your project direct from a nonlinear editor (NLE).

digital encoding Referring to the transformation of any analog information into digital values.

digital recording A method of recording in which the recorded signal is encoded on the tape as binary digits and then is decoded during playback.

digitally record To convert analog video and audio signals to digital signals.

digitize Also known as capture. To input video and/or audio into a digital nonlinear editor (NLE) format. The process of converting analog signals to digital values. In some cases, a process of transferring digital values from one storage medium to another. Can also refer to any type of capture of media into a digital format, such as scanning a photograph into a JPEG file.

direct digital interface The interconnection of digital audio or video equipment without analog conversion of the signal.

direction handle A line extending from a control point that controls the direction of a Bézier curve.

disk The medium used to store digital data. Also called hard disk or drive.

display A device that presents images to an observer. Could be a monitor, television, etc.

dissolve An effect between video or audio sources in which one source is faded out overlapping another source as it is faded in.

D-mode A linear method of assembling an edit decision list (EDL). In D-mode assemblies, the editing system performs edits in the order in which they will appear on the master with the exception of multiple source events (dissolves, effects, wipes, graphic overlays) that are performed at the end.

DNR Acronym for digital noise reduction. An option used in telecine that can virtually eliminate all sources of noise on the film. Potentially hazardous to use because it can also remove grain.

dongle A hardware device used as a key to control the use of licensed software. Most modern dongles are USB-based.

double-perf film Film stock with perforations along both edges of the film.

double system Any film- or video-recording system in which picture and sound are recorded on separate media. A double system requires the resyncing of picture and sound during postproduction.

drop frame A timecode-counting method that reflects real time. To compensate for the base 30 timecode count and the actual frame rate of National Television Standards Committee (NTSC) video (29.97 fps), drop-frame timecode skips ahead two frames in the count at the top of every minute, excepting the tenth minutes of time. Does not exist in phase alternating line (PAL) video.

drop shadow A shadow that is offset from a title or shape and superimposed onto a background to give the sense of spatial dimension.

DTV Digital television. DTV is a standard for broadcast that incorporates transmission of a digital signal vs. traditional analog. Often confused with high-definition television (HDTV).

dubbing In videotape production, the process of copying video or audio from one tape to another. In film production, the process of replacing dialog on a sound, as in automated dialog replacement (ADR) or foley recording. Can also refer to foreign language translations on audio tracks.

dubmaster A second-generation copy of a program master used for making additional copies, thereby protecting the master from use.

dupe A duplicate. When one or more frames are used twice in an edited sequence. Short for "duplicate," as in duplicate frames. Dupe lists are generated to determine which frames will need to be duplicated before a list is conformed. The neg is copied onto an interpositive, which is then duplicated. See also IP.

dupe reel A reel used for recording and playback of duplicate shots during videotape editing. Dupe reels are used in linear edits, in which a transition must occur from two different shots that occur on the same reel. One of the shots is dubbed to the dupe reel.

duration The length of time (in hours, minutes, and seconds; or in feet and frames) that a particular effect or section of audio or video material lasts.

DV Acronym for digital video. Video that is transferred through equipment conforming to IEEE Standard 1394 or FireWire.

DVE Acronym for digital video effect. Usually refers to a specific device that creates digital video effects, such as Ampex ADO, Grass Valley Kaleidoscope, and others. Originally used as a trademarked name by NEC, which introduced its DVE the same year Ampex introduced its similar-in-function ADO.

dynamic range An audio term that refers to the range between the softest and loudest levels that a source can produce without encountering distortion. Also refers to the color depth or possible pixel values for a digital image— the number of possible colors or shades of gray that can be included in a particular image. Eight-bit images represent up to 256 colors; 24-bit images represent approximately 16 million colors.

edge code A broad classification of film frame numeration that can be either key numbers or ink numbers. Printed numbers on the edge of film that identify frames; a method of keeping track of edits through a simple numbering process. There are two types of edge numbers. Acmade or ink numbers can be printed on the edge of synced workprint and mag track by an inkjet printer. Key numbers (also called latent edge numbers) appear on the edge of the film when it is developed. Key numbers are more commonly used with nonlinear editors (NLEs).

edge filter A filter that applies anti-aliasing to graphics created in the Title tool, thus preventing jaggies.

edit bench The place in which much of the nondigital work takes place. Synchronizing and conforming are done here. Also known as the bench or workbench. Typically contains rewinds, a gang sync, and a splicer.

edit controller An electronic device, usually computer-based, that allows an editor to precisely control playback, shuttling, and recording to various videotape machines.

edit rate Also called fps or frames per second. The number of frames per second that a specific type of media uses. Film is 24fps, phase alternating line (PAL) video is 25fps and National Television Standards Committee (NTSC) video is 29.97fps (sometimes referred to as 30fps).

EDL Acronym for edit decision list. A list of edits in a sequence showing timecode numbers for both source and record tapes as well as source tracks for each edit. Used for online video editing, sound conforming, spotting, and mixing, and in some cases, for comparison with telecine logs for matchback. Can be used with some computerized video-editing equipment for automatic conforming.

effects The manipulation of an audio or a video signal. In video, can include keys, dissolves, Picture In Picture, morphing, and others. In audio, some possible effects include reverb, pitch shifting, and flanging.

electronic editing The assembly of video in which scenes are joined together electronically instead of physically splicing tape.

E-mode In linear editing, a C-mode edit decision list (EDL) in which all effects (dissolves, wipes, and graphic overlays) are performed at the end.

equalization The balancing of various frequencies to create a desired sound. Can also refer to the balancing of color and luminance in color correction.

event An edit number assigned by a linear editing system in an EDL (edit decision list).

Evertz A manufacturer of motion picture equipment. Also refers to a telecine log format whose files end with an .ftl suffix.

exposure The quantity of light that is captured by a receptor such as film or a video camera charged coupling device (CCD).

extract The process of removing a specific section from an edited sequence and closing the resulting gap.

eyedropper A tool used for sampling a color from a screen image that can be used with titles or color correction.

facing pages Pages printed on the back of three-hole punch paper used in conjunction with a script so that the editor can see both script pages and script supervisor notes. Contain scene, take, camera, and other details recorded while on location.

fade A dissolve from video to black or from audio to silence, or vice versa.

FAT Acronym for File Allocation Table. A type of file system used on Windows computers.

FCC Acronym for Federal Communications Commission. The governing body for radio and television transmission in the United States.

feedback A loud squeal or howl caused when the sound is looped through a source to itself and reamplified.

field In interlaced video formats, a single scan of the raster that includes every other line of resolution, comprising one-half of an interlaced video frame.

file system A way of organizing directories and files on a computer.

filler clip A segment of a sequence that contains no audio or video information.

film timecode Timecode added to the film negative during a film shoot via a film timecode generator. Used much like key code and edge numbers for counting film frames.

FireWire The international hardware and software standard for transporting data at speeds of up to 400 megabits per second (Mb/s) (1394a) or up to 800 megabits per second (Mb/s) (1394b). Also known as iLink (Sony trademark) 1394 or IEEE 1394.

flare Stray light that is usually reflected from a medium, but is not part of an image.

flash frame Short unwanted frames. Also refers to an effect in which a small number of frames are added for impact. With an Avid system, an editor can use the Find Flash Frame command to find these bits.

flatbed A film-editing system for playing back conformed workprint. Flatbeds are flat tables with viewing screens attached. Most common are KEMs and Steenbecks.

flex Also known as flex files or Aaton files, a telecine log format whose files end with an .flx suffix.

foley The background sounds and effects added by foley artists during audio sweetening to increase realism.

format 1. To prepare a disk drive or floppy disk for use. 2. A specific form that a sequence must follow, or a show format used in a television series, such as a tease, three acts, and a conclusion.

formatting The transfer and editing of material to form a complete program, including any of the following: countdown, test patterns, bars and tone, titles, credits, logos, space for commercial, closed captioning, and so forth.

4:1:1 Subsampling rate of NTSC DV, DVCAM, DVC PRO, and PAL DVCPRO.

4:2:0 Subsampling rate of PAL DV and DVCAM.

4:2:2 A subsampling rate used in video images. The higher the number, the better the sample. Higher numbers also create higher data rates, larger file sizes, and more complex pictures. The first number refers to the luminance of the picture. Second and third numbers refer to color. Sometimes a fourth number is also included, which refers to a key or alpha channel. See subsampling. 4:2:2 is the subsampling rate for formats such as Digital Betacam, DVCPro50, and D9.

fps Acronym for frames per second. Used to measure video or film playback rates.

frame One complete video picture. A frame normally contains two video fields, scanned at the NTSC rate of approximately 30 fps or the PAL rate of 25 fps.

frame offset 1. A way of indicating a particular frame within the group of frames identified by the edge number on a piece of film. For example, a frame offset of +12 indicates the 12th frame from the frame marked by the edgecode or key code. 2. The number of frames needed to delay the playback of a FireWire-based signal to maintain sync with an external monitor. 3. In master-slave terms, the number of frames of timecode that differ in the master-slave relationship.

frame pulse A pulse emitted to the control track signal.

frame synchronizer A device that converts nonsynchronous video sources into timed sources through capture of entire frames. Also referred to as a frame shaker.

freeze frame A video or film effect that appears to stop the action through continuous playback or integration of the same single frame.

gamma 1. The slope of the straight line portion of a CRT that relates log luminance to log voltage. 2. The portion of an image that normally defines the midtones. Adjustable by a colorist to create more contrast in lower luminance areas or higher luminance areas.

gamut The complete range for a set of colors within a given color space.

gamut boundary The outermost boundary of a color space.

gang 1. The combination of multiple tracks that are grouped together. 2. Slaving of a source clip to a sequence in Xpress Pro.

gang sync A gang synchronizer. Used to synchronize a picture with one or more sound tracks on an edit bench. Measures footage and frames.

gate The aperture assembly in which film is exposed in a camera or projector.

generation Refers to the iteration of recordings, usually in analog recordings, in which the sharpness of the electronic signal wanes with each recorded pass. For example, a camera master would be a first-generation recording. An edited piece would technically be second generation. Any duplication of the edited piece would be third generation, and so on. This assumes that no duplication is done digitally, where generational loss is actually minimal.

genlock A system whereby the internal sync generator of a device (such as a deck) locks onto and synchronizes itself with an external sync generator.

gigabyte (GB) Approximately one billion bytes of information.

GPI Acronym for general-purpose interface. In computerized linear editing systems, A GPI is a simple switch used to a send a start or stop command at a specific time to various remote components, such as digital video effects (DVEs), character generators, video switchers, and automated audio boards.

grading The process of adjusting color balance for each scene from a conformed negative. Also called timing or color timing.

grayscale A progression of achromatic values from black to gray to white, usually indicated on a chart.

GUI Acronym for graphical user interface. The graphical representation on a monitor of the software interface. Frequently pronounced "gooey."

GVG Acronym for Grass Valley Group. A manufacturer of video and television production equipment. Also an edit decision list (EDL) file format. GVG EDLs usually refer to their software versions. Most commonly used are 4.0–7.0.

hamburger Slang term for the Fast menu used to access preview mattes in an Avid.

handles Material immediately before the in point and immediately after the out point of a clip in a sequence. Handles are used when consolidating, redigitizing, or otherwise moving media just in case slight adjustments need to be made to the final sequence.

hard disk A magnetic data disk that is mounted within a drive enclosure.

hard matte Term used when shooting original camera negative (OCN) with a matte in place. As opposed to a soft matte, where no physical matting is done during the production phase.

HDTV Acronym for high-definition television. A system having greater spatial resolution than that of standard-definition television (SDTV) whose standards are recommended by the Advanced Television Systems Committtee (ATSC). Currently there are 18 different formats for HDTV.

head frame The first frame in a clip of film or in a segment of video.

headroom 1. Visually, the amount of room that should be between the top of a person's head and the top of the image in frame composition. 2. Technically, the amount of gain allotted before distortion or clipping of an audio or video signal is encountered.

heads out Film or tape wound on a reel with the beginning of the media on the outside of the reel.

Hertz (Hz) A unit of frequency equal to one cycle per second.

hi-con An 8-bit, grayscale representation of an image that determines masked areas for keys. Also referred to as alpha channel, holdout, cookie cutter, key channel, matte, and mask.

HIIP Acronym for Host Image Independence Protocol. A system that allows the Avid system to import and export files in various standard formats. Also called Image Independence.

histogram In color correction, a graph that plots the distribution of pixels in an image based on their brightness. Histograms plot luminance on the x axis and recurrence of pixels on a y axis.

H phase Horizontal phase. The horizontal blanking interval of a given video source. H-phase is measured between sources and calibrated to prevent shifting of the video image in analog composite video.

hue An attribute of a visual sensation that defines a specific shade of color. Hue is mapped on a vectorscope, which indicates degrees of red, green, blue, yellow, cyan, and magenta.

ICC Acronym for the International Color Consortium, formed in 1993. The ICC promotes interoperability of color imaging systems.

IEEE 1394 The international hardware and software standard for transporting data at speeds of up to 400 megabits per second (Mb/s) (1394a) or up to 800 megabits per second (Mb/s) (1394b). Also known as iLink (Sony trademark) 1394 and FireWire.

illuminant A source that reflects or transmits light.

ink numbers Also called Acmade numbers. Inkjet numbers that are added to a workprint and mag stock for reference. Can be used in some nonlinear editors (NLEs). Also used for preview code. Key numbers are more commonly used for digital editing.

in point The starting point of an edit.

insert edit An electronic edit in which the control track and longitudinal timecode (LTC) timecode are not replaced during the editing process.

interlock projector The projector used for screening workprint and dailies. It consists of a film projector and mag track player that can be "interlocked" and remain in sync.

IP Acronym for interpositive print. Created from the original camera negative (OCN), this positive print is used to duplicate a negative. IPs are created for items on a dupe list.

IRE A unit of measurement on a National Television Standards Committee (NTSC) waveform monitor for the measurement of video levels, originally established by the Institute of Radio Engineers.

ISO 1. International Organization for Standardization 2. Refers to a video feed of a single isolated camera, used frequently in multicamera production.

ITU Acronym for International Telecommunications Union, a United Nations organization that regulates all form of communication.

ITU-R BT 601 A document issued by the ITU that recommends specifications for digital component video. Formerly referred to as CCIR-601.

ITU-R BT-709 A document issued by the ITU that recommends specifications high-definition television (HDTV) signals. Formerly referred to as CCIR-709.

jaggies The rough edges around computer-generated graphic objects and titles. Can be adjusted through anti-aliasing.

jam syncing The process of synchronizing a secondary timecode generator with a selected master timecode.

JFIF Acronym for JPEG File Interchange Format. A file format that contains JPEG-encoded image data, which can be shared among various applications.

jogging The process of moving forward or backward through media one frame at a time. Also called stepping.

JPEG Acronym for Joint Photographic Experts Group. A form of image compression for both still and motion graphic images.

jutter Also called judder. A stopping and stuttering motion of video caused by pull-down in the telecine process. 2:3 produces the most telecine jutter. PAL B pull-down produces very little.

kerning Adjustment of the spacing between text characters.

key The combining of a selected image from one source with an image from another source.

key channel An 8-bit, grayscale representation of an image which determines masked areas for keys. Also referred to as hi-con, hold-out, cookie cutter, alpha channel, matte, and mask.

key code Refers to the barcode reference which is machine readable and is placed adjacent to key numbers on a film. Key code can be read by a telecine to generate a database of numbers during a telecine transfer. Commonly confused with key numbers.

key code reader A machine used in telecine that reads the latent bar code on film. Key code readers are located on the telecine scanner, usually connected to a character generator which can put key number burn-in windows onto a transferred videotape.

key color The solid color used to key when using blue screen or chroma key. Also used in luma keys.

keyframes Points in time where you have set effect parameter values. The system uses the values set at keyframes and interpolates changes between keyframes to create effects and animation.

key numbers Latent edge numbers that appear along the edge of the film near the sprocket holes. The numbers are adjacent to Key Code, a bar code system used in telecines to identify the frames. Not to be confused with ink or acmade numbers, which are printed on the edge of film after the film is processed. Key numbers are generally used for digital editing more often than ink numbers.

keyscope A telecine log format using files that end with .ksl.

kilobyte (KB) Approximately one thousand bytes of information.

kilohertz (kHz) One thousand cycles per second.

layback The process of transferring a finished audio track back to the master videotape.

L-cut A type of sync edit in which the transition of audio and video from a source does not occur at the exact same time. Also called a delay, split, or overlap edit.

leader Film-like materials that are attached to head and tail of a reel of film. The clear leader is used as a protecting agent and threading guide for a reel and is attached at the head and tail. The picture leader contains writing that identifies the reel and its contents. The picture leader is usually placed at the head and tail. The Society of Motion Picture and Television Engineers (SMPTE) or Academy leader provides a countdown before the picture content of a film begins. The SMPTE or Academy leader is placed at the head of a reel adjacent to picture content.

lift The process of removing selected frames from a sequence and leaving a black space in their place.

light That portion of the electromagnetic spectrum between 380 and 780 nm that is visually detectable by a normal human observer.

light source A physical emitter of electromagnetic energy between 380 and 780 nm.

linear editing A type of tape editing in which you assemble the program chronologically from beginning to end.

lined script A script prepared by the script supervisor, marked with vertical lines to determine coverage of a shot, indicating which characters are on camera for a given take at a given time. Used by editors for easy reference.

line feed A recording of a program that is switched between camera sources by a technical director. Also known as line cut.

liquid gate A process in which film is immersed in a suitable liquid at the moment of exposure to reduce scratches and abrasions. Also known as wet gate.

locator In Avid, a mark added to a selected frame that can be annotated with information.

log The entering of information about clips that could include timecode, audio and video tracks, key numbers, and so forth. Can also refer to a medium on which the logging data is placed, such as a file or paper.

looping The recording of multiple takes of dialog or sound effects. Also a term for automated dialog replacement (ADR).

lossless compression A compression scheme in which no data is lost. In video compression, lossless data files are very large.

lossy compression A compression scheme in which some pertinent data is thrown away, resulting in loss of image quality. The degree of loss depends on the specific compression algorithm used.

LTC Acronym for longitudinal timecode. A type of Society of Motion Picture and Television Engineers (SMPTE) timecode that is recorded on an assigned address track of a videotape.

luma The achromatic part of a video signal that refers to a quantity of light.

luminance The measure of an object that correlates with the perception of brightness.

luminance contrast The apparent change from lighter to darker areas of an image.

M & E track A single or stereo pair audio track that contains music and sound effects.

magenta A subtractive primary that absorbs green light and reflects red and blue light.

magnetic track A sound track recorded on magnetic sound recording film. Mag track has sprocket holes and resembles film stock in shape and size, but is coated with magnetic oxide.

married print A positive film print with both picture and sound.

mask To cover unwanted parts of an image. In film production, the U.S. common mask is 1.85:1. Also used in alpha channels to mask unwanted elements, such as in keys.

master 1. The tape resulting from a camera shoot or camera master. 2. The tape resulting from editing, also known as an edited composite master (ECM).

master clip In the bin, the media object in the database that points to complete or whole media files.

master shot The shot that serves as the overview of a scene and into which all cutaways and closeups will be inserted during editing. A master shot is usually a wide shot showing all characters and action.

master-slave A video-editing procedure in which one or more decks (the slaves) are set to follow along with another in terms of its location (the master). The difference in timecode between master and slave is called the master-slave offset. Also called chase.

matchback A process that allows generation of a film cut list from a 30 fps video-based project. Matchback lists can be + or − 1 frame accuracy per edit. A method of converting from one frame rate to another; that is, from 30 fps video to 24 fps film. Matchback provides ease of use with the ability to generate both edit decision lists (EDLs) for video and cut lists for a telecined film. Commonly used process for television where a conformed print will be required for distribution in other formats. Can also refer to the application that generates a matchback list.

match-frame edit An edit in which the last frame of the outgoing clip is in sequences chronologically with the first frame of the incoming clip so as to continue the picture or sound seamlessly without interruption. In an Avid Timeline, this is indicated by a small equal sign (=) across the edit between two clips. In linear systems, match frames are used to extend an existing edit or continue through a transition effect, such as a dissolve.

matte key A video effect comprised of three components: the background video, the foreground video, and the matte (also called holdout, hi-con, cookie cutter, or alpha channel), which allows one portion of the image to be superimposed on the other.

media Video, audio, and graphics.

media files Digital files stored on a computer containing audio and video data.

megahertz (MHz) One million cycles per second.

Meta speed An option used on Cintel telecines that allows for an extraordinary variety of frame rates during telecine transfers. Meta speed transfers can range from −30 fps to +96 fps.

MIDI Acronym for Musical Instrument Digital Interface. A standard protocol that allows a user to control electronic music equipment from a computer.

MII format A now obsolete component videotape format created by Panasonic.

millivolt One one-thousandth of a volt. A unit of measurement on a PAL waveform monitor for the measurement of video levels. In NTSC, the unit of measurement for video is IRE.

mix To combine video or audio signals.

mixdown audio The process that allows the user to combine several tracks of audio onto a single track.

monitor A device or interface used to view video or listen to audio.

monochromatic Having a single hue. Electromagnetic energy of a single wavelength. Frequently confused with achromatic (without color).

MOS From the pseudo-German, "Mit Out Sprechen," a shot that is recorded without sound.

motion effect An effect that speeds up or slows the media in a track.

motion tracking The process of generating position information of motion in a clip. Motion-tracking data is used to control the movement of effects.

multicamera A method of recording in which an event is recorded from more than one camera simultaneously.

multitrack Magnetic tape recording process in which more than one track can be recorded at any given time.

mute print A print with no sound. Picture-only print.

NAB Acronym for National Association of Broadcasters. Also commonly used to refer to an annual trade show and convention put on by this organization.

Nagra A brand of reel-to-reel audiotape recorder widely used in the film production and postproduction industries.

neutral Achromatic; without hue.

NLE Acronym for nonlinear editor. A digital computer system application that features editing in a nonlinear method. Also known as DNLE or digital nonlinear editor. Manufactured by Avid Technology, Media 100, Lightworks, Apple (Final Cut Pro) and others.

noise 1. Any aberration of a video picture which appears to be fine specks, not smooth, noisy. 2. Audio recording term for any undesired sound, particularly excess hissing.

non–drop frame A timecode-counting method that reflects 30 fps instead of the more accurate 29.97 fps of National Television Standards Committee (NTSC) video. As a result, this method of counting frames is not duration accurate, but each number correctly accounts for each frame without skipping ahead, as drop frame does. See drop frame. Phase alternating line (PAL) timecode is technically non–drop frame because it is precisely 25 fps, hence no need for drop-frame timecode.

nonlinear Pertaining to the ability to assemble materials from any point in the sequence.

nonlinear editing A nondestructive, random-access type of editing in which you do not need to assemble the program chronologically from beginning to end.

NTFS Acronym for New Technology File System. A file system used on Windows computers.

NTSC Acronym for National Television Standards Committee. The group that developed the standard for color television in the United States. NTSC signals have 525 lines of vertical resolution at a frame rate of 29.97 fps.

OCN Acronym for original camera negative. See original camera negative (OCN).

offline Pertaining to items that are not currently recognized by the computer, such as offline media files.

offline edit Usually refers to a rough or creative cutting of a sequence. Traditionally, offline edits were assembled on simple non-computerized video equipment, so these sequences were literally offline and edited without regard to broadcast standards. With the advent of nonlinear systems, the line between offline and online has been blurred and defined only by resolution standards and broadcast acceptance.

OMFI Acronym for Open Media Framework Interchange. A file format that is used primarily for transferring audio files (but is capable of containing video files as well) and sequences from one work station to another. Platform-independent.

online edit Usually the final edit using the master tapes and (sometimes but not always) an edit decision list (EDL) to produce a finished program ready for distribution or broadcast. Usually associated with high-quality computer editing and digital effects.

opticals The separate creation of dissolves, fades, and superimpositions by an optical house. A-roll conformed films must create opticals of all such effects. A/B-roll conformed films must create opticals of any effects that are not lab standard durations.

original camera negative (OCN) The original film shot on location. Most films are shot with negative (not reversal) film.

outtake A take that is not selected for inclusion in the finished product. Frequently associated with comedic production and performance errors.

overwrite An edit in which existing video and/or audio is replaced by new material.

oxide A metallic coating used for electronic recording that is magnetized during the recording process.

PAL Acronym for phase alternating line. A standard that is used in many different countries (as opposed to NTSC or SECAM). Features 625 vertical lines of resolution and a frame rate of 25 fps.

palette 1. A central location for color selection. 2. A central location for user-selectable buttons, as in the Command palette.

pan and scan A method of transferring widescreen images to standard-definition television (SDTV), in which the telecine operator can zoom into a part of the widescreen image and pan across it, filling the SDTV screen but eliminating some elements of the wider original picture. Pan and scan is a time-consuming and expensive method of transfer.

partition Dividing of hard disk space to create two or more virtual drives on a single physical drive.

patching The routing of audio or video from one channel or track in the sequence to another. Traditionally from patch bays, in which audio and video signals were routed through cables and connectors.

phantom telecine A system that plays back previously telecined films from a drive storage array. Used for color correction on motion pictures.

phosphors Materials on the screen of a cathode ray tube that emit light to form an image when irradiated by an electron beam.

picture leader Placed adjacent to SMPTE or Academy leader, picture leader has information written on it that consists of project name, reel number, and running time.

pixel Contraction of "picture element." A single point of an image.

position indicator A vertical blue line that moves in position bars and in the Timeline to indicate the time location of the frame displayed in the monitor. In other applications, frequently referred to as the play head or CTI (current time indicator). Also known as the blue position indicator, or BPI.

postroll A preset period of time during previews when a sequence or other media will continue to play past the out point before pausing.

precomputes An effect stored as a media file. Applications must precompute effects that they cannot create during playback.

prelay The phase of audio postproduction during which tracks are added to the master before a final mix.

preroll The process of shuttling media to a predetermined cue point (for example, six seconds) so the media is stable when it reaches a selected edit point, usually when recording or digitizing from a video deck.

preview To rehearse an edit without actually performing it.

primary color correction Color correction that applies to every part of a video image, or to every part of a video image that falls within a defined range.

print A positive copy of a film negative.

process shot A shot photographed specifically to be part of a special effect.

progressive media Media composed of whole deinterlaced frames.

project Database that contains all your clips, sequences, effects, and media file pointers.

project folder The folder containing an Avid project.

protection master A copy or clone of a master tape, usually made immediately after the master has been recorded. It is used as a backup if the master is damaged and also can be used as a dubbing master.

pulldown A process in which extra fields are added or "pulled down" during the conversion of 24 fps material to 30 fps NTSC or 25 fps PAL videotape.

primaries The base colors used to make other colors additively or subtractively.

radio frequency (RF) The high-frequency portion of the electromagnetic spectrum used for transmitting television and radio signals.

RAID Acronym for Redundant Array of Independent Disks. A storage device standard that helps to increase data speed and assist in fault tolerance of data.

RAM Acronym for random-access memory. Computer memory that is volatile.

random access The ability to move to a single point instantly without having to shuttle.

real time The actual measured time in which events occur.

record To copy video and audio signals from one medium to another.

region of interest The target for a motion tracking effect. Also known as the search pattern.

release print A film print that is ready for release to a general audience.

rendering The combining of effect layers to create one stream of digital data for playback in real time.

replace edit An edit in which a clip in the sequence is overwritten or replaced with source material of matching duration.

resolution The amount and degree of detail of an image, usually measured in dots per inch (dpi) or horizontal lines.

RGB Red, green, and blue. The primary additive colors; also can refer to a specific color space.

ripple The process in edit decision list (EDL) management of adjusting the times of all edits following an edit that has been altered in overall length.

rod A photoreceptor in the retina of the eye that receives achromatic information that initiates luminance perception.

roll A length of film wound on a core. Generally, a spool of film is referred to as a roll, and a spool of tape is referred to as a reel.

rolling text Text that moves vertically across the screen, particularly end credits. Also called credit roll.

room tone Also referred to as ambience or presence, production sound used where there is no dialogue to establish a setting. More

traditionally, *ambience* refers to outdoor locations, whereas *room tone* refers to interiors.

rough cut A preliminary edit of a program, usually the result of an offline edit.

RS-170A Created by the Electronic Industries Association (EIA), RS-170A specifies the timing of scans and blanking required to decode color signals.

RS-232C Created by the Electronic Industries Association (EIA), RS-232C is the standard interface for connecting serial devices.

RS-422 Created by the Electronic Industries Association (EIA), RS-422 is an enhancement of the RS-232C standard. It allows for higher data rates and an extended line length. Used by nonlinear and computer editing systems to control videotape recorders and other devices.

rushes The results of a single day of shooting. Usually refers to workprint made from a single day of shooting, but can also refer to a videotape transfer of the footage. Referred to as rushes because of the traditional method of shooting, developing, and printing quickly for editorial use. Same as dailies.

R–Y One of the color difference signals in an analog component color system of the National Television Standards Committee (NTSC) video standard. The signal formula is as follows:

R–Y = 0.701R (red) – 0.587G (green) – 0.114B (blue)

safe action area, safe title area The regions of the video image considered safe from cropping for either the action or on-screen titles.

safe color limiting The process of adjusting color values in a finished program so that they do not exceed broadcast standards.

sample data The media data created by recording or digitizing from a physical source. A sample is a unit of data that the recording or capturing device can measure.

sample plot The representation of audio as a sample waveform.

sample rate The frequency of the sampled units.

saturation The amount of chroma in an image. Colorfulness.

scale bar A control in the Timeline window that allows you to expand and contract the Timeline area centered around the blue position indicator.

scanner Also known as a film scanner, flying spot scanner, or telecine scanner. The physical machine where the film passes through a scanner and is converted to video.

scene-by-scene telecine A method of telecine transfer in which color is carefully corrected for best exposure of a film, and continuity between scenes is also carefully calibrated. Unnecessarily expensive for editing, a scene-by-scene is sometimes used after a cut has been made of a film for video distribution or promotion.

SC phase Subcarrier phase—the color burst portion of a composite video signal.

SC/H phase In composite video, subcarrier to horizontal phase. The phase relationship between subcarrier burst and the horizontal blanking reference point in a video signal. Used to time two or more video signals to prevent horizontal picture shifts.

screening Any viewing of a film program, a video program, or raw footage.

script supervisor The person responsible for maintaining script notes and circled takes. Produces facing pages and notes for editing.

scrubbing The process of shuttling through and monitoring segments of audio at various speeds. Originates from earlier analog audio days when audiotape media was "scrubbed" against the play head of an ATR to monitor cue points.

SDTV Acronym for standard-definition television. Refers to current television standards, such as NTSC, PAL, PAL-M, and SECAM. Opposite of high-definition television (HDTV).

sequence Another term for an edited master, cut, or program created in a nonlinear editor (NLE).

search pattern The target for a motion tracking effect, also known as the region of interest.

SECAM Acronym for Séquential Couleur à Memoire. The second color television standard developed (after NTSC) and used in France and its former colonies, Eastern Europe, and the Middle East.

secondary color correction Color correction that applies to specific parts of an image defined by hue and saturation values. Secondary color correction allows the user to affect colors within a specific range without altering any other colors in the image.

segment A section of a track or clip in the Timeline.

sequence Avid term for an edited composition. Can also refer to a series of shots or scenes within a film.

serial timecode A type of SMPTE timecode that is recorded on an assigned address track of a videotape. Also called longitudinal timecode (LTC) or address track timecode.

setup A reference point in the North American version of the National Television Standards Committee (NTSC) analog video signal. It is the blackest point in the visible picture. Also called black level or pedestal.

shared volume segmentation A method of transferring media files to a workgroup in segments so that users can begin using the files without the entire file having been sent. Also called chunking.

shot log A listing of information about a roll of film or a reel of videotape, usually in the order in which it was shot.

shuttling Reviewing footage at speeds greater than the normal playback rate.

sifting Searching for and displaying clips that meet specific criteria in a bin.

signal-to-noise (S/N) ratio The ratio of a wanted signal to an unwanted noise within the signal. The higher the S/N ratio, the better.

silence Blank space in the audio tracks in a Timeline that contains no audio material. Not the same as ambience, which contains background noise.

single-perf film Film stock that is perforated along one edge only; generally 8mm and 16mm stock.

slate 1. An identification board held briefly in front of the camera at the beginning of a take that displays information about the take. The clapper on top of the slate allows for the editor to properly synchronize sound and picture when using a double system. 2. An identification screen preceding between bars and tone and program content on a videotape master.

slewing The synchronizing of decks in computerized editing systems.

sliding A form of trimming where a clip is "slid" in its entirety along the outgoing (A-side) and incoming (B-side) shots.

slipping A form of trimming where the head and tail frames of the clip change proportionately, for example, if two frames are removed from the head of a clip, they are added to the tail of the clip.

smart slate A slate held in front of a camera which also includes a timecode and/or user bit LED display that is fed from the sound recorder for easier synchronization purposes.

SMPTE Acronym for Society of Motion Picture and Television Engineers. A society that develops standards used for television and film.

SMPTE DAT A digital audiotape (DAT) machine that uses Society of Motion Picture and Television Engineers (SMPTE) timecode. SMPTE DATs are far more expensive than a conventional non-timecode DAT.

SMPTE leader Countdown leader placed at the head of each built film reel. Society of Motion Picture and Television Engineers (SMPTE) leader counts from 8 to 2 seconds. When the first "2" frame appears, a 1000 Hz tone pops with it (called the 2-pop, or sync pop), and an additional 47 frames of black are shown before the reel starts. As opposed to Academy leader, which counts from 11 to 3.

SMPTE timecode The timecode standard approved by the Society of Motion Picture and Television Engineers (SMPTE), as opposed to other standards such as VISCA timecode. The most commonly used format of timecode.

soft matte Term used when shooting without a matte, with the intention of inserting one during negative printing. Soft matting allows for adjustments to be made to the frame, optically if necessary. Also allows for a 1.33:1

aspect frame to be displayed on videotape or DVD.

soft wipe A wipe effect from one image to another that has a diffused edge.

sorting The displaying of clips in a bin column in alphanumeric order of the selected heading.

Sound Designer II (SD2) An audio file format used for import and export of digital audio on Macintosh-based editing systems.

source mode A method of linear auto-assembly that determines in what order the edit controller reads the edit decision list (EDL). B-mode assemblies are generally referred to as source mode.

sound report A report issued for each sound roll by the sound department of a motion picture production. Includes scene numbers, takes, circled takes, Society of Motion Picture and Television Engineers (SMPTE) timecode, and other information. A copy should be sent to the editorial department.

speed The point at which playback or recording reaches a stable speed and all servos are locked.

splice An edit in which the material already on the video or audio track is lengthened by the addition (editing) of new material spliced in at any point in the sequence.

split edit A type of sync edit in which transition of audio and video from a source do not occur at the exact same time. Also called L-cut, delay, or overlap edit.

split-screen The video special effect that displays two images separated by a horizontal or vertical wipe line. Also a monitoring tool to view an effect before and after it is applied to a segment.

spot color correction A color adjustment made to a specific part of a video image that is identified using geometric drawing tools.

stabilization A specialized form of motion tracking used to eliminate unwanted motion such as camera movement from a clip. Stabilization works by tracking a theoretically unmoving object in the clip and by repositioning each frame or field of video to keep that object stationary.

startup disk The disk that contains the operating system files. The computer needs an operating system to run.

stepping The process of moving forward or backward through media one frame at a time. Also called jogging.

storyboard A series of pictures (traditionally sketches) designed to show the look and order of events of a production.

streaming A technology that allows users to watch a video transmission, usually over the Internet.

striped stock Blacked and timecoded videotape stock.

subcarrier (SC) The sine wave signal used for color reference.

subclip A subsection or smaller part of a clip or sequence, created for easier reference. Subclips are made and categorized to prevent long searches across entire reels of tape or long media clips. As a metadata in a bin, it points to only part of a Master clip.

subsampling (chroma) A method of reducing data within image files for transmission, usually to videotape. Subsampling is represented by a ratio of three or four digits, where the leading digit, usually 4, is representative only as a luminance sample relative to the amount of horizontal and vertical color samples. A fourth digit can be added to this notation to indicate the alpha channel. Alpha channel sampling, when used, always matches luminance sampling. Examples of subsampling rates include 4:2:2, 4:4:4, 4:1:1, and 4:2:0.

subtractive color The color formed by the subtraction of light by absorption. CMYK primaries work as subtractive colorants.

Super 16 A special formatting technique using 16mm film that creates an enlarged picture area. Super 16 was originally designed to be printed to 35mm film for release.

surround The area surrounding an image.

surround effect An effect that is caused by brightness adaptation of surrounds where an image is perceived as having lower or higher luminance contrast.

sweetening Mixing sound effects, music, and announcer audio tracks with the audio track of the edited master tape, usually during the mixing stages of a production. Also called audio sweetening.

sync (synchronization) The process of maintaining correct correlation between picture and sound.

sync pop A 1000 Hz tone emitted for one frame 47 frames before a reel begins. Used to establish sync with a Society of Motion Picture and Television Engineers (SMPTE) leader "2" frame. Also called a 2-pop.

sync word The portion of Society of Motion Picture and Television Engineers (SMPTE) timecode that indicates the end of each frame and the direction of tape travel. Can also refer to timecode phase.

tail frame The last frame in a clip.

tail slate The slate information recorded at the end of the take instead of at the begin-

ning; usually recorded with the slate upside down. Tail slates are frequently used in documentaries in which the beginning of a shot is spontaneous and there is no time to slate the event.

tails out Film or tape wound on a reel with the end of the media on the outside of the reel.

take Filming a single shot.

TBC Acronym for time-base corrector. An electronic device that improves video signal stability by correcting time-base errors that are inherent on mechanical videotape recorders.

telecine The process of transferring film to videotape. A telecine maintains a consistent relationship between film and video frames. Not to be confused with a film chain, which is not as accurate.

telecine log converter An application within Trakker's Slingshot matchback suite. Converts telecine files to NLE-usable import files. Could generically refer to all telecine log converters as well, including Avid Log Exchange.

telecine logger A computer system used to database the relationship between key code from an original camera negative to video timecode recorded on a telecine transfer videotape.

1394 The international hardware and software standard for transporting data at up to 400 megabits per second (Mb/s) (1394a) or 800 megabits per second (Mb/s) (1394b). Also known as iLink (Sony trademark), FireWire, or IEEE 1394.

three perf (3-perf) A 35mm system that records a single frame using only three perfs instead of the traditional four. Used mostly for television production, three perf requires a specially equipped camera and a telecine with metaspeed or other speed-alteration device.

three-point editing The principle that any edit requires only three marks between the source and record sides to automatically calculate the fourth mark and thus complete the edit.

three-stripe Magnetic film stock containing three rows of magnetic oxide coating.

TIFF Acronym for Tag Image File Format. A graphics format.

time-base error A variation in the stability of picture information, color information, and video sync pulse during playback on a video-tape recorder (VTR).

timecode A numbering system used to measure frames of video. Non–drop frame is most commonly used on film and has a direct number to frame correspondence, but is not completely time-accurate due to the actual video rate of 29.97 fps (NTSC). Drop frame does not have a direct frame-to-frame numbering correspondence, but it is time-accurate.

timecode reader A machine used in telecine that reads timecode, usually connected to a timecode character generator that can put timecode burn-in windows onto a transferred videotape.

timecode window Refers to character-generated timecode numbers superimposed on video images for reference to timecode of a master tape.

Timeline The graphical representation of edits made to a sequence.

tone A constant audio frequency signal recorded at the start of a tape at 0 VU (volume units) to provide a reference for later use. Usually recorded in conjunction with SMPTE color bars.

track A single channel of audio or video.

tracker In motion tracking, a structure associated with a specific region of interest that contains a single set of data points.

tracking The adjustment of video heads during playback of a tape to ensure the strongest possible constant signal.

tracking edit A zero-duration edit used during transition edits (dissolves, wipes, and so forth) on computerized linear editing systems.

track selector An interface function of selecting an active track in the Timeline.

TransferManager The Avid application that allows you to transfer media from one work-group to another.

transition Any form of edit between two pictures. Can be a cut, dissolve, or other representation of what is to take place as one segment ends and the next one begins.

transition effect An effect that can be applied to an edit transition.

transition play loop The loop that plays in Avid's Trim mode, which allows the editor to see slightly before and slightly after a transition. Plays in a continuous loop.

trichromatic Three-color, such as RGB.

trim The process of adjusting transitions in a sequence. Used for fine-tuning and cleaning up sequences.

24p 24-fps progressive frames. 24p frames are created by deinterlacing two video fields into a single full, reconstructed frame.

25p 25-fps progressive frames. 25p frames are created by deinterlacing two video fields into a single full, reconstructed frame.

2:3 pulldown The process in telecine created when a film, shot at 24 fps, is transferred to video at 30 fps. Every other frame of film is held for an extra field of video, thus the fields run in a 2:3 order. Used in NTSC telecine only.

2-pop A 1000 Hz tone emitted for one frame 47 frames before a reel begins. Used to establish sync with a SMPTE leader "2" frame. Also called a sync pop.

U-matic ¾″ analog videocassette recorder and tapes.

uncompressed video A recorded or digitized video stream that is not processed by a data-compression scheme.

up cut In editing, to cut off the end of the previous scene, often by mistake.

upright A vertical viewing system for film. Also used for cutting. Moviolas are the most common uprights used. Vaguely resembles a sewing machine with two pedals attached: one for sound, and the other for the picture.

user bits The portion of the timecode data available for encoding data chosen by the user; for example, footage count and key code numbers. Frequently used in music videos for take and scene numbers.

U-type A recorder format that uses ¾″ U-matic videotape.

variable-speed play A process of shifting easily between the playing, stepping (jogging), and shuttling of footage. When images remain stable, sometimes referred to as dynamic tracking.

VBV Acronym for Video-Black-Video. A preview mode in linear editing systems that displays a previously recorded scene, a black

segment where footage is to be inserted, and then an adjacent recorded scene on the other side of the edit. Frequently used to check for flash frames on either side of a previewed edit.

VCR Acronym for videocassette recorder.

vector Term that refers to a specific color and hue on a vectorscope.

vectorscope A visual display that shows the electronic pattern of the color portion of the video signal. It is used to adjust the color saturation and hue by using a reference such as color bars.

vertical blanking interval The period during which the television picture goes blank as the electron beam returns (retraces) from scanning the bottom of one field of video to begin scanning the topline of the next. The vertical blanking interval is sometimes used for inserting timecode, for automatic color tuning, and for closed captioning.

vertical sync Sync pulses that control the vertical field-by-field scanning of the video picture by the electron beam.

VHS Acronym for video home system. The ½″ consumer videocassette format developed by JVC.

video slave driver A hardware component that synchronizes audio frame rates and pulldown of video frames.

videotape Oxide-coated, Mylar-based magnetic tape used for recording and playback of video and audio signals.

viewing conditions A description of the characteristics of an area where images are viewed.

VITC Acronym for vertical interval timecode. Refers to timecode that is inserted in the vertical blanking interval. Not all video use VITC.

V-LAN An upgradable software protocol, developed by Videomedia, for video device control used by proprietary hardware between the computer and the controlled device.

VLX A series of controllers developed by Videomedia that control and synchronize professional video equipment for animation, video editing, high-definition television (HDTV), and broadcast television production. Uses V-LAN software as control protocol.

VTR Acronym for videotape recorder.

VU meter Volume unit meter. An instrument used to measure audio levels.

VVV Acronym for Video-Video-Video. A preview mode that shows a previously recorded scene, the new insert video, and the adjacent scene after the inserted video. Most common form of preview on linear edit systems.

WAVE RIFF Waveform Audio File Format. A widely used format for audio data.

wild lines Dialogue that is recorded without the camera rolling.

wild sound Sounds that are recorded without the camera rolling.

window dub Refers to character-generated numbers superimposed on video and telecine transfers. Typical window dubs could include video timecode, audio timecode, and key numbers.

wipe A shaped transition between video sources in which a margin or border moves across the screen, wiping out the image of one scene and replacing it with another.

workprint Positive prints (workprint) of film created from the original camera negative (OCN). Usually consist of only the takes that the director orders printed. (Hence the director's on-location phrase, "Print it!") Workprint is disposable and used for editing. It gets cut, hung in a bin, spliced and unspliced together, cursed at, and abused. If destroyed, it can be reordered from the lab. If additional takes need to be printed, the editor can order them from the lab.

X axis The horizontal axis in a three-dimensional graph or system.

Y The luminance signal of the component color system in the National Television Standards Committee (NTSC) video standard. The signal is composed of the following proportions of red, green, and blue:

$$0.299R + 0.587G + 0.114B$$

Y axis The vertical axis in a three-dimensional graph or system.

Y, R–Y, B–Y The luminance and color difference signals of the component color system in the NTSC video standard.

yellow One of the subtractive primaries that absorbs blue light and transmits green and yellow light.

Z axis The zooming axis that is perpendicular to the X and Y axes in a three-dimensional system.

zero-duration dissolve The method of editing two scenes end-to-end simultaneously within a single edit.

Index

Note to the Reader: Throughout this index **boldfaced** page numbers indicate primary discussions of a topic. *Italicized* page numbers indicate illustrations.

C

keyframes. *See* keyframes
rate of, 68, 289
size of, **193–194**, *193–194*
slipping, 181
snapping to, 158–159
in trimming, 178
frames per second (fps), 301
FreeDV requirements, **22–23**
freeze frames, 246, **248–249**, *248*, 301
full resolution, 158

G

game shows, rhythm in, 170
gamma, 302
gamut, 302
gamut boundary, 302
gang sync, 302
gangs, 302
gates, 302
GBs (gigabytes), 302
Gee Three Stealth card, 32
general-purpose interfaces (GPIs), 302
General settings, 100, *100*
generation, 302
Generic deck option, 233
genlock system, 302
geometric buttons, 251
gigabytes (GBs), 302
Go To (Cue) option, 62
Go To In button, 185
Go To Next Edit button, 115
Go To Out button, 185
Go To Previous Edit button, 115
GPIs (general-purpose interfaces), 302
grading, 302

Graphic Converter, 192
Graphic Documents option, 201
Graphic Export menu, 211
Graphic Files option, 201
Graphical User Interface (GUI), **83–87**, *84*
    defined, 302
    toolsets for, **87–92**, *87–92*
graphics
    alpha channels for, **200–201**, *201*
    color levels and color space for,
        197–198
    exporting, **208–212**, *210*
    field dominance in, **199–200**
    field ordering in, **198–199**, *198*
    frame size for, **193–194**, *193–194*
    importing, **201–208**, *202–205*, **238**
    pixel aspect in, **195–197**, *195–197*
    preparing, **192–193**
    still, **192**
grayscale, 302
grayscale images, 200
green color with Vectorscope, 44
ground signal, 34
GUI (Graphical User Interface), **83–87**, *84*
    defined, 302
    toolsets for, **87–92**, *87–92*
GVG (Grass valley Group), 302

H

H phase, 303
hamburger menu, 93, 109, 302
hand tool, 251
handles
    benefits of, 66
    in capturing and logging, 28
    defined, 302

DV, 194, *194*
in exporting, 210
frames in, 198
SDTV, 195
NuBus systems, **6–8**, *6–7*
nudging effects, 178
Number of Tracks setting, 150, 239
numerical entry for trimming, **178**, *178*, 189
NuVista card, 6

O

Object menu for titles, **250–251**
OCNs (original camera negatives)
defined, 308
resolution for, 29
offline edits, 308
offline items, 308
OMF (Open Media Framework) files, importing, **207–208**
OMFI (Open Media Framework Interchange) files
defined, 308
exporting, **223–225**, *224*
on the fly capture, **63**
on the fly trimming, **179**, *179*, **190**
1:1 (Uncompressed Resolution) option, *52*
online edits, defined, 308
online media in exporting, 217
opacity for titles, *255*
Open Media Framework (OMF) files, importing, **207–208**
Open Media Framework Interchange (OMFI) files, exporting, **223–225**, *224*
opticals, 308
Optimize For Speed option, 70

order
field, **198–199**, *198*
in nesting, **281**
original camera negatives (OCNs)
defined, 308
resolution for, 29
outgoing clips in trimming, *171*
output
audio settings, **152**, *153*
bitstream, **286–287**, *287*
calibrating for, **243**
in editing workflow, **19–20**, *20*
outtakes, 308
Override Clip Settings With Current Settings option, 205
Overwrite button, 115
overwrite edits, **130–131**, 308
oxide, 308

P

Page folds, 282, *282*
PAL standard
capturing in, 38
defined, 308
in exporting, 210
frames in, 193, *194*, 198
SDTV, 195
palettes and palette effects, **256–260**, *256*, *258–259*, 308
pan and scan method, 308
partitions, 308
pasting keyframe parameters, **270**
patching
defined, 308
in timeline capturing, 66
tracks, **141–142**, *141*

for timeline, 65–66

for trimming, 180

projects

  defined, 309

  prepping, **126**

protection masters, 309

pulldown process, 309

Q

QT codec, 216

quality

  audio, 46

  video, **35–36**, *35–36*, **157–158**

Quick Transition button, **121–122**, *122*

QuickTime files

  codecs for, **215–216**, *216*

  exporting, **214–220**, *214*, *216*

  importing, **206–207**, 238

  for video streaming, **221–222**, *222*

QuickTime folder, 216

R

R-Y signal, 36, 310

radio frequency (RF), 309

ragged edges, 253, *253*

RAID standard, 54, 309

RAM, 309

RAM buffers, **273–275**, *274*

random access, 309

rate of frames, 68, 289

RCA connectors, **33–34**, *34*, 36

real time, 310

real-time DV-25 bitstream output, **286–287**, *287*

real-time effects, 122

  playing back, **273**

    building the pipes in, **273**

    RAM buffer in, **273–275**, *274*

Record Deck time option, 236

record decks. *See* decks

Record Monitor, *84*, *86*, 115, *115*

Record Sequence and Timecode display, *84*, 86

Record Timeline, *84*, 86

Record track indicators, **119–120**, *120*

Record Track panel, *84*, 87, **137–138**, *137*

Record window, 107

recording

  buttons for, **109–110**, *109*

  in capturing, **78–79**

  crash, **230–231**

  defined, 310

red bars stress indicator, 274

red color with Vectorscope, 44

reference levels for audio, **148–149**

regions of interest, 310

reimporting graphics, **205–206**, *205*

release prints, 310

Remove Effect button, 123

Remove Marks button, 123

removing effects, **257**

renaming sequence tracks, **147**

Render Effect button, **122–123**

Render settings, 101, *101*

rendering

  defined, 310

  for digital cuts, **228**, **241–242**, *241–242*

  ExpertRender for, **275**

  for exporting, 217

S

Undo buffer, 131, **133**

Undo keys, 131

unlocking tracks, 144

up cutting, 316

upright system, 316

upsampling audio, 46, 154

Use Enabled Tracks option, 211, 218–220

Use Marks option, 210–212, 219–220

Use Source Compression For OMFI
option, 205

Use Video Compression Logged For Each
Clip option, 72

user bits, 316

V

V button, 253

V-LAN protocol, 317

Variable Speed heading, 249

variable-speed play process, 316

VBV (Video-Black-Video) mode, 316

VCRs (videocassette recorders), 316

vectors, 316

Vectorscope tool, **43–45**, *43*, 316

vertical blanking interval, 316

vertical effects, **272–273**

vertical interval timecode (VITC), 316

vertical position for effects, 265, *265*

vertical sync, 316

VHS decks, 41

VHS systems, 316

video

capturing, 49

channels for, 78

connectors for, **33**

fields in, 6

levels for, **75–76**, 217

monitoring, **139**

organizing, **51–52**

previewing quality, **157–158**

settings for

for exporting, **220–221**, *221*

for real-time DV-25 bitstream
output, 287, *287*

Video Display, **102**, *103*, 274, *274*

splitting from audio, 54

streaming, **221–222**, *222*

tracks for, **144**, *144*

Vectorscope sources, 44

Video-Black-Video (VBV) mode, 316

Video Only option, 189

Video Quality button, 286

video slave drivers, 316

Video-Video-Video (VVV) mode, 317

videotape, 69, 316

viewing conditions, 316

views

bin, **116–119**, *116–119*

Timeline, **167**, *167*

VITC (vertical interval timecode), 316

VLX controllers, 317

VTR-Style interpolation method, 247–248

VTRs (videotape recorders), 317

VU meters, 317

VVV (Video-Video-Video) mode, 317

W

wash between transparencies, 255

WAV files, 213

WAVE format, 317

Waveform tool, **43–45**, *43*

weather shows, rhythm in, 170

wild lines, 317

wild sounds, 317

window dubs, 317

Windows systems

    image export settings for, 208–209

    requirements for, **22–23**

wipes, 317

workprints, 317

Workspace settings, 106, *106*

WYHIWYG (what you hear is what you get), 48, 213

WYSIWYG (what you see is what you get), 261

X

X axis

    defined, 317

    for effect scaling, 264

Xpress Pro requirements, **23–24**

Y

Y axis

    defined, 317

    for effect scaling, 264

Y/C video, 36

Y signal, 36, 317

yellow bars stress indicator, 275

yellow color

    defined, 317

    with Vectorscope, 44

Z

Z axis

    for 3D space, 282

    defined, 317

zero-duration dissolves, 317

zoom tools for effects, 272

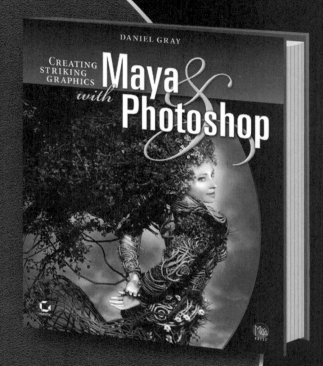

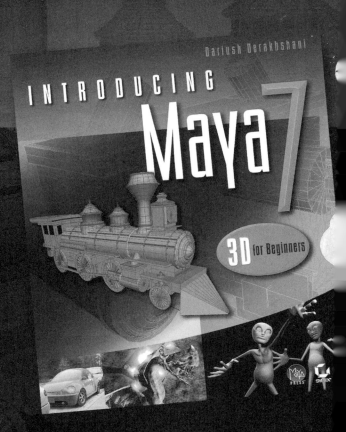